Computational Macroeconomics for the Open Economy

Computational Macroeconomics for the Open Economy

G. C. Lim and Paul D. McNelis

The MIT Press
Cambridge, Massachusetts
London, England

This book was set in Palatino on 3B2 by Asco Typesetters, Hong Kong.

Library of Congress Cataloging-in-Publication Data

Lim, G. C. (Guay C.)
Computational macroeconomics for the open economy / G. C. Lim and Paul D. McNelis.
    p.   cm.
Includes bibliographical references and index.
ISBN 978-0-262-12306-8 (hbk. : alk. paper)
ISBN 978-0-262-55283-7 (pbk) 1. Econometric models. 2. Macroeconomics—
Mathematical models. I. McNelis, Paul D. II. Title.
HB141.L54   2008
339.01′5195—dc22   2008011200

Contents

Preface

This study comes from the conviction that policy makers need quantitative, not simply qualitative, answers to pressing policy questions. Policy makers have to make decisions in the real world, and it is often useful, if not imperative, to augment qualitative advice with specific numerical ranges for operational targets in the short and medium run. For example, while it is useful for economic advisors to inform policy makers about the need for a competitive real exchange rate, or a sustainable trade deficit, it would be even more useful for the advice to include some benchmark numerical values of the competitive real exchange rate, or the sustainable trade balance (given the magnitudes of the key characteristics of the economy and external conditions)

Quantitative answers have often come from ad hoc back-of-envelope calculations, or cursory eyeballing of charts and graphs, based on incomplete partial equilibrium models with simple backward-looking expectations. Today quantitative policy-useful recommendations can come from a rigorous analysis of well-specified, internally coherent macroeconomic models, calibrated to capture key characteristics of particular real world situations. Good economic policy evaluation today is thus about providing quantitative, not simply qualitative, answers to pressing questions.

The way toward more effective quantitative policy analysis is through the use of computational stochastic nonlinear dynamic general equilibrium models. This study shows how such models may be made accessible and operational for confronting policy issues in highly open economies.

Wider use of computational experiments or simulation-based policy evaluation, based on stochastic nonlinear dynamic general equilibrium models, is now possible due to recent advances in computational methods, as well as faster, less costly, and more widely available computers. Newer algorithms permit the analysis of models which are not only *sufficiently complex* so that interesting questions may be explored, but also *tractable enough* so that one may be able to assess the sensitivity of results to particular assumptions and initial conditions.

Furthermore, it is no longer necessary to think linearly. For many years it was necessary to linearize the nonlinear first-order conditions of such models around a long-run steady state in order to make these models operational for estimation, computer simulation, and subsequent policy evaluation. Physicist Richard Feynman, for example, asks the question, why are linear systems so important? There is only one answer, and that answer, he states, is simply that we can solve them (see Feynman, Leighton and Sands 1963).

While such linearization makes estimation and simulation relatively fast, it frequently throws out the baby with the bath water, since many of the interesting questions in macroeconomic adjustment—such as asymmetric response of asset prices to shocks, or the effects of risk on economic welfare—necessitate explicit nonlinear approaches. For example, why do currencies crash spectacularly fast but recover much more slowly? Such phenomena do not take place in linear symmetric environments.

More to the point, many of the changes in external or internal environments facing decision makers in small highly open economies hardly represent small or local departures or movements around a steady state. Similarly the movements of key financial variables, such as asset-market returns, have hardly been linear and symmetric. As Franses and van Dijk (2000, p. 5) point out, such returns display erratic behavior, in the sense that "large outlying observations occur with rather high-frequency, large negative returns occur more often than large positive ones, these large returns tend to occur in clusters, and periods of high volatility are often preceded by large negative returns."

Miranda and Fackler (2002, p. xv) point out that economists have "not embraced numerical methods as eagerly as other scientists" perhaps "out of a belief that numerical solutions are less elegant or less general than closed-form solutions." However, the development of parameterized expectations, collocation methods, neural network approximation, and genetic algorithms, as well as other methods, have opened the way to use relatively complex nonlinear models for policy analysis and evaluation. As Kenneth Judd reminds us in his book, *Numerical Methods in Economics*, models, to give meaningful insight to policy makers, must be simple, but the models should not, and need not be, too simple. This study shows how state-of-the-art tools may be used to apply sufficiently complex models in computational experiments to give meaningful insights, under realistic assumptions about the underlying economic environments.

This book is, in part, a stand-alone research treatise and a stand-alone graduate textbook. It is like a research treatise in the sense that it contributes to current research knowledge in the area, but in a more extensive format than would be common in an academic journal article. It is like a graduate textbook, in the sense that it aims to help students and researchers get up to speed on computational methods and to apply these techniques to interesting questions. Finally, it is a policy-oriented book, intended to help researchers at central banks build their own models for ongoing analysis and evaluation.

Of course, all models are limited. As Martin Feldstein observes, in his tribute to Otmar Issing (when he departed as a member of the Board of the European Central Bank), our computational models are "only useful as heuristic devices to help clear our thinking" rather than for specifying real time policies, and that we are "particularly poor at open economy issues" (Feldstein 2006). We hope that this book contributes to clear thinking about open economy issues, as well as the design of better policies even in real time.

While remaining a stand-alone book, this study may also be seen as a distillation of several ideas coming from *Numerical Methods in Economics* and *Foundations of International Macroeconomics*. Both of these books are widely used sources for learning the literature in computational methods and open economy macroeconomics respectively.

We stress at the outset that this book is concerned with monetary and fiscal policy, for a prototype small open economy. We do not try to capture the environment of any economy in particular, through methods for "matching moments" of simulated and actual data, or with Bayesian estimation. Rather, we intend to show the important trade-offs in the conduct of policy under familiar and realistic scenarios taking place in small open economies throughout the world.

The organization of the material in the book is influenced by our experience with graduate students and with policy researchers. As professors, both of us recognize that students and researchers face significant learning setup costs (including psychological adjustment costs!) when they contemplate the implementation of computational algorithms. Common reactions among many of our current and former students and colleagues include feelings that they are delving into a "black box," that they have to learn the "art and science" of programming cumbersome code, that they have to wait long hours or even days for computer programs to "converge," and finally, that they have to live with the lingering uncertainty about the "accuracy" and "uniqueness" of the numerical results, as well as their policy relevance, once they have taken the time and trouble to do the computational work. Small wonder, then, that many prefer to work with simplified, linear, analytically tractable models, even if the assumptions are at times highly artificial and abstract.

We wish to show that the "black box" is not as dark as many think when viewed through the lens of a "random search" solution algorithm, that popular algorithmic methods can be understood rather quickly and are well worth the investment in time and energy, that "convergence waiting time" is often not that much longer than the "programming cost" of setting up linear models with equally cumbersome log-linear algebraic approximation, that "accuracy checks" for models are easily implemented, and that these models yield important new insights into dynamic macroeconomics for open economies.

Acknowledgments

McNelis is grateful to the Melbourne Institute of Applied Economic and Social Research at the University of Melbourne for hospitality and research support for several extended visits between 2004 and 2007, for purposes of collaboration with Professor Lim on this project. He also thanks the Research Visitors Program of the European Central Bank and the Research Visitor Program of the National Bank of the Netherlands for support and hospitality during 2004–2005 academic year in Frankfurt and Amsterdam, while he continued to work on projects closely related to material appearing in this book.

Lim thanks the Bendheim Scholar Program of the Department of Finance of Fordham University Graduate School of Business for research support and hospitality in New York in January 2007. She also thanks Georgetown University and Boston College for facilitating various visits to the United States for the purpose of collaboration with Professor McNelis.

We wish to acknowledge that MathWorks Inc. has provided recent versions of MATLAB® for this project. In the appendix we list the programming codes for the results appearing in chapter 2 of this book, in order to get readers started in developing their own computer algoritms.[1]

Lim and McNelis are grateful to Elizabeth Murry, formerly of The MIT Press, for her encouragement at the start of this project, and to Jane McDonald of The MIT Press as this book came to its present form.

McNelis dedicates this book to the newest member of the latest generation of his family, Samantha Nicole Snyder, born February 23, 2004.

Computational Macroeconomics for the Open Economy

1 Introduction

The focus of this book is on a computational approach to the analysis of macroeconomic adjustments in an open or globalized economy. Specifying, calibrating, solving, and simulating a model for evaluating alternative policy rules can appear to be a cumbersome task. There are, of course, many different types of models to choose from, alternative views about likely parameter values, multiple approximation methods to try, and different options about simulation.

In this chapter we give a brief overview of the issues arising from the agenda we set for this book and the rationale for the structure of the book, the methodology adopted, and the economic experiments considered. Since the same solution method will be used throughout the book, to minimize repetitions, we provide more details here about the solution method, the approximating functions and the optimization algorithms used.

1.1 The Open Economy Setting

This book uses computational experiments to obtain insights about macroeconomic adjustments in the open economy setting. These analyses can then inform the design of policies such as the best inflation targeting program or the best tax regime.

Benigno and Woodford (2004) have pointed out, that too often monetary and fiscal policy rules have been discussed in isolation from each other, but they opt to work in a closed economy setting, within a linear quadratic framework to yield analytical closed form solutions for monetary and fiscal policy rules. In contrast, we adopt the open economy setting for our discussion of monetary and fiscal policies and abandon the quest for analytical results in favor of numerical approaches. In so doing, we also extend our discussion of policy issues to encompass inflation targeting and the problem of recurring deficits or surpluses in the fiscal and current-account deficits.

Incorporating the open economy setting, of course, raises issues about international trade and finance, external borrowing conditions and assumptions about "closing" the open economy. As Schmitt-Grohé and Uribe (2003) have pointed out, there are many alternative ways to do this, all of which involve further complications to the standard models used for monetary and fiscal policy analysis.

Discussions about monetary policy, by their very nature, involve assumptions about price stickiness. In the closed economy setting such stickiness can come about either in wage or price-setting behavior in monopolistically competitive markets. Once we move to an open economy environment, we face stickiness in the pricing of imported goods, and thus the case of incomplete pass-through of exchange-rate changes to the prices of imported goods.

The variety of shocks or exogenous forces affecting the economy also expands when we move to the open economy setting. In addition to the usual productivity changes driving a business cycle, there are terms of trade shocks, foreign interest rate developments, and global demand variables to consider. The open economy setting is much more exposed to varying types of shocks.

Discussions of optimal policy in the open economy, then, involve much more complexity than corresponding discussions in the closed economy setting. The models need to be closed, and there are different ways to do this (including the use of a two-country model). Furthermore a reasonable case can be made for "stickiness" in the pricing of imported goods, as well as in domestic price-setting behavior, which in turn involves both forward and backward-looking behavior in the imported-goods sector of the economy.

The models we use in this book are in the class of so-called open economy new neoclassical synthesis (NNS) models. Such models, as Goodfriend (2002) reminds us, incorporate classical features such as the real business cycle, as well as Keynesian features, such as monopolistically competitive firms and costly price adjustment. As Canzoneri, Cumby, and Diba (2004) note, such models have been routinely used to revisit the central issues of stabilization policy.

Different general equilibrium models can generate different effects, so it is essential to have a good strategy for developing a good dynamic stochastic general equilibrium (DSGE) model. As McCallum (2001) points out, it is desirable for a model to be consistent with both economic theory and empirical evidence, but this "dual requirement" is only a starting point for consideration of numerous issues. McCallum also points out that "depicting individuals as solving dynamic optimization problems," as is done in general equilibrium settings, is "useful in tending to reduce inconsistencies and forcing the modeler to think about the economy in a disciplined way" (McCallum 2001, p. 15). But adhering to dynamic general equilibrium models still leaves room for enormous differences, as the reader will see as the chapters unfold.

In this book we focus on variations of one prototype model of the open economy; complexity is introduced, by adding extra economic features, chapter by chapter. While there are many unresolved issues about macroeconomic adjustments and the conduct of policy in the open economy, the differing positions rest on specific assumptions in the models. Rather than review a myriad of conflicting positions based on differing models, we work with increasingly complex versions of the prototype model. The same productivity shock is considered in each case. However, to gain further insight, we also compare the dynamic responses of key variables to other shocks, such as exports and the terms of trade. The progressive addition of complexity highlights the contribution of each added economic feature and aids in the understanding of the economic results and the derived implications for policy rules in an open economy setting.

The model is calibrated rather than estimated—the recent development of estimation techniques for DSGE models deserves a separate book. However, the parameters are based on estimates which are widely accepted. Thus our model is not only completely based on underlying optimization decisions of economic agents, at the household, firm, and policy-making level, it is also meant to be reasonably realistic. To put this point another way, following Canova (2007), what is relevant for us is the extent to which our series of "false" models yield coherent explanations of interesting aspects of data, while maintaining highly stylized structures (Canova 2007, p. 251). Thus the models we use are widely shared, if not consensus, benchmarks of how to model an open economy for policy evaluation.

1.2   Solution Methods

DSGE models, no matter how simple, do not have closed form solutions except under very restrictive circumstances (e.g., logarithmic utility functions and full depreciation of capital). We have to use computational methods if we are going to find out how the models behave for a given set of initial conditions and parameter values. However, the results may differ, depending on the solution method. Moreover there is no benchmark exact solution for this model, against which we can compare the accuracy of alternative numerical methods.[1]

There are, of course, a variety of solution methods. Every practicing computational economist has a favorite solution method (or two). And even with a given solution method there are many different options, such as the functional form to use in any type of approximating function, or the way in which we measure the errors for finding accurate decision rules for the model's control variables. The selection of one method or another is as much a matter of taste as well as convenience, based on speed of convergence and the amount of time it takes to set up a computer program.

Briefly, there are two broad classes of solution methods: perturbation and projection methods. Both are widely used and have advantages and drawbacks. We can illustrate these differences with reference to the well-known example of an agent choosing a stream of consumption c_t that maximizes her utility function U, which then defines the capital k accumulation, given the production function f and productivity process z_t,

$$\max_{c_t} \sum_{t=1}^{\infty} \beta^t U(c_t), \tag{1.1}$$

$$k_{t+1} = f(z_t, k_t) - c_t, \tag{1.2}$$

$$z_t = \rho z_{t-1} + e_t, \qquad e_t \sim N(0, \sigma^2). \tag{1.3}$$

The first-order condition for the problem is

$$U'(c_t) = \beta U'(c_{t+1}) f'(k_{t+1}). \tag{1.4}$$

The system has one forward-looking variable for the evolution of c_t, and one state variable k_t that depends on the values of the forward-looking variable, c_t, and the previous period's values k_{t-1}. The key to solving the model is to find ways to represent functional forms ("decision rules")[2] for these controls, as these rules depend on the lagged values of the state variables. Once we do this, the system becomes fully recursive and the dynamic process is generated (given an initial value for k).

1.2.1 Perturbation Method

The first method—the perturbation method—involves a local approximation based on a Taylor expansion. For example, let $h(x_t)$ represent the decision rule (or policy function) for c_t based on the vector of state variables $x_t = [z_t, k_t]$ around the steady-state x_0:

$$h(x_t) = h(x_0) + h'(x_0)(x_t - x_0) + \frac{1}{2}h''(x_0)(x_t - x_0)^2 + \cdots.$$

Perturbation methods have been extensively analyzed by Schmidt-Grohé and Uribe (2004). The first-order perturbation approach (a first-order Taylor expansion around the steady state) is identical to the most widely used solution method for dynamic general equilibrium models, namely linearization or log linearization of the Euler equations around a steady state (for examples, see Uribe 2003). The linear model is then solved using the methods for forward-looking rational expectations such as those put forward by Blanchard and Kahn (1980) and later discussed by Sims (2001).

Part of the appeal of this approach lies with the fact that the solution algorithm is fast. The linearized system is quickly and efficiently solved by exploiting the fact that it can be expressed as a state-space system. Vaughan's method, popularized by Blanchard and Khan (1980), established the conditions for the existence and uniqueness of a rational expectations solution as well as providing the solution. Canova (2007) summarizes this method as essentially an eigenvalue–eigenvector decomposition on the matrix governing the dynamics of the system by dividing the roots into explosive and stable ones.

This first-order approach can be extended to higher order Taylor expansions. Moving from a first to a second-order approximation simply involves adding second-order terms linearly in the specification of the decision rules. Since the Taylor expansion has both forward-looking and backward-looking state variables, these methods also use the same Blanchard-Kahn (1980) method as the first-order approach. Collard and Julliard (2001a, b) offer first- and second-order perturbation methods in their DYNARE software system.

Log-linearization is an example of the "change of variable" method for a first-order perturbation method. Fernández-Villaverde and Rubio-Ramírez (2005) take this idea one step further within the context of the perturbation method. The essence of the Fernández-Villaverde and Rubio-Ramírez approach is to use a first or second-order perturbation method but with transformation of the variables in the decision

rule from levels to power-functions. Just as a log-linear transformation
is easily applied to the linear or first order perturbation representation,
these power transformations may be done in the same way. The process simply involves iterating on a set of parameters for the power
functions, in transforming the state variables, for minimizing the Euler
equation errors. The final step is to back out the level of the series from
the power transformations, once the best set of parameters is found.
They argue that this method preserves the fast linear method for efficient solution while capturing model nonlinearities that would otherwise not be captured by the first-order perturbation method.

We note that the second-order method remains, like the first-order
method, a local method. As such, as Fernandez-Villaverde (2006, p. 39)
observes, it approximates the solution around the deterministic steady
state and it is only valid within a specific radius of convergence. Overall, the perturbation method is especially useful when the dynamics of
the model consists of small deviations from the steady-state values of
the variables. It assumes that there are no asymmetries, no threshold
effects, no types of precautionary behavior, and no big transitional
changes in the economy. The perturbation methods are local approximations, in the sense that they assume that the shocks represent small
deviations from the steady state.

While these methods are fast and easy to implement, they suffer
from one important drawback: the shocks must be small.[3] First- and
second-order perturbation methods go beyond linearization by making
use of first- and second-order Taylor expansions of the Euler equations
around the steady state. However, both linearization and perturbation
methods leave out any possibility of asymmetric behavior widely
observed in the adjustment of asset prices and other key macroeconomic variables. While this is fine for discussion of very small shocks,
it is limiting for large or recurring disturbances.

1.2.2 Projection Methods and Accuracy Tests

This book applies the projection method to solve the DSGE models.
The solution method seeks decision rules for c_t that are "rational" in
that they satisfy the Euler equation (1.4) in a sufficiently robust way.
It may be viewed intuitively as a computer analogue of the method of
undetermined coefficients. The steps in the algorithm are as follows:

• Specify decision rules for the forward looking variables; for example,
$\hat{c}_t = f(\Omega, x_t)$, where Ω are parameters, x_t are explanatory variables and
f is an approximating function.

• Obtain the Euler error from the Euler equations

$$\epsilon_t = U'(\hat{c}_t) - \beta U'(\hat{c}_{t+1}) f'(k_{t+1}).$$

• Estimate Ω using various optimizing algorithm so that the Euler equation residuals, or the difference between the left- and right-hand sides of the Euler equation, is close to zero.

• Perform accuracy tests to check on the robustness of the results.

Approximating Functions For the example discussed here, the approximating function for consumption c_t, expressed as a function of the state variable known at time t, is

$$\hat{c}_t = \psi^c(\Omega^c, z_t, k_{t-1}). \tag{1.5}$$

The function ψ^c can be any approximating functions, and the decision variables are typically observations on the shocks and the state variable. In fact approximating functions are just flexible functional forms parameterized to minimize Euler equation errors that are well defined by a priori theoretical restrictions based on the optimizing behavior of the agents in the underlying the model.

Neural network (typically logistic) or the Chebychev orthogonal polynomial specifications are the two most common approximating functions used. The question facing the researcher here is one of robustness. First, given a relatively simple model, should one use a low-order Chebychev polynomial approximation or are there gains to using slightly higher order expansion for obtaining the decision rules for the forward-looking variable? Will the results change very much if we use a more complex Chebychev polynomial or a neural network alternative? Are there advantages to using a more complex approximating function, even if a less complex approximation does rather well? In other words, is the functional form of the decision rule robust with respect to the complexity of the model?

The question of using slightly more complex approximating functions, even when they may not be needed for simple models, illustrates a trade-off noted by Wolkenhauer (2001, p. ii): more complex approximations are often not specific or precise enough for a particular problem while simple approximations may not be general enough for more complex models. As a rule, the "discipline" of Occam's razor still applies: relatively simple and more transparent approximating functions are to be preferred over more complex and less transparent functions. Canova (2007) recommends starting with simple approximating functions such as a first- or second-order polynomial, and later checking the robustness of the solution with more complex functions.

In this book we use neural networks throughout. Sirakaya, Turnovsky, and Alemdar (2006) cite several reasons for using neural networks as approximating functions. First, as noted by Hornik, Stinchcombe, and White (1989), a sufficiently complex feedforward network can approximate any member of a class of functions to any degree of accuracy. Second, neural networks allow fewer parameters to be used to achieve the same degree of accuracy as orthogonal polynomials, which require an exponential increase in parameters. While the curse of dimensionality is still there, its "sting"—to borrow an expression from St. Paul, and expanded by Kenneth Judd[4]—is reduced. Third, neural networks, with logsigmoid functions, easily deliver control bounds on endogenous variables. Finally, such networks can be easily applied to models that admit bang-bang solutions [Sirakaya, Turnovsky, and Alemdar (2006): p. 3]. For all these reasons, neural networks can serve as a useful and readily available alternative or robustness check to the more commonly used Chebychev approximating functions.

While the outcomes of different approximating functions will not be identical since we cannot obtain closed form solutions for these models, we would like the results to be sufficiently robust, in terms of basic dynamic properties. In this book we also assess the performance of the function using accuracy tests. Before discussing these tests, we digress to present a brief overview of the neural network function.

Logistic Neural Networks   Like orthogonal polynomial approximation methods, a logistic neural network relates a set of input variables to a set of one or more output variables, but the difference is that the neural network makes use of one or more hidden layers in which the input variables are squashed or transformed by a special function, known as a logistic or logsigmoid transformation. The following equations describe this form of approximation:

$$n_{j,t} = \omega_{j,0} + \sum_{i=1}^{i*} \omega_{j,i} x_{i,t}^*, \tag{1.6}$$

$$N_{j,t} = \frac{1}{1 + e^{-n_{j,t}}}, \tag{1.7}$$

$$y_t^* = \gamma_0 + \sum_{j=1}^{j^*} \gamma_j N_{j,t}. \tag{1.8}$$

Equation (1.6) describes a variable $n_{j,t}$ as a linear combination of a constant term $\omega_{j,0}$ and input variables observed at time t, $\{x_{i,t}\}$, $i = 1, \ldots, i^*$, with coefficient vector or set of "input weights" $\omega_{j,i}$, $i = 1, \ldots, i^*$. Equation (1.8) shows how this variable is squashed by the logistic function and becomes a neuron $N_{j,t}$ at time or observation t. The set of j^* neurons are then combined in a linear way with the coefficient vector $\{\gamma_j\}$, $j = 1, \ldots, j^*$, and taken with a constant term γ_0 to form the forecast $\hat{y}_t^*$ at time t.

This system is known as a feedforward network, and when coupled with the logsigmoid activation functions, it is also known as the multilayer perception (MLP) network. It is the basic workhorse of the neural network forecasting approach, in the sense that researchers usually start with this network as the first representative network alternative to the linear forecasting model. An important difference between neural network and orthogonal polynomial approximation is that the neural network approximation is not linear in parameters.

Optimizing Algorithm   The parameters Ω_c are obtained by minimizing the squared residuals ϵ:[5]

$$\epsilon_t^c = U'(\hat{c}_t) - \beta U'(\hat{c}_{t+1}) f'(f(z_t, k_t) - \hat{c}_t). \tag{1.9}$$

To obtain the parameters, we use an algorithm similar to the parameterized expectations approach developed by Marcet (1988, 1992), and further developed in Den Haan and Marcet (1990, 1994) and in Marcet and Lorenzoni (1999). We solve for the parameters as a fixed-point problem. We make an initial guess of the parameter vector $[\Omega^c]$, draw a large sequence of shocks (e_t), and then generate time series for the endogenous variables of the model (c_t, k_t). We next iterate on the parameter set $[\Omega^c]$ to minimize a loss function $\mathscr{L}$ based on the Euler equation errors ϵ for a sufficiently large T.[6] We continue this process until convergence.

Note that the projection method does not require linearization, nor does it need the Blanchard-Khan algorithm. Instead, once expressions can be found for determining the forward-looking variables, the nonlinear model is solved for the other endogenous variables given the exogenously determined variables. A variety of optimization methods can be used to obtain the global optimum.[7] Fortunately optimization methods are becoming more effective for finding the global minima.

There are, however, drawbacks of this approach, as Canova (2005, p. 64) points out. One is that for more complex models, the iterations may take quite a bit of time for convergence. Fernández-Villaverde and Rubio-Ramírez (2006) also note that this is expensive in terms of computing time. We have found that with the right set of initial values the speed can be greatly reduced.

There is also the ever-present curse of dimensionality. The larger the number of state variables, the greater is the number of parameters needed to solve for the decision rules. There is no guarantee the Euler equation errors will diminish as the number of iterations grows when we deal with a very large number of parameters. The method relies on the sufficiency of the Euler equation errors. If the utility function is not strictly concave, for example, then the method may not give appropriate solutions. As Canova (2005) suggested, minimization of Euler equations may fail when there are large number of parameters or when there is a high degree of complexity or nonlinearity.

Heer and Maußner (2005) note another type of drawback of the approach. They point out that the Monte Carlo simulation will more likely generate data points near the steady-state values than far away from the steady state in the repeated simulations for estimating the parameter set $[\Omega_c]$ (Heer and Maußner 2005, p. 163). Fernández-Villaverde and Rubio-Ramírez (2006) have elaborated on this point. We want to weight the Euler equation errors by the percentage of time that the economy spends at those points. More to the point, we want to put more weight on the Euler equation errors where most of the action happens and less weight on the Euler equation errors that are not frequently realized. The problem, of course, is that we do not know the stationary distribution until we solve the model—that is, minimize the Euler equation errors.

That criticism is true, of course, if the innovations to the model represent small normally distributed disturbances around the steady-state equilibrium. If we simulate out for large sample, we are just staying close to the steady state. However, if we use, as Fernández-Villaverde (2005) suggests, either distributions with fat tails or with time-varying volatility, then the repeated simulations will be less likely to generate realizations concentrated near to the steady state. Similarly, if the process for the innovation distributions are realistic, based on well-accepted empirical results, then we are more than likely to stay in regions of the state space likely to be realized.

We have used normally distributed errors for most of this book, in order to show the effects of increasing model complexity and non-linearity in the structural relations in the model. But we note that fat tails and volatility clustering are pervasive features of observed macro-economic data, so there is no reason not to use wider classes of distributions for solving and simulating dynamic stochastic models. As Fernandez-Villaverde (2005) and Justiniano and Primiceri (2006) emphasize, there is no reason for a stochastic dynamic general equilibrium model not to have a richer structure than normal innovations. However, for the first-order perturbation approach, small normally distributed innovations are necessary. That is not the case for projection methods.

In summary, we work with one basic approach for solving models: the projection method, which is closely related to the Wright and Williams (1982, 1984, 1991) smoothing algorithm. We show that this method may be viewed as a computerized analogue of the method of undetermined coefficients commonly used to solve rational expectations models. With this method, as noted by Canova (2007), the approximation is globally valid as opposed to being valid only around a particular steady-state point as is the case for perturbation methods. The method is computationally more time-consuming than the perturbation method. But it has the advantage in that it is very useful for analyzing dynamics involving movements of key variables far away from their steady-state variables. And, of course, it allows us to incorporate asymmetries, threshold effects, and precautionary behavior. As Canova notes, the advantage of using this method is that the researcher or policy analyst can undertake experiments that are far away from the steady state, or involve more dramatic regime changes in the policy rule. Canova further notes two specific advantages of this approach: first, it can be used when inequality constraints are present, and second, it has a built-in mechanism to check if a candidate solution satisfies the optimality conditions of the model. These advantages are important when we take up open economy issues, such as constraints on foreign debt accumulation or the zero bound on nominal interest rates.

Another important reason for staying with the projection method is that it is a natural starting point for introducing learning on the part of the policy makers or on the part of the private decision makers in the model. Learning can be straightforwardly introduced and contrasted with the rational expectations when the setup comes from projection methods. Such learning represents stickiness in information in contrast to stickiness in price-setting behavior. As Orphanides and Williams (2002) put it, learning adds an additional layer of dynamic interactions between macroeconomic policies and economic outcomes.

Finally, Oveido (2005) argues, for us, convincingly, that the projection method is the appropriate approach to use for open economy models. The reason is that the net foreign asset position can deviate quite a bit from its steady-state value, since access to nearly frictionless world financial markets effectively separates saving from investment decisions. Since first- and second-order perturbation methods assume only small deviations of state variables from their steady-state variables, solutions based on these methods will overstate the volatility of macroeconomic aggregates.

Accuracy Tests   To test the accuracy of stochastic simulation results, we have to work with the Euler equations. Since the model does not have any exact closed form solution against which we can benchmark numerical approximations, we have to use indirect measures of accuracy. Too often these accuracy checks are ignored when researchers present simulation results based on stochastic dynamic models. This is unfortunate, since the credibility of the results, even apart from matching key characteristics of observable data, rests on acceptable measures of computational accuracy as well as theoretical foundations. The accuracy tests used throughout the book are those due to Judd and Gaspar (1997) and to den Haan and Marcet (1994). They are based on the Euler equation errors.

Judd-Gaspar Statistic   A natural way to start is to check to see if the Euler equations are satisfied, in the sense that the Euler equation errors are close to zero. Judd and Gaspar (1997) suggest transforming the Euler equation errors as follows:

$$JG_t^c = \frac{|\epsilon_t^c|}{C_t};\tag{1.10}$$

that is they suggest checking the accuracy of the approximations by examining the absolute Euler equation errors relative to their respective forward looking variable. If the mean absolute values of the Euler equation errors, deflated by the forward-looking variable c_t, is 10^{-2}, Judd and Gaspar note that the Euler equation is accurate to within a penny per unit of consumption.

Den Haan-Marcet Statistic   A drawback of the Judd and Gaspar criterion is that it is not based on any statistical distribution. It is purely a numerical method. At which point do the errors become statistically significant? For this reason we use another commonly used criterion, due to den Haan and Marcet (1994). This test is denoted $DM(m)$ and is defined as

$$DM(m) = T\mathbb{Q}'A^{-1}\mathbb{Q} \sim \chi^2(m), \tag{1.11}$$

$$\mathbb{Q} = \frac{1}{T}(\epsilon'x), \quad A = \frac{1}{T}\sum x_t x_t' \epsilon_t^2,$$

where the vector ϵ represents the vector of Euler equation errors, x is the instrument matrix with m columns. Under the null hypothesis of an accurate solution, $E(\epsilon'x) = 0$.

The authors recommend the following procedure for implementing this test: first, draw a sample of size T of den Haan and Marcet test of accuracy, with m degrees of freedom, repeatedly, say 500 times and calculate the DM statistics; second, compute the percentage of the DM statistics that is below the lower or above the upper 5 percent critical values of the $\chi^2(m)$ distribution. If these fractions are noticeably different from the expected 5 percent, then we have evidence for an inaccurate solution. They also recommend performing a "goodness-of-fit" type of test and to compare the empirical and theoretical cumulative density $\chi^2(m)$ function.

One of the goals of this book is to promote the reporting of accuracy statistics in computationally based research publications. We are no longer in the world of closed form solutions. However intuitively plausible the results of any research endeavor may be, it is important to know that they pass a minimum degree of computational accuracy.

1.3   Policy Goals, Welfare, and Scenarios

Whenever we discuss optimal policy, we have to specify the objectives of policy makers. Central banks, of course, have low inflation goals, and fiscal authorities may be concerned with fiscal sustainability. However, when we evaluate the overall performance of particular policy rules or stances of policy makers over the medium to long run, the overarching criterion for the performance of policy should be the welfare of households in the economy. By welfare, we mean an intertemporal index or measure of current and future consumption and leisure available to households.

Of course, policy is not made in a vacuum: the economy is subject to a variety of change, from external and internal sources, such as productivity, foreign interest rates, foreign demand, and terms of trade, all well beyond the control of any policy maker. So the measures of welfare, resulting from alternative rules for fiscal and monetary policy, also depend on factors beyond the scope of policy decisions. How can we evaluate the welfare consequences of specific policy rules when changes beyond the scope of policy are also taking place?

We make our case for computational approaches to policy evaluation precisely on this issue. With computational methods we can evaluate the distribution of welfare measures over a wide variety of realizations of shocks or exogenous changes affecting the economy, for different monetary and fiscal policy settings. We can specify a functional form for household utility and develop an intertemporal index, and compute this measure over a variety of policy settings. There is no need to substitute these direct welfare measures with quadratic loss functions or other ad hoc measures, since we are not linearizing the welfare function.

Moreover, whenever we discuss welfare, we present a histogram of welfare distributions. Given that any welfare index is based on realizations of one set of random shocks based on a given seed to a random number generator, it is important to know the dispersion of this welfare index for a wide set of realizations based on different seeds. We hope that this book will promote more widely the use of welfare distributions for assessing the payoff of different policy rules.

All chapters contain an alternative scenario or policy experiment, intended to motivate our readers to engage in computational experiments on their own. Many of the results come from one important difference between the open and closed economy setting. In the open economy consumers have access to international financial markets to smooth their consumption over time, when they face distortions in the domestic economy in the form of price or wage stickiness.

1.4   Plan of the Book

This book has eleven chapters. The goal of the computational experiments is to find robust conclusions regarding policy response to external and internal disturbances, under alternative assumptions about the structure of the economy and how agents react to new developments and policy change. We start with a very simple setting with no distortions or rigidities and gradually incorporate more distortions (e.g., in the form of price and wage stickiness, taxes, real rigidities in investment, financial frictions, and habit persistence in consumption).

Chapter 2 lays out the basic theoretical framework or model with fully flexible prices and with a simple Taylor rule for monetary policy. The model is closed by allowing for a debt elastic interest rate. We discuss how we calibrate the model and solve for the steady-state initial conditions of the model. Overall, we show that even this very simple framework involves forward-looking behavior and requires carefully constructed approximation methods for solution and simulation. Following the traditional literature, we show how the model can be solved for a given productivity shock with the projection method. We also present the results of the suggested accuracy checks. This chapter includes discussion about impulse-responses in response to a once-only shock as well as discussion of results from stochastic simulations resulting from recurring changes in productivity.

We believe that it is useful to consider simple flexible models because they are the benchmarks to evaluate welfare gains and loses of policy approaches under different types of rigidities and distortions. Consequently from the simulations we obtain benchmark welfare distributions under fully flexible prices for domestic and foreign goods, but bearing in mind that in these benchmark scenarios the monetary authority follows a simple Taylor rule aimed simply at inflation targets. The experiment conducted in this chapter is for the case of recurring changes in foreign demand. The results are compared with those obtained in response to changes in domestic productivity.

Chapter 3 takes up stickiness in domestic price setting. We examine how this form of stickiness reduces welfare, relative to the benchmark welfare distribution under fully flexible prices. We also explore more extensive Taylor rules responding not only to inflation targets but also to output gaps. The output gap is the difference between the actual level of output and the output which would occur in the flexible price economy. This chapter illustrates the effects of alternative policy targets.

The first few chapters were only concerned with monetary policy. In chapter 4 we analyze the welfare effects of alternative fiscal systems or tax bases, when there are recurring productivity shocks, for a given inflation-targeting monetary regime. We compare the case where the income tax rate is greater than the consumption tax rate with the reverse case where the income tax rate is less than the consumption tax rate.

The issue of domestic debt leads naturally to a consideration of the "twin" deficits in chapter 5. Here we let export demands react to the real exchange rate, and we explore the sensitivity of the relationship between the fiscal and current account deficits as the export elasticity of demand range from low to high for a productivity shock. Collectively, chapters 4 and 5 illustrate the sensitivity of results to alternative base case and alternative parameters.

Chapter 6 introduces capital accumulation into the basic models and considers the role of Tobin's Q in policy analysis. While the earlier chapters dealt with nominal stickiness associated with prices, this chapter is concerned with real rigidities and other types of distortions.

Chapter 7 expands the model to two sectors, which then allows us to broaden our scenario analysis to a consideration of a terms-of-trade shock. In particular, this chapter examines the case of productivity versus terms-of-trade shocks for an economy with a rich natural resource sector.

Chapter 8 introduces financial frictions by allowing for banking and financial frictions. This type of model is also called a limited participation model, since households are now restricted on the types of assets they can hold. In this chapter we compare the case of inflation targeting with a flexible exchange rate with the case of no inflation targeting with an effectively fixed exchange rate (which is akin to imported goods inflation targeting).

Chapter 9 is concerned with wage rigidities as a source of stickiness. Scenarios are simulated to explore how labor–leisure choices affect the outcomes of the productivity shock.

Chapter 10 introduces habit persistence into the consumption decision and considers the simulated results for two sets of comparisons: inflation targeting and no-inflation targeting, and productivity and terms-of-trade shocks.

The final chapter, chapter 11, makes use of the model with all of the bells and whistles and simulates a sudden stop as well as a large continuing capital inflow (and increasing external deficit) for an economy. Sudden stops have plagued emerging market economies in the last two decades, while the United States has experienced large and continuing external debt accumulation. This final chapter brings into sharp focus the advantages of using our nonlinear approximation algorithm for solving and simulating open economy stochastic dynamic models with sudden large shocks or increasing external debt levels. The aim of this chapter is to highlight, once again, the insights that can be obtained from simulating (nonlinear) DSGE models.

Of course, the order in which we have progressed, with increasing complexity—from the flexible price model, to sticky prices, to distortionary taxes, to capital accumulation, to sectoral production, to financial frictions, to sticky wages, to habit persistence—is a matter of taste. We are not suggesting that there is any deep evolutionary pattern in the ordering we have chosen, just that it follows roughly the development of the literature in open economy business-cycle analysis. Also as a final comment, we note that while we cover a range of topics familiar to students of open economy macroeconomics, this book is about methods for policy evaluation and not about policy evaluation itself.

Computational Exercises

At the end of chapters 2 through 10, we have added computational exercises. The MATLAB codes for the base flexible price model discussed in chapter 2 appears in the appendix at the end of the book.[8] This program estimates the decision rule coefficients as well as generates the impulse-response paths and the stochastic simulations for the model presented in chapter 2. As we move from chapter to chapter, the reader is invited to modify the codes from the base flexible price model to more complex extensions. Quite apart from programming to suit one's personal style and taste, we believe that the act of programming is an integral part of open economy macro research as it enhances the comprehension of the models and the simulated results.

2   A Small Open Economy Model

2.1   Introduction

This chapter contains the simplest version of the small open economy model to illustrate the computational methods for solving and simulating DSGE models. The basic framework contains equations that describe the behavior of the private sector for consumption, labor, production, the pricing decisions, the setting of monetary policy, and the closure conditions of the open economy.

The model is very simple: there are no rigidities in the form of price or wage stickiness, nor any form of adjustment costs. It is a fully flexible price model, but it is nevertheless a useful model because it can serve as the benchmark for assessing the welfare effects of alternative policy arrangements when there are sticky prices or other distortions in the economy. The flexible price model is a convenient starting point and the dynamics are easier to understand. The model is presented in section 2.2.

However, the model, simple as it is, does not have a closed form solution, and we have to use computational methods to find out how this model behaves for a given set of initial conditions and parameter values. In section 2.3 we apply the projection method to solve this model, for the case of a productivity shock. We also present the accuracy tests. Section 2.4 discusses the simulated results for the case of a one-off shock and for the case of many stochastic simulations. The final section 2.5 presents simulations for an alternative scenario, the case of a demand shock (coming from exports) as a contrast to the case of a supply shock (coming from productivity).

2.2 Flexible Price Model

The economy has five main groups of economic agents. The first group are households who consume goods and supply labor services. They also own the capital that is rented to firms. The second group are firms that combine capital and labor to produce goods that are demanded for domestic use and by foreigners. The firms also set prices, which, in this chapter, are assumed to be fully flexible. The third group are the authorities, in effect a monetary authority that sets monetary policy and a fiscal authority that sets fiscal policy. The fourth group are the foreigners who supply imports and demand domestically produced goods (the exports). Foreigners also lend to the home country. The fifth group are the financial institutions, but in this chapter, there is no explicit financial sector. In other words, there is no financial intermediation: households lend and borrow directly. We start with the simplest intertemporal dynamic model and gradually relax many of the simplifications.

A major difference between working with a closed and a open economy model is the need to "close" the model. Since the closure condition affects the optimizing behavior of all the agents, it is useful to discuss the closure condition first.

2.2.1 Closure Condition

The purpose of the closure is to induce stationarity in the debt process of the economy. If the consumers of the economy can borrow risk-free debt ad infinitum, there is no reason for them to limit their consumption. There are many ways to close an open economy model. Schmitt-Grohé and Uribe (2003) examine alternatives such as endogenous discounting for the utility function or adjustment costs for foreign debt accumulation. Using a real business-cycle open economy model without exchange rates or aggregate prices, they conclude that given the same calibration, the quantitative predictions regarding key macro variables, as measured by unconditional second moments and impulse response functions, are "virtually identical" (Schmitt-Grohé and Uribe 2003, p. 183).

In this book we adopt the debt–elastic risk premia approach to close the economy; that is, we introduce a risk premium term Φ_t that has the following symmetric functional form:

$$\Phi_t = \text{sign}(F_{t-1}^*) \cdot \varphi[e^{(|F_{t-1}^*| - \overline{F^*})} - 1], \tag{2.1}$$

where $\overline{F^*}$ represents the steady-state value of the international asset (denominated in foreign dollars). If the debt is greater (less) than the steady state, we assume that foreign lenders exact an international risk premium (discount).[1] This will have the desired effect of increasing the debt service of borrowing, and it will bring about the desired adjustment in consumption. Note when $F^*_{t-1} = \overline{F^*}$, then $\Phi(\overline{F^*}) = 0$.

2.2.2 Consumption and Labor
A representative household, at period 0, optimizes the intertemporal welfare function

$$V = E_0 \sum_{t=0}^{\infty} \beta^t U_t(C_t, L_t),$$

$$U_t(.) = \frac{C_t^{1-\eta}}{1-\eta} - \frac{L_t^{1+\varpi}}{1+\varpi},$$

where β is the discount factor, C_t is an index of consumption goods, L_t is labor services, η is the coefficient of relative risk aversion, and ϖ is the elasticity of marginal disutility with respect to labor supply. There is no habit persistence in this simple model—this feature will be introduced later.[2] Utility is additively separable in consumption and labor. The household's utility depends positively on the level of consumption and negatively on the hours of labor supplied.[3]

In this simple example the household is assumed to consume only domestic goods, which is a bundle of differentiated goods

$$C_t = \left[\int_0^1 (C_{j,t})^{(\zeta-1)/\zeta} dj\right]^{\zeta/(\zeta-1)},$$

where j denotes the domestic goods and the elasticity of substitution between differentiated goods is given by $\zeta > 1$. The price index P is given by

$$P_t = \left[\int_0^1 (P_{j,t})^{1-\zeta} dj\right]^{1/(1-\zeta)}.$$

The household sector also include entrepreneurs who own the capital stock K_t and hold shares in all the firms in the economy. There is no capital accumulation or depreciation in this simple case and all capital goods are imported:

$$K_t = I_t,$$ (2.2)

where I is imported investment goods. The price of the imported intermediate goods P_t^f is

$$P_t^f = P_t^* S_t,$$ (2.3)

where P_t^* describes the price set by foreigners. The rental price of capital is P_t^k.

Household Euler Equations The household intertemporal budget constraint is of the form

$$\begin{bmatrix} W_t L_t + \Pi_t + P_t^k K_t \\ + (1 + R_{t-1})B_{t-1} + S_t F_t \end{bmatrix} = \begin{bmatrix} P_t C_t + P_t^f I_t + B_t \\ + (1 + R_{t-1}^* + \Phi_{t-1})S_t F_{t-1}^* + Tax_t \end{bmatrix},$$

where W is the wage rate, Π is distributed profits, F is one-period foreign bonds, B is one-period domestic bonds, S is the nominal exchange rate (defined as the home currency per unit of foreign), R^* is the foreign interest rate, and R is the domestic interest rate. Tax is lump-sum tax and Φ_t is a risk premium term that is a function of debt. Note that without an explicit financial sector, we have assumed that households lend directly to the government as well as borrow directly from foreigners. There is no financial sector frictions or "limited participation" restrictions on households.

In this simple example the household takes the wage as given, and each household chooses consumption, labor, capital (investment), bonds, and foreign debt to maximize utility subject to the budget constraint. We assume that each household chooses nontrivial solutions in that $C_t > 0$, $L_t > 0$, $K_t > 0$, $B_t > 0$, and $F_t > 0$. The Lagrangian problem, which is to maximize utility subject to the budget constraint

$$\mathcal{L} = \sum_{t=0}^{\infty} \beta^t \left\{ U(C_{t+t}, L_{t+t}) - \Lambda_{t+t} \begin{bmatrix} P_{t+t}C_{t+t} + P_{t+t}^f K_{t+t} + B_{t+t} \\ + (1 + R_{t-1+t}^* + \Phi_{t-1+t})S_{t+t}F_{t-1+t}^* \\ + Tax_{t+t} - W_{t+t}L_{t+t} \\ - \Pi_{t+t} - P_{t+t}^k K_{t+t} \\ - (1 + R_{t-1+t})B_{t-1+t} - S_{t+t}F_{t+t} \end{bmatrix} \right\},$$

yields the first-order conditions:

$$\frac{\partial \mathscr{L}}{\partial C_t} = C_t^{-\eta} - \Lambda_t P_t = 0,$$

$$\frac{\partial \mathscr{L}}{\partial L_t} = -L_t^{\varpi} + \Lambda_t W_t = 0,$$

$$\frac{\partial \mathscr{L}}{\partial K_t} = -\Lambda_t P_t^f + \Lambda_t P_t^k = 0,$$

$$\frac{\partial \mathscr{L}}{\partial B_t} = -\Lambda_t + \Lambda_{t+1}\beta(1 + R_t) = 0,$$

$$\frac{\partial \mathscr{L}}{\partial F_t} = -\Lambda_{t+1}\beta(1 + R_t^* + \Phi_t + \Phi_t' F_t^*)S_{t+1} + \Lambda_t S_t = 0,$$

$$\Phi_t' = \varphi[e^{(|F_{t-1}^*| - \overline{F^*})}].$$

We assume all households face the same interest rate and wages—so these conditions are identical across all households and hold in aggregate:

$$C_t^{-\eta} = \Lambda_t P_t, \tag{2.4}$$

$$L_t^{\varpi} = \Lambda_t W_t, \tag{2.5}$$

$$P_t^f = P_t^k, \tag{2.6}$$

$$\Lambda_t = \Lambda_{t+1}\beta(1 + R_t), \tag{2.7}$$

$$\Lambda_t S_t = \Lambda_{t+1}\beta(1 + R_t^* + \Phi_t + \Phi_t' F_t^*)S_{t+1}. \tag{2.8}$$

Note that in the Euler equation given by equation (6.6) we do not assume $E_t[\Lambda_{t+1}S_{t+1}] = E_t[\Lambda_{t+1}][E_t S_{t+1}]$, where E_t is the expectation conditional on information at time t, nor do we log-linearize this equation, as is common in linear approximation methods. The standard interest parity relationship can be derived by log-linearization and by imposing the condition of statistical independence. Our nonlinear solution algorithm acknowledges the joint distribution of the endogenous variables in the determination of the exchange rate.

These equations are standard Euler results. Note that equation (2.6) indicates that the full effect of exchange rate changes are passed through to the domestic price of imported capital goods.

2.2.3 Production and Pricing

We assume that each firm j produces differentiated goods using a constant elasticity of substitution production function:

$$Y_{j,t} = Z_t[(1 - \alpha_1)(L_{j,t})^{\kappa_1} + \alpha_1(K_{j,t})^{\kappa_1}]^{1/\kappa_1}. \tag{2.9}$$

The symbol L_j denotes the labor services hired by the firm and K_j represents capital; $0 < \alpha_1 < 1$ is a share parameter and $0 < \kappa_1 < 1$ determines the degree of substitutability of the inputs. The elasticity of substitution of capital and labor is given as $1/(1 - \kappa_1)$. Z_t is the aggregate productivity shock, which follows a stochastic log-linear autoregressive process with the disturbance term ϵ_t assumed to be normally distributed with mean zero and variance σ_z^2:

$$\ln(Z_t) = \rho \ln(Z_{t-1}) + (1 - \rho) \ln(\overline{Z}) + \varepsilon_t; \qquad \varepsilon_t \sim N(0, \sigma_z^2). \tag{2.10}$$

In all of our analyses, productivity Z_t is assumed to be an exogenous stochastic process.

Aggregating over all firms yields:

$$Y_t = \left[\int_0^1 (Y_{j,t})^{(\zeta-1)/\zeta} \, dj \right]^{\zeta/(\zeta-1)},$$

$$L_t = \left[\int_0^1 (L_{j,t})^{(\zeta-1)/\zeta} \, dj \right]^{\zeta/(\zeta-1)},$$

$$K_t = \left[\int_0^1 (K_{j,t})^{(\zeta-1)/\zeta} \, dj \right]^{\zeta/(\zeta-1)},$$

where Y is the aggregate domestic output comprising the composite bundle of differentiated goods produced by monopolistically competitive producers. The demand for good $Y_{j,t}$ is given by the following expression:

$$Y_{j,t} = \left(\frac{P_{j,t}^d}{P_t^d} \right)^{-\zeta} Y_t,$$

where $\zeta > 1$ is the elasticity of substitution. These results are derived by Chari, Kehoe, and McGrattan (2000) who assume the artifice of a bundler, who buys output $Y_{j,t}$ at price $P_{j,t}$, and sells the composite good Y_t at price P_t, under the assumptions of cost minimization and zero competitive profits.

Aggregate production Y of domestic goods is demanded by households (C), government (G), and by foreigners (exports X) so in aggregate, the market-clearing equation is

$$Y_t = C_t + G_t + X_t \tag{2.11}$$

Pricing Behavior   There are two input costs: the price of labor and the price of capital. The wage rate is determined competitively. The firm sells the goods at the price P_t and remits Π_t to households:

$$\Pi_t = P_t Y_t - P_t^k K_t - W_t L_t.$$

Minimizing costs subject to the production relation

$$\mathscr{L} = W_t L_t + P_t^k K_t + \lambda(Y_t - Z[(1 - \alpha_1)(L_t)^\kappa + \alpha_1 (K_t)^\kappa]^{1/\kappa})$$

and taking into account the firm's demands for labor and capital yields the pricing equations

$$A_t = \left\{ \begin{array}{l} \left(\dfrac{1}{Z}\right) \left[\begin{array}{l} (1 - \alpha)(\alpha W)^{\kappa/(\kappa-1)} \\ + \alpha((1 - \alpha)P^k)^{\kappa/(\kappa-1)} \end{array} \right]^{-1/\kappa} \\ \times \left[\begin{array}{l} W(\alpha W)^{1/(\kappa-1)} \\ + P^k((1 - \alpha)P^k)^{1/(\kappa-1)} \end{array} \right] \end{array} \right\}, \tag{2.12}$$

$$P_t = A_t, \tag{2.13}$$

where A_t is the marginal cost. As in the usual analysis when prices are fully flexible, the aggregate domestic price P_t is equal to the marginal cost A_t.

2.2.4   Monetary and Fiscal Authorities

Monetary Policy and Taylor Rule   Throughout the book we assume that the central bank follows a very simple Taylor (1993) rule aimed solely at inflation stabilization. Following Woodford (2003, p. 39), we set the long-run interest rate equal to the foreign interest rate R^*. Desired interest rate $\tilde{R}_t$ is related to the foreign rate and the difference between the actual and target rate of inflation:

$$\tilde{R}_t = R^* + \phi_1(\pi_t - \tilde{\pi}), \qquad \phi_1 > 1.$$

The restriction $\phi_1 > 1$ is known as the "Taylor principle." As Carl Walsh (1998) points out, a greater than one-for-one response of the interest rate ensures that the economy has a unique, stationary, and rational expectations equilibrium (Walsh 1998, p. 547). Actual interest rate follows a partial adjustment mechanism:

$$R_t = \phi_2 R_{t-1} + (1 - \phi_2)[R^* + \phi_1(\pi_t - \tilde{\pi})], \tag{2.14}$$

where the inflation rate is defined as

$$\pi_t = \left(\frac{P_t}{P_{t-1}}\right)^4 - 1.$$

This formulation of the Taylor rule is similar to the rule estimated by Judd and Rudebusch (1998), but in our specification we leave out, for the time being, any interest rate reaction to measures of an output gap. The symbol ϕ_2 is called the "smoothing parameter," and it allows lagged interest rates to play a significant role in the determination of the current interest rate.[4] The target rate of inflation, in the case of fully flexible prices, is simply zero. Hence $\tilde{\pi} = 0$.[5]

Such a Taylor rule is needed, as Woodford points out, in order to avoid the Sargent and Wallace (1975) indeterminacy problem. Citing McCallum (1981), Woodford notes that such indeterminacy only applies if the interest rate rule is set as an exogenous process, but it does not apply when the interest rate is a function of endogenous variables.

For the simple flexible price example discussed in this chapter, there is no compelling case for a Taylor-type monetary policy. Indeed, given the small open economy assumption, the activities of international arbitrageurs would ensure global financial integration. Hence the domestic interest rate R_t follows the foreign rate R^*, and we can implement this scenario by setting $\phi_1 = \phi_2 = 0$.

However, although in theory, there is no role for monetary policy in a flexible price world, in practice, because central banks are not all-knowing about the state of the economy, they may well implement monetary policy. In fact there is a growing literature that recognizes that agents in the economy as well as policy-makers "learn" about economic behavior.[6]

We have deliberately set up the Taylor rule framework based on current inflation in this chapter for two reasons. The first reason is that monetary policy has an important role to play when we start to introduce distortions and rigidities in later chapters, and the Taylor rule is the most common way to model monetary policy. The second reason is that adopting a Taylor rule in the flexible price case introduces a type of informational rigidity, and comparing results from a model with the rule to a model without the rule allows us to assess how this type of behavior affects dynamic adjustments in the economy.

Taxes and Domestic Debt   Government spending G is assumed to be fixed in this chapter:

$$G_t = \bar{G}. \tag{2.15}$$

The Treasury receives lump-sum taxes Tax_t and borrows B_t, where B is a one-period domestic bond. The evolution of bonds is

$$B_t = (1 + R_{t-1})B_{t-1} + P_t G_t - Tax_t. \tag{2.16}$$

For this chapter, G is set at zero and B is fixed. The presence of a domestic debt instrument is a necessary device to facilitate the conduct of monetary policy operating on the domestic interest rate. Hence taxes can be thought of intuitively as the amount necessary to support monetary policy. The household sector holds government bonds and is taxed in a lump-sum fashion to service the debt.

2.2.5   Exports and Foreign Debt
Exports X_t^* in this chapter are determined exogenously:

$$X_t = \bar{X}. \tag{2.17}$$

The current account in this model is rather simple. Exports are exogenous while imports are simply intermediate goods for production of domestic goods. In later chapters we will examine the effects of exogenous stochastic export demand, as well endogenous exports, that are dependent on the real exchange rate. For now, given the exogenously determined exports X_t^* and the imports of intermediate goods K_t, the change in foreign debt evolves as follows:

$$S_t F_t^* = (1 + R_{t-1}^* + \Phi_{t-1})S_t F_{t-1}^* + (S_t P_t^* I_t - P_t X_t). \tag{2.18}$$

2.2.6   Calibration
The calibrated parameter values are shown in the appendix at the end of the book. The values for σ, β, ϖ, and α are the values suggested by

Smets and Wouters (2002). The Taylor rule parameters, the values for θ and ϕ_π, are set to allow for some inertia. There is nothing controversial about these values.

Solving for the steady-state values is relatively easy, given the coefficients of the model and our choice of normalizations. The foreign interest rate R^* is fixed at the annual rate of 0.04, and the foreign price $\bar{P}^*$ is normalized at unity. Productivity Z and labor $\bar{S}$ are also normalized at unity. At steady state, the inflation rate is zero, so domestic interest rate $\bar{R}$ is equal to R^*. In the stochastic simulations where we examine the moments of key endogenous variables, the effect of initialization is mitigated by discarding the first 15 percent of the sample size.

2.3 Solution: Projection Method

The projection solution method used here may be seen as a computational extension of the method of undetermined coefficients.

2.3.1 Approximating Functions

The first task is to specify approximation functions (or decision rules ψ^c, ψ^s) for the forward-looking variables (consumption C_t and the exchange rate S_t) as functions of the state variables x_t known at time t:

$$\hat{C}_t = \psi^c(\Omega^c; x_t),$$

$$\hat{S}_t = \psi^s(\Omega^s; x_t),$$

$$x_t = \{(Z_t - \bar{Z}), (F_{t-1} - \bar{F}), (R_{t-1} - \bar{R})\}.$$

The state variables are typically observations on the shocks (in this case, productivity Z_t), stock variables (in this case, foreign debt F_{t-1} predetermined at time t), and policy variables (in this case, the interest rate R_t).[7] The functions ψ^c and ψ^s may be any approximating functions. In this book we use a relatively simple neural network:

$$\Delta_t^c = \Omega_1^c(Z_t - \bar{Z}) + \Omega_2^c(F_{t-1} - \bar{F}) + \Omega_3^c(R_{t-1} - \bar{R}),$$

$$\hat{C}_t = \bar{C}\left(\frac{1}{1 + \exp(-\Delta_t^c)} - 0.5\right),$$

$$\Delta_t^s = \Omega_1^s(Z_t - \bar{Z}) + \Omega_2^s(F_{t-1} - \bar{F}) + \Omega_3^s(R_{t-1} - \bar{R}),$$

$$\hat{S}_t = \bar{S}\left(\frac{1}{1 + \exp(-\Delta_t^s)} - 0.5\right).$$

We use a neural network specification with one neuron for each of the decision variables. After taking exponents, we multiplied the function values by their steady-state values to ensure steady-state convergence.

2.3.2 Euler Errors

Optimization algorithms are used next, to find the estimates of the parameter set Ω^c, Ω^s that yields the minimum values for the sum of squared Euler errors. The Euler errors are defined as

$$\epsilon_t^c = \frac{\hat{C}_t^{-\eta}}{P_t}\left[\frac{1}{(1 + R_t)}\right] - \beta\left[\frac{\hat{C}_{t+1}^{-\eta}}{P_{t+1}}\right],$$

$$\epsilon_t^s = \frac{\hat{C}_t^{-\eta}}{P_t}\left[\frac{\hat{S}_t}{(1 + R_t^* + \Phi_t + \Phi_t' F_t^*)}\right] - \beta\left[\hat{S}_{t+1}\frac{\hat{C}_{t+1}^{-\eta}}{P_{t+1}}\right].$$

As described in chapter 1, we solve for the parameters as a fixed-point problem. We make an initial guess of the parameter vector $[\Omega^c, \Omega^s]$, draw a large sequence of shocks (ε_t), and then generate time series for all the endogenous variables of the model. We next iterate on the parameter set to minimize a loss function $\mathscr{L}$ based on the Euler equation errors ϵ for a sufficiently large T. We continue this process until convergence.

2.3.3 Accuracy Checks

Once we have obtained the decision rules for consumption C and the exchange rate S for our model, by the projection method, the next step is to check that the approximations are robust. Figure 2.1 shows the distribution of the Judd-Gaspar statistics for the consumption and exchange-rate Euler equation errors, for 500 realizations of sample size 200. We see that the average cost for both the consumption Euler errors and the exchange-rate Euler errors are less than one cent per dollar. Table 2.1 shows the mean and standard deviation of the Judd-Gaspar statistics.

Figure 2.2 and table 2.2 presents the results using the Den-Hann-Marcet test statistics. In this application we stack the Euler equation errors for consumption and the exchange rate from the simulated model. As Heer and Maußner (2005) note, any deviation of these errors from zero is simply a consequence of the shocks driving the model, so

Table 2.1
Judd-Gaspar statistic ($\times 10^{-2}$)

	$\dfrac{\lvert \epsilon_t^c \rvert}{C_t}$	$\dfrac{\lvert \epsilon_t^s \rvert}{S_t}$
Mean	0.2541	0.6937
Standard deviation	0.0287	0.0400

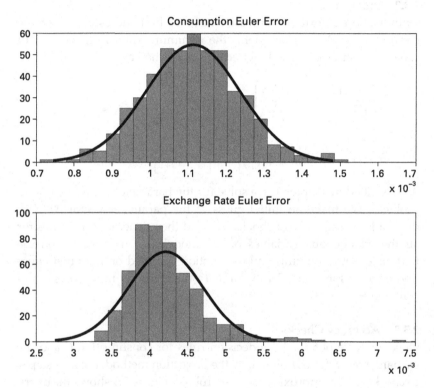

Figure 2.1
Judd-Gaspar statistic

Table 2.2
DenHann-Marcet test

	Lag order			
	1	2	3	4
Lower region ($p < 0.05$)	0.054	0.056	0.036	0.052
Upper region ($p > 0.95$)	0.042	0.042	0.034	0.040

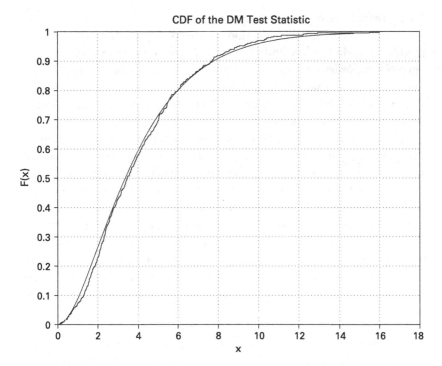

Figure 2.2
DenHann-Marcet test for accuracy

it should not be possible to predict these deviations from past information on shocks. The results for various order of lags are shown in table 2.2. This set of results conveys good news. Theoretically we would expect 5 percent of the p-values to be below 5 percent, and another 5 percent to be greater than 95 percent. The results in table 2.2 support this. Figure 2.2 shows the cumulative distribution function of the empirical analysis (one lag) against the theoretical cumulative density function (CDF) for the chi-square distribution. As shown, the CDF's are very close.

Overall, the projection errors are quite small, and the approximations appear accurate as evaluated by the Judd-Gaspar and the Den Hann-Marcet statistics. We can be reasonably certain that dynamic results for the case of productivity shocks based on these approximations are robust.

2.4   Stochastic Dynamic Simulations

2.4.1   Impulse-Response Analysis

We turn now to an examination of the dynamic properties of the model. How do the key endogenous variables behave in response to a one-off temporary change in the productivity index? Is the model stable, in the sense that the endogenous variables return to their steady-state values after the one-off change? Do these variables return to the steady state within a reasonable time frame?

In this section we will first use impulse-response analysis to examine the properties of the model. Impulse-response analysis allows us to see which variables display more complicated (or more interesting) dynamics in their response to a one-period shock, such as under- and/ or overshooting the long-run steady state. For a given parameter configuration this type of simulation allows us to see which variables display greater or lesser response and which variables have more volatile or oscillatory dynamics. To be sure, the "real world" has many recurring changes, but these simple impulse-responses help us isolate key dynamic properties of the model that we would not otherwise be able to do.

Taylor Rule   For the impulse-response analysis we work with the equation governing the evolution of the logarithm of the productivity index. The productivity shock follows a stochastic log-linear autoregressive process, with the disturbance term ε_t normally distributed with mean zero and variance σ_z^2. Starting from steady-state values, we shock productivity by the value of one standard deviation, and then set it to zero in succeeding periods:

$$\varepsilon_t = \begin{cases} \sigma_z, & T = 25, \\ 0, & T > 25. \end{cases}$$

To see the impulses more clearly in the figures, we let the length of the simulation run to $T = 200$ with the shock occurring at period $T = 25$. Of course, we can specify σ_z at arbitrarily large or small values to see if

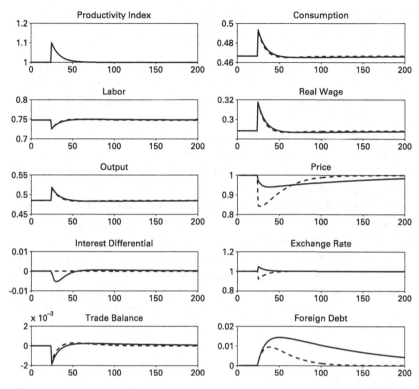

Figure 2.3
Impulse responses following a productivity shock: with Taylor rule (*solid line*) and without Taylor rule (*dashed line*)

there are different dynamic responses to the magnitude of the exogenous change. Since the model as well as the decision rules are nonlinear, there is no reason to expect proportionality in the response paths of endogenous variables, relative to small or large impulses. In our impulse-response analysis, we set $\sigma_z = 0.1$.

Figure 2.3 shows the impulse-response paths for selected key variables (solid lines). The exogenous productivity index appear in the top left-hand panel. The figure shows that productivity has a positive effect on output and a negative effect on price, which then encourages more consumption. The improvement in productivity also results in a fall in labor and an increase in the real wage. Foreign debt initially increases with the fall in the trade balance (imports increase with the increase in production but exports remain fixed). In this case the interest rate falls with the fall in price, and with the domestic rate less than the foreign interest rate (a fall in interest differential), the exchange rate first depreciates and then appreciates back to the steady-state value.

No Taylor Rule Figure 2.3 also shows the impulse responses for the case where the monetary authority did not adopt a Taylor rule (dashed lines). As shown since the domestic rate is now fixed to the foreign rate, the interest differential between these two rates is zero. However, international financiers in this model are sensitive to the size of the domestic debt F^* and the risk premium accordingly increase with the increase in foreign debt. To induce capital inflows, the exchange rate has to appreciate. Note too the magnitude and the speed of convergence of price to its steady-state value. Relative to the case with interest rate "stickiness," the price without an active monetary policy falls by more and reverts faster to its steady state.

Figure 2.3 includes an important point about monetary neutrality. Comparing the response of the real variables under the Taylor rule with those under a fixed interest rate rule, we see almost identical paths for consumption, output, labor, and the real wage. In a flexible price world, the behavior of real variables is unaffected by the conduct of monetary policy.

2.4.2 Recurring Shocks

Following the impulse-response analysis, we now conduct dynamic simulations with recurring shocks. The aim here is to examine the behavior of the variables for the case where the productivity index follows an autoregressive stochastic process. The time paths of these simulations may then be examined for static or dynamic cross-correlations as well as overall variability. Obviously the choice of statistics we compute and evaluate from these artificial data depends on the particular reasons for doing the simulation in the first place. As Anthony A. Smith Jr. (2004) of Yale University reminds us in his tips for computational work in economics, the goal of computational research is insight (see the Web page cited in the bibliography of this book).

Figure 2.4 shows the evolution of the exogenous productivity index as well as consumption, output, price, foreign debt, and the exchange rate for one realization of the stochastic process in the Taylor rule framework. Note that all variables are well behaved in that they display mean-reverting behavior. We also note that the price level, due to the assumption of full flexibility in price-setting behavior, is much more volatile than the exchange rate. Clearly, this behavior does not

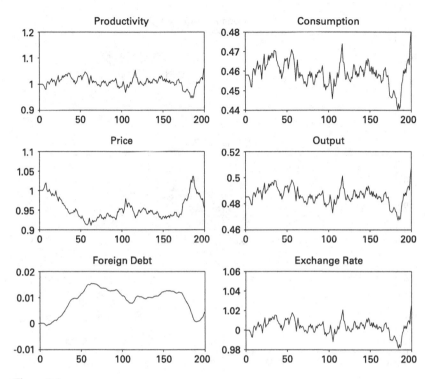

Figure 2.4
Simulated time series

match the relatively sluggish real world behavior of goods prices relative to asset prices. The issue of sticky prices will be considered in chapter 3.

After this initial simulation, it is useful to perform additional simulations, for different draws of the random shocks driving the model to check for robustness. This would also allow us to generate distributions for key summary statistics of the model. For example, key properties of the model can be assessed by examining the autocorrelations and correlations among key variables. We will first examine the time-series property for consumption, the exchange rate and price based on 500 simulations of productivity shocks and where each simulation contains a run of 200 observations.

Figure 2.5 shows the distributions of the autocorrelation coefficients with the raw "artificial" data.[8] All the autocorrelation correlations are high and close to unity indicating high persistence, which is a feature of real world data.[9]

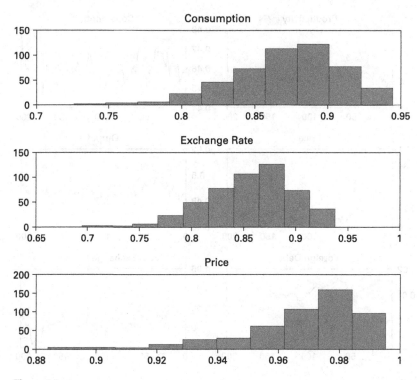

Figure 2.5
First-order autocorrelations

Figure 2.6 shows some more properties of the model as revealed by the distributions of key economic correlations among the variables. The top panel shows that productivity Z and output Y are strongly positively correlated, as expected, when there is a supply shock. The results shows that productivity Z and employment L are negatively related, which is in line with Galí (2004) who found a decline in hours worked following a technology shock. In contrast, Christiano, Eichenbaum, and Vigfusson (2003) found that a positive technology shock drives hours worked up, which is more in line with a central tenet of the real business-cycle literature, namely the comovement of technology shocks and output and labor. We note, however, that the model in this chapter is different from the standard real business-cycle model in that there is no capital accumulation and that it is moreover an open economy model. We will see whether the positive correlations between productivity and the exchange rate and the negative correlations be-

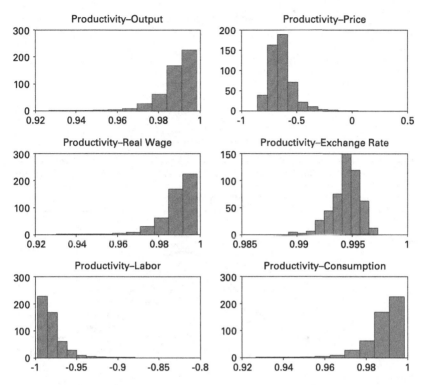

Figure 2.6
Correlations among key economic variables

tween productivity and price hold as we add more frictions to this basic model.

2.4.3 Welfare Distributions

Although the flexible price model is clearly unrealistic for replicating key features of real world data, it serves one important purpose for economic policy evaluation. The welfare distributions (across 500 different realizations of the productivity shocks), obtained under the flexible price and full market-clearing conditions, represent the benchmark or reference distributions for policy analysis. We use these distributions to assess the effectiveness of monetary policy under the distorted conditions of sticky prices, conditional on the same distribution of underlying productivity shocks. The rationale is that the best that the economy can achieve, in terms of welfare, comes under fully flexible prices and perfect market-clearing conditions. Once we introduce price

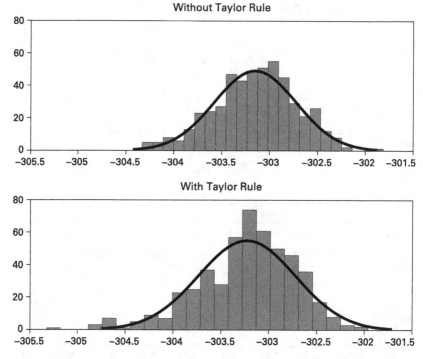

Figure 2.7
Distribution of the welfare index

stickiness, we reduce welfare. The aim of optimal monetary policy, and other forms of government intervention, then, is to bring the welfare distributions of the economy operating under the distortions of price stickiness as close as possible to the welfare distributions under perfect price flexibility.

Figure 2.7 shows the welfare measure of the representative household over a given time horizon for a variety of possible outcomes or realizations of the stochastic processes. To be sure, the numbers in the figure do not have any particular meaning. By way of comparison, the figure also includes the welfare distribution for the case with a Taylor rule—the shocks are identical to the case without active monetary policy. As can be seen, there are more outcomes on the lower end of welfare. In later chapters we will examine how alternative forms of price stickiness and other distortions cause further deviations of welfare from the benchmark case.

2.5 Effects of a Demand Shock

Until now we have only examined the dynamic effects of an exogenous change in productivity. Since Kydland and Prescott (1982), productivity or technology changes have been extensively examined as the major source of business cycles, at least in industrialized or developed countries. So it is natural to use productivity changes as the exogenous variable for our first series of computational experiments or simulation studies with our model. But of course, countries are subject to (or vulnerable to) a wide variety of exogenous factors. In this section we examine the effects of one alternative factor—exogenous changes in foreign demand for the export goods of the domestic country. We use the same model, only this time, a demand factor, rather than a supply factor, is the key variable forcing the dynamic response of the economy. This is a natural juxtaposition, since we can readily compare the effects of demand with supply impulses, and check to see, in this simple framework, if they agree with widely shared intuition about how the macroeconomic variables should respond to underlying changes in demand as well as supply.

Of course, in the real world both factors help to drive the evolution of the economy. We do not enter into any discussion of the relative importance of supply versus demand factors as determinants of fluctuations in real or financial-sector variables. We just want to see how differently the model responds, through the way the decision rules are formed, when demand factors rather than supply factors drive the economy.

2.5.1 Scenario: Export Shock

For the sake of simplicity, we assume that the foreign demand of exports X_t is mean-reverting to its steady-state value $\overline{X}$. Like productivity, the stochastic process for X_t follows a stochastic log-linear autoregressive process, with the disturbance term ε_t assumed to be normally distributed with mean zero and variance σ_x^2:

$$\ln(X_t) = \rho \ln(X_t) + (1 - \rho) \ln(\overline{X}) + \varepsilon_t, \qquad \varepsilon_t \sim N(0, \sigma_x^2).$$

Similar to the evolution of the productivity index, we set $\rho = 0.9$, with standard deviation $\sigma_x = 0.01$. During these experiments we suppress changes in the productivity index so that $Z_t = 1$ $\forall t$. Note that the demand variable affects production directly through the identity $Y = C + G + X$. It also affects the economy through the current account, the accumulation or decummulation of foreign assets and its subsequent effects on the risk premium demanded by foreign investors.

The approximation functions (or decision rules ψ^c, ψ^s) for the forward-looking variables (consumption C_t and the exchange rate S_t) are as above, except for the state variables x_t known at time t:

$$\hat{C}_t = \psi^c(\Omega^c; x_t),$$

$$\hat{S}_t = \psi^s(\Omega^s; x_t),$$

$$x_t = \{(X_t - \overline{X}), (F_{t-1}^* - \overline{F^*}), (R_{t-1} - \overline{R})\}.$$

The Judd-Gaspar Euler equation error statistics are quite small—about a fraction of a penny per unit of expenditure. The accuracy of the function is also confirmed by the CDF of the DM statistics for 500 realizations, with $T = 200$, for the case with one lag for the instrument set. The percentage rejections at the tails are all under the 5 percent levels for lags of order one to four.

2.5.2 Stochastic Dynamic Simulations

Impulse-Response Analysis As in the case of a productivity shock, we start from steady-state values and then shock the demand for export by one standard deviation for one period only. Of course, we can specify σ_x at arbitrarily large or small values, to see if there are different dynamic responses to the magnitude of the exogenous change. Since we would like to compare supply and demand effects, we set σ_x to 0.1 for both scenarios.

Figure 2.8 shows the effects of these two shocks on consumption. Note that while a productivity (supply) shock causes an increase in consumption, an export (demand) shock has negligible effect on consumption. The effect on labor and real wage are also relatively small. As expected, the demand shock causes an increase in price and the interest rate rises to forestall the inflationary effects of the increase in demand. The interest differential encourages capital inflows while the positive export shock improves the trade balance. The overall adjustment of the exchange rate is a real appreciation. As expected, the debt

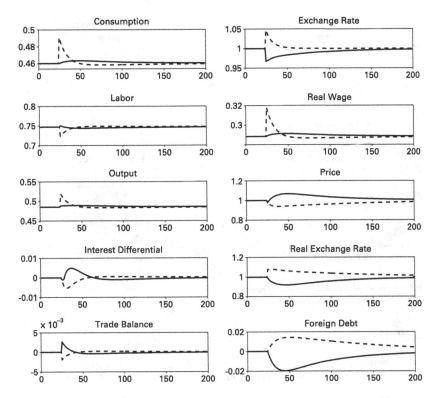

Figure 2.8
Impulse response functions: comparing demand (*solid line*) and supply shocks (*dashed line*)

response is negative, since the foreign demand shocks led to an increase in foreign assets. These results contrast with the effects of the productivity shock, which led to an increase in debt.

Macroeconomic Correlations The correlations between prices and outputs and between the shocks and employment appear in Figure 2.9. We note that the correlations between output Y and price P when the economy is subjected to productivity (supply) shocks is negative, but it becomes positive when the economy is subjected to export (demand) shocks. This result illustrates the fact that in a supply–demand framework, shifts to the supply curve trace out the negative relationship between price and quantity, whereas shifts to the demand curve trace out the positive relationship between price and quantity. In our

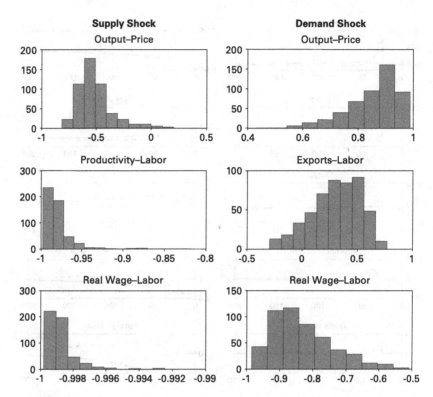

Figure 2.9
Correlations

flexible price version of the model, the computational results are delivering precisely what we should expect on theoretical grounds.

As shown earlier, the correlations between productivity shocks and employment are negative while the correlations between export shocks and employment are positive. Interestingly, while the correlation between real wage and labor is negative for both supply and demand shocks, the dispersion of correlations is wider under the demand scenario. This result conforms intuitively with our understanding that whereas an improvement in productivity has an immediate and direct effect on output (and hence labor), an improvement in export demand has an effect on output (and hence labor) via changes in price.

In this section we examined the dynamic effects of an exogenous change in foreign demand rather than in domestic productivity. Obviously an economy is subject to a variety of ever-changing exogenous factors, beyond domestic productivity and foreign demand. We studied the effects of each of these in isolation to show how the model performs, based on computational criteria, as well as to see if our theoretical intuitions are confirmed.

2.6 Concluding Remarks

In summary, this chapter shows how to check the accuracy of a model as well as how to apply the model once we have obtained the decision rules for C and S. Of course, the model used in this chapter is extremely simple and is not meant to replicate key properties of any economy, particularly with respect to persistence in pricing behavior. However, the use of impulse-response analysis as well as stochastic simulations enables us to validate our intuition about how flexible-price economies should behave in response to ongoing changes in productivity. The simulations and scenario analysis also yield insights about dynamic macroeconomics in a small open economy setting.

To replicate more interesting issues observed in actual economies, we have to make the model more complex, which of course, means more variables and parameters to estimate in order to obtain the decision rules. But the simplest model is not necessarily the least important. As we discussed above, the welfare distribution generated by this model (for the case with no Taylor rule) is, under special circumstances, a benchmark by which we can assess the optimality of proposed policy rules.

Computational Exercise: Stochastic Processes

The results of this chapter were based on random normal shocks to productivity or to export demand. As mentioned in the previous chapter, Fernandez-Villaverde (2005) and Justiniano and Primiceri (2006) have noted that there is no reason for a stochastic dynamic general equilibrium model not to have a richer structure than normal innovations. Specifically, they note that fat tails and volatility clustering are pervasive features of observed macroeconomic data.

Figure 2.10 shows the simulated paths of alternative shock processes. As can be seen, compared to the standard normal case, more extreme observations are generated under a t-distribution, and more clustering of observations are generated under a ARCH/GARCH schema. How would the time path of the productivity index Z be

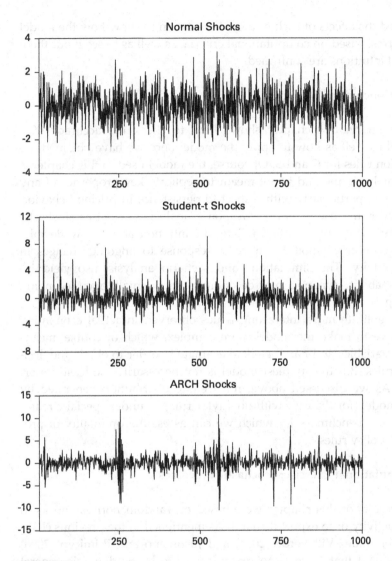

Figure 2.10
Alternative shock processes

affected if we change the innovation generating process for ε_t from a standard normal to a t-distribution to a ARCH/GARCH process?

It is easy to incorporate these types of shocks into the model. An obvious robustness check of the results of this chapter is to redo the estimation of the decision rules, and evaluate the impulse-response functions, the dynamic simulations, and the accuracy checks when the fundamental shocks come from distributions with fat tails or with ARCH/GARCH processes. It should be noted, that the productivity index Z is the appropriate state variable, and it follows an autoregressive process with a large persistence parameter. Hence the effects of alternative types of innovations may be somewhat muted.

3   Sticky Domestic Prices

3.1 Introduction

This chapter extends the model of chapter 2 by introducing sticky price setting in the domestic-goods producing sector. The model so far is unrealistic, and it cannot serve as a tool for replicating key stylized facts, such as the persistence in goods prices. However, we spent time with the flexible price model for one important reason: its welfare distribution represents a benchmark to compare, under certain conditions, the welfare distributions generated by models with distortions due to different forms of stickiness.

There are, of course, many ways to specify stickiness in price setting. Prior to the rational expectations revolution of the 1970s, expectations of future inflation (which in turn generated wage changes) were backward-looking, usually following an error-correction process in which the change in expected inflation was a fraction of the difference between last period's expected inflation and actual inflation. The fractional error-correction factor was a pre-specified coefficient, so that expectations could be modelled as adjusting quickly or slowly to past forecast errors.

The backward-looking error-correction approach was challenged on a number of grounds. First, it is a pure backward-looking approach, in the sense that we only learn from past errors—we do not exploit information available in the full structure of the model at the time we form expectations. Second, because the fractional error-correction coefficient is a pre-specified constant, the designer of the model is given a "free parameter." A modeler can thus produce almost any type of desired dynamics, depending on the specification of the value of this coefficient, since there are no restrictions or a priori constraints on the value of this parameter. The rational expectations critique to having such free parameters in a model is that a model that is capable of explaining almost any type of dynamics really explains no type of dynamics at all. More to the point, the mantra against such backward-looking approaches soon became "beware of economists bearing free parameters."

A strong implication of the pure backward-looking models, of course, is that there is a role for activism or discretion in stabilization policy. In particular the presence of short-run nominal rigidities allow changes in nominal monetary policy variables, such as the interest rate or the money supply, to have temporary real effects. The rational expectations revolution challenged this policy view. In the ensuing rules versus discretion debate, the rational expectations revolution called for a return to rules for monetary policy; that is, monetary policy, at best, should only target inflation, and overall, it eschewed policy activism.

The new neoclassical synthesis models, or new Keynesian open economy models, represent a response to the rational expectations revolution. In this latest paradigm, economic agents are modeled as forward-looking, and information is gleaned from the structure of the macroeconomy. However, this approach also contends that agents can be backward-looking, meaning there is inertia in price setting (and wage setting) due to institutional constraints such as overlapping contracts. The new Keynesian macroeconomics thus synthesizes the forward-looking role inherent in rational expectations models with backward-looking inertia effects in price setting behavior. Not surprisingly, this approach allows greater scope for monetary policy beyond pure inflation targeting, and the focus of much of the research in this framework is on the "optimal degree" of discretion for monetary policy.

Of course, there is empirical debate about the degree of backward-looking behavior in actual price-setting behavior and about how well this assumption helps us to replicate key stylized facts. For example, Chari, Kehoe, and McGrattan (2000) contend that monetary shocks interacting with sticky prices generate real exchange rate behavior that is volatile and persistent, but not as persistent as in the data. However, there is no question that staggered or sticky price setting is the default model for discussions of both closed and open-economy monetary policy (e.g., see Woodford 2003; Benigno and Woodford 2004; Galí and Monacelli 2005). Embedding sticky price-setting behavior in the domestic-goods sector is the task of this chapter.

In section 3.2, we lay out the modifications of the model and note that associated with the sticky price mechanism is the price dispersion index, which represents the resource costs of sticky prices. This section extends the consideration of decision rules for consumption and the exchange rate to the consideration of decision rules for expected domestic prices. In section 3.3, we examine the impulse response paths of key variables under this form of price stickiness and compare these paths with those generated under full price flexibility. We also examine the adjustment of key variables in full stochastic simulations and compare the welfare distributions under price stickiness with the corresponding distributions under flexible prices. The scenario considered in this chapter deals with the case where the Taylor rule includes a measure of the output gap. Welfare distributions for the case of Taylor rules with and without the output gap are compared.

3.2 Model with Calvo Pricing

In this section we add to the simple small open economy described in chapter 2, as well as to the household and foreign sectors following optimizing behavior and the monetary authority setting the interest rate using a Taylor rule. We now allow the firms to adopt Calvo-style price-setting behavior.

3.2.1 Households—Consumption and Labor
The Euler equations for this sector are, as in chapter 2,

$$C_t^{-\eta} = \Lambda_t P_t, \tag{3.1}$$

$$L_t^{\varpi} = \Lambda_t W_t, \tag{3.2}$$

$$P_t^f = P_t^k, \tag{3.3}$$

$$\Lambda_t = \Lambda_{t+1}\beta(1 + R_t), \tag{3.4}$$

$$\Lambda_t S_t = \Lambda_{t+1}\beta(1 + R_t^* + \Phi_t + \Phi_t' F_t^*)S_{t+1}. \tag{3.5}$$

Note, again, that the interest on international asset R_t^* is augmented with a risk premium term Φ_t, which has the symmetric functional form

$$\Phi_t = \text{sign}(F_{t-1}^*) \cdot \varphi[e^{(|F_{t-1}^*|-\overline{F^*})} - 1], \tag{3.6}$$

where $\overline{F}^*$ represents the steady-state value of the international asset. All capital is imported as investment goods,

$$K_t = I_t, \tag{3.7}$$

and the price of the imports P_t^f is still

$$P_t^f = P_t^* S_t \tag{3.8}$$

3.2.2 Production and Calvo Pricing

As in chapter 2, each firm j produces differentiated goods using a constant elasticity of substitution production function, and the aggregate product Y is demanded by households C, by the government sector G, and by foreigners (exports) X. The aggregate equations are

$$Y_t = Z_t[(1 - \alpha_1)(L_t)^{\kappa_1} + \alpha_1(K_t)^{\kappa_1}]^{1/\kappa_1} \tag{3.9}$$

$$\ln(Z_t) = \rho \ln(Z_{t-1}) + (1 - \rho) \ln(\overline{Z}) + \epsilon_t, \qquad \epsilon_t \sim N(0, \sigma_z^2), \tag{3.10}$$

$$Y_t = C_t + G_t + X_t \tag{3.11}$$

However, unlike the firms in chapter 2, we now assume that firms set prices according to the Calvo (1983) staggered pricing system. Each firm chooses the optimal price $P_{j,t}^a$ by maximizing the expected discounted profits

$$E_t \sum_{i=0}^{\infty} \xi^i \beta^i ((1 + \varkappa) P_{j,t}^a Y_{j,t+i} - A_{t+i} Y_{j,t}) = 0$$

subject to the demand for its product, where A represents the marginal cost that is identical across firms:

$$Y_{j,t} = \left(\frac{P_{j,t}^a}{P_t}\right)^{-\zeta} Y_t.$$

Each firm is given a subsidy $\varkappa$ whose value is determined to eliminate the effect of a price markup[1]

$$E_t \sum_{i=0}^{\infty} \xi^i \beta^i \left((1 + \varkappa) P_{j,t}^a \left(\frac{P_{j,t}^a}{P_{t+i}}\right)^{-\zeta} - A_{t+i} \left(\frac{P_{j,t}^a}{P_{t+i}}\right)^{-\zeta} \right) Y_{t+i}.$$

Taking derivatives yields the optimal price as

$$P_{j,t}^a = \left(\frac{\zeta}{\zeta-1}\right)\frac{1}{(1+\varkappa)}\frac{E_t\sum_{l=0}^{\infty}\xi^l\beta^l(A_{t+l}(P_{t+l})^{\zeta})Y_{t+l}}{E_t\sum_{l=0}^{\infty}\xi^l\beta^l((P_{t+l})^{\zeta})Y_{t+l}},$$

$$P_{j,t}^a = \frac{Y_{j,t}(P_t)^{\zeta}A_{j,t}+\sum_{l=1}^{\infty}\xi^l\beta^lY_{j,t+j}A_{j,t+j}(P_{t+l})^{\zeta}}{Y_{j,t}(P_t)^{\zeta}+\sum_{l=1}^{\infty}\xi^l\beta^lY_{j,t+l}(P_{t+l})^{\zeta}}.$$

The optimal price is chosen before the realization of the shock at time t, and only a fraction $(1-\xi)$ can set the prices optimally. Note that the optimal markup factor ψ is equal to $[\zeta/(\zeta-1)]$, the so-called markup distortion created by monopolistic competition, and this leads firms to produce too little. We assume the subsidy $\varkappa$ is chosen to eliminate the effect of the markup.[2] For simplicity too, the likelihood that any price will be changed in a given period is $(1-\xi)$ and it is independent of the length of time since the price was set and the level of the current price. As Woodford (2003) notes, while these assumptions are unrealistic, they drastically simplify equilibrium inflation dynamics as well as reduce the state space required to solve for the dynamics (Woodford 2003, p. 177).[3]

The numerator and the denominator of the optimal price have current and forward-looking variables. Rather than work with infinite forward sums, following Schmidt-Grohé and Uribe (2004), we retain the nonlinear structure of the optimal pricing system by using a recursive framework with two auxiliary variables A_t^{p1} and A_t^{p2}, in the following way:

$$A_t^{p1} = Y_t(P_t)^{\zeta}A_t + \beta\xi A_{t+1}^{p1}, \tag{3.12}$$

$$A_t^{p2} = Y_t(P_t)^{\zeta} + \beta\xi A_{t+1}^{p2}, \tag{3.13}$$

$$P_t^a = \frac{A_t^{p1}}{A_t^{p2}}. \tag{3.14}$$

This simplification allows us to write the Calvo pricing equation in a form similar to the Euler equations, which we then exploit in the computational section. Note that when all firms set their prices optimally $(\xi = 0)$, the optimal price collapses to the flexible price noted in chapter 2, namely that the price is then equal to marginal cost. The term A_t is the marginal cost and is defined below:

$$A_t = \left\{ \begin{array}{c} (\frac{1}{Z})[(1-\alpha)(\alpha W)^{\kappa/(\kappa-1)} + \alpha((1-\alpha)P^k)^{\kappa/(\kappa-1)}]^{-1/\kappa} \\ \times [W(\alpha W)^{1/(\kappa-1)} + P^k((1-\alpha)P^k)^{1/(\kappa-1)}] \end{array} \right\}. \tag{3.15}$$

The aggregate price index is given by the following Dixit-Stiglitz aggregator:

$$P_t = [\xi(P_{t-1})^{1-\zeta} + (1-\xi)(P_t^a)^{1-\zeta}]^{1/(1-\zeta)}. \tag{3.16}$$

Overall, the major implication of price stickiness is that it creates distortion, and hence it generates real resource allocation costs leading to a reduction in production (and hence demand for labor services). Briefly, the real resource cost of relative price dispersion—the greater the dispersion of price in the economy, the lower is the level of consumption for a given level of aggregate output and export demand. Alternatively, to maintain consumption at a particular level (for a given export demand), the greater the dispersion, the greater is the demand for labor and intermediate goods, which in turn implies increases in disutility (reduction in welfare) and increases in the current account (and foreign debt).[4]

3.2.3 Government Sector

Monetary Policy As in chapter 2 we assume that the central bank follows a very simple Taylor (1993) rule aimed solely at inflation stabilization:

$$R_t = \phi_2 R_{t-1} + (1-\phi_2)[R^* + \phi_1(\pi_t - \tilde{\pi})], \qquad \phi_1 > 1, \tag{3.17}$$

$$\pi_t = \left(\frac{P_t}{P_{t-1}}\right)^4 - 1,$$

where ϕ_2 is the smoothing parameter and ϕ_1 measures the influence of the inflation gap in monetary policy. In passing, we note a point made by Laxton and Pesenti (2003) who remarked on how the impossible trinity of fixed exchange rates, full capital mobility, and independent monetary policy has now yielded center stage to a new trinity, which Taylor (2000) calls flexible and desirable: the trinity of flexible exchange rates, inflation targeting, and a monetary policy rule. Our analysis is set in the world of this new trinity.

Taxes and Domestic Debt Government spending G is assumed to be fixed at zero:

$$G_t = \bar{G}. \tag{3.18}$$

The Treasury/central bank receives lump-sum taxes, and the evolution of the bonds is

$$B_t = (1 + R_{t-1})B_{t-1} + P_t G_t - Tax_t, \tag{3.19}$$

where B is a one-period domestic bond. As in chapter 2, taxes adjust each period to fully repay any government debt from the previous period: $R_{t-1}B_{t-1} = Tax_t$. So debt remains constant.

3.2.4 Exports and Foreign Debt
Exports are exogenously determined in this chapter:

$$X_t = \bar{X}. \tag{3.20}$$

Given the exports X_t and the imports of intermediate goods K_t, the evolution of the foreign debt is as follows:

$$S_t F_t^* = (1 + R_{t-1}^* + \Phi_{t-1})S_t F_{t-1}^* + (S_t P_t^* I_t - P_t X_t). \tag{3.21}$$

3.3 Computational Analysis

3.3.1 Approximating Functions
We have four decision rules, one for consumption C, one for the exchange rate S, and two for the price (one for the numerator A^{p1}, and one for the denominator A^{p2}):

$$\hat{C}_t = \psi^c(\Omega^c; \mathbf{x}_t),$$

$$\hat{S}_t = \psi^s(\Omega^s; \mathbf{x}_t),$$

$$\hat{A}_t^{p1} = \psi^{p1}(\Omega^{p1}; \mathbf{x}_t),$$

$$\hat{A}_t^{p2} = \psi^{p2}(\Omega^{p2}; \mathbf{x}_t),$$

$$\mathbf{x}_t = \{(Z_t - \bar{Z}), (F_{t-1} - \bar{F}), (R_{t-1} - \bar{R})\}.$$

The state variables are the productivity, foreign debt, and interest rate. The approximating functions ψ^c, ψ^s, ψ^{p1}, and ψ^{p2} are again neural network functions.

3.3.2 Euler Errors

Overall, we seek to determine decision rules for consumption C_t, the exchange rate S_t, as well as for the numerator and denominator of the forward-looking Calvo price P_t. The errors we minimize are the three intertemporal Euler equation errors, given below:

$$\epsilon_t^c = \frac{\hat{C}_t^{-\eta}}{\hat{P}_t}\left[\frac{1}{(1+R_t)}\right] - \beta\left[\frac{\hat{C}_{t+1}^{-\eta}}{\hat{P}_{t+1}}\right],$$

$$\epsilon_t^s = \frac{\hat{C}_t^{-\eta}}{P_t}\left[\frac{\hat{S}_t}{(1+R_t^*+\Phi_t+\Phi_t'F_t^*)}\right] - \beta\left[\hat{S}_{t+1}\frac{\hat{C}_{t+1}^{-\eta}}{P_{t+1}}\right],$$

$$\epsilon_t^P = \frac{\hat{A}_t^{p1}}{\hat{A}_t^{p2}} - \frac{Y_t(P_t)^\zeta A_t + \beta\xi\hat{A}_{t+1}^{p1}}{Y_t(P_t)^\zeta + \beta\xi\hat{A}_{t+1}^{p2}}.$$

Under a Monte Carlo approach we make an initial guess of the parameter vector of the parameter values, draw a large sequence of shocks, and then generate time series for the endogenous variables of the model. We then iterate on the parameter set to minimize a loss function based on the sum (or weighted sum) of squared Euler equation errors. We continue to iterate until the Euler equation errors are minimized and the results satisfy the accuracy tests.

3.3.3 Accuracy Checks

The accuracy test are based on a very large number of shocks, 500 runs with sample run of $T = 200$. Table 3.1 and figure 3.1 present the Judd-Gaspar statistics, which are shown as distributions of the means of the absolute values of the Euler equation errors, divided by the respective forward-looking variables. These statistics represent the cost of the Euler equation errors in terms of a unit of expenditure. We see that the distribution of these errors are centered around mean values of almost zero, or less than a penny per dollar of expenditure for the case of consumption.

The Den Haan-Marcet test results are presented in table 3.2 for various order of lags and the plot of the CDF of the test is shown in figure 3.2.

Table 3.1
Judd-Gaspar statistic ($\times 10^{-2}$)

	$\dfrac{|\epsilon_t^c|}{C_t}$	$\dfrac{|\epsilon_t^s|}{S_t}$	$\dfrac{|\epsilon_t^p|}{P_t}$
Mean	0.2344	0.7619	0.0168
Standard deviation	0.0133	0.0439	0.0027

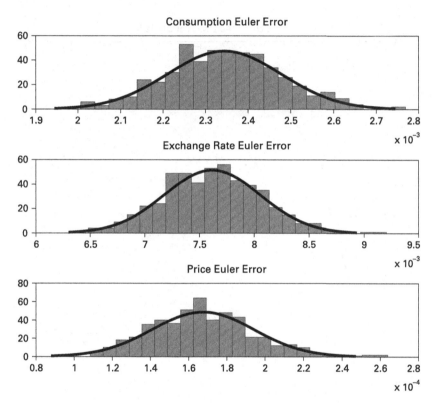

Figure 3.1
Judd-Gaspar statistics

Table 3.2
DenHann-Marcet test

	Lag order			
	1	2	3	4
Lower region ($p < 0.05$)	0.042	0.048	0.058	0.054
Upper region ($p > 0.95$)	0.046	0.038	0.050	0.054

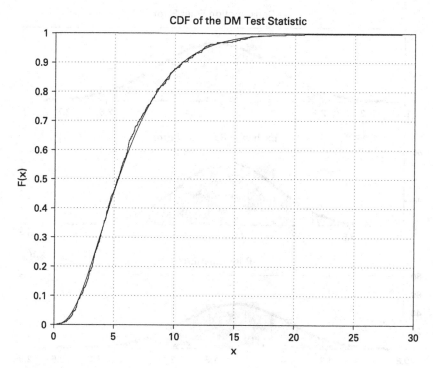

Figure 3.2
DenHann-Marcet test of accuracy

Again, these tests indicate that we have little or no reason to doubt the accuracy of our numerical approximations.

3.4 Stochastic Simulations

3.4.1 Impulse-Response Analysis
This section compares the impulse-responses for the sticky price case against the benchmark flexible price scenario for an economy subjected

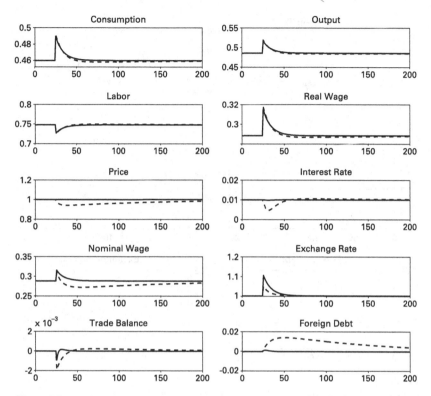

Figure 3.3
Impulse responses following a productivity shock: with (*solid line*) and without (*dashed line*) sticky prices

to a one-off positive shock to productivity. For the flexible price case, we assumed that all firms price optimally and hence that $\xi = 0$; for the sticky price case, we set $\xi = 0.85$. Note that we have eliminated the steady-state effects of the markup by introducing subsidies.

Figure 3.3 shows the impulse functions for the real variables (consumption C, output Y, labor services L, and real wage W/P) and some nominal variables (prices P, interest rate R, exchange rate S, and the nominal wage W) for the two cases of flexible and sticky prices. We see small dynamic differences with the real variables: the adjustment paths for consumption, output, labor and the real wage are slower relative to the flexible price case. However, the behavior of the nominal variables in a sticky price setting are very different from their behavior under flexible prices. Prices are hardly affected by the shock in the sticky price case, which implies, according to the Taylor rule, hardly

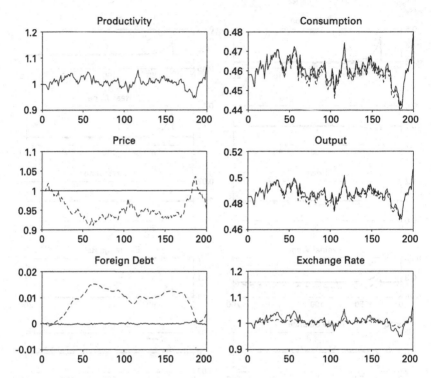

Figure 3.4
Simulated time series under sticky prices (*solid line*) and flexible prices (*dashed line*)

any change to the nominal interest rate. Adjustments in the economy work through income rather than price effects. Compared to the flexible price economy, the nominal wage rate increases by more to ensure that households have sufficient income to demand the increased output.

The deterioration in the trade balance comes from the increase in the value of imports associated with an exchange-rate depreciation. When prices are sticky, the foreign debt worsens only slightly because the value of exports is relatively stable.

3.4.2 Macroeconomic Correlations

Figure 3.4 shows the time series for key economic variables for the same single simulated run of 200 observations of the productivity index considered in chapter 2. The main point to note is that the volatility of the exchange rate is greater under sticky prices.

Figure 3.5 shows some macroeconomic correlations under sticky prices. Compared to the flexible price case, the high positive correla-

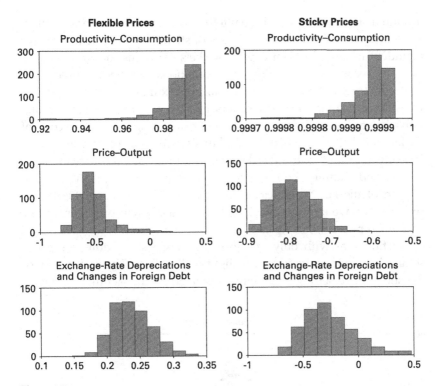

Figure 3.5
Macroeconomic correlations

tions between productivity and consumption are unchanged, while the negative correlations between prices and outputs vary over a smaller range. However, the correlations between changes in the exchange rate (depreciations) and changes in foreign debt are reversed. When prices are flexible, adjustments to clear the product market operate through prices; when prices are sticky, adjustments to clear the product market mainly operate through adjustments in quantity demanded. In this latter case the exchange rate has to depreciate significantly to induce a decrease in imports (recall exports are fixed in this scenario) to stabilize the current account. Hence with recurring shocks, on balance, the foreign debt falls.

3.4.3 Welfare Analysis
Many studies analyzing the welfare costs of price stickiness use a closed economy framework, and the results of such models come from first- or second-order Taylor approximations of the Euler equations,

around a steady state. In this chapter we use an open economy setting, since households can offset the losses of sticky prices by acquiring foreign debt in more efficient capital markets. Also, instead of relying on first- or second-order Taylor approximations, we have employed a projection method based on nonlinear approximations for the decision rules for consumers and price setters, and we use exact welfare calculations. We followed the usual custom of calculating the welfare costs of sticky price behavior when the markups are re-adjusted by compensating subsidies and taxes. We thus set aside the long-term steady state effects, and examine how sticky price behavior changes the laws of motion of the key variables of interest for policy making. Figure 3.6 presents the welfare distributions for the case when prices are sticky and when prices are flexible.

We find that with only one form of stickiness, in domestic price-setting behavior, there is only a slight welfare loss. The inefficiency of the sticky price-setting behavior is mitigated by the fact that the repre-

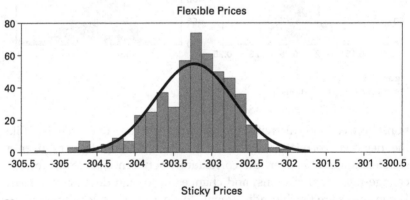

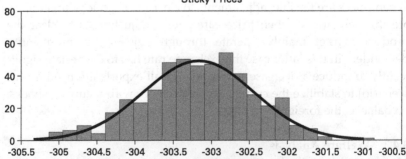

Figure 3.6
Welfare comparisons: sticky and flexible prices

sentative household can offset a great deal of the welfare losses due to sticky prices, through acquiring foreign assets in efficiently functioning international capital markets. The household can thus afford to work less, and take more leisure, in order to compensate for the welfare losses in reduced consumption, coming from the distortions of the sticky price system.[5]

One well-known way to evaluate monetary policy is to compare the welfare of the sticky price economy to the welfare of a fully flexible price and wage economy; that is, the loss function of monetary policy is

$$\ell_t^w = \frac{V_0^s - V_0^{flex}}{V_0^{flex}}, \tag{3.22}$$

where V^{flex} is welfare under flexible prices and V^s is welfare under sticky prices. This loss function, of course, is measured in terms of a utility function. Following Schmitt-Grohé and Uribe (2004), the differences in the two welfare indexes may be re-expressed as the percentage of consumption that the household in the sticky price economy should be compensated in order to make the household indifferent between the sticky and flexible price economies. With our utility function we calculate this consumption compensation percentage as

$$\lambda\% = 100 \left[1 - \left(\frac{V_0^s - V_0^{flex}}{\tilde{C}^{flex}} + 1 \right)^{1/(1-\eta)} \right], \tag{3.23}$$

$$\tilde{C}^{flex} = \frac{1}{1-\eta} \mathrm{E}_0 \sum_{t=0}^{\infty} \beta^t (C_t^{flex})^{1-\eta}. \tag{3.24}$$

The term λ is the welfare compensation, expressed in consumption units, where a value of 0 indicates indifference between the two states. For this study, the overall loss (due to price stickiness) is less than one percentage point of consumption (0.0249 percent). Estimating the welfare costs of business cycles was addressed by Lucas (1993), who contends that such costs are relatively minor, about 0.05 percent or 0.0005, with the implication that further macroeconomic fine-tuning through activist stabilization policies should have a low priority both for policy makers and for academic researchers. Canzonieri, Cumby, and Diba (2004) have taken issue with this finding, and argue that the costs of business cycles, obtained from a new neoclassical synthesis (NNS) model with price and wage stickiness, range between 1 and 3 percent of consumption. They argue that stabilization based on output gap targets as well as on inflation targets may reduce these welfare losses. We take up this issue in the next section.

3.5 Output Gaps and Sensitivity Analysis

We have thus far only been concerned with backward-looking Taylor rules and with strict inflation targeting. To be sure, many central banks operate this way. For example, the Reserve Bank of New Zealand is bound by law to deliver inflation below a given target. If the bank fails to meet this target for a given time horizon, the governor is expected to resign.

However, there is a very rich literature that deals with rules that include the output gap. This is because central bankers can have little effect on short-term inflation as current prices and even prices for the next quarter or two may be pre-set. Hence the central bank has to look at indicators of demand pressure that will lead to future inflation over an annual or two-year horizon. For this reason the output gap has emerged as a useful target of monetary policy.

More to the point, if actual output is greater than potential output, the central bank should tighten monetary policy by raising interest rates because there is excess demand or medium to longer term inflationary pressure in the economy. Alternatively, even when there is some inflation, if the output gap is negative, the central bank should ease financial conditions by reducing interest rates because the economy is becoming slack and inflationary pressure is falling or negative.

3.5.1 Output Gap Environment

The output gap measure is an outgrowth of the earlier literature on the Phillips curve where inflation was considered to be a function of unemployment. Soon the relationship became one between inflation and the difference between unemployment and the natural rate of unemployment, after Milton Friedman's famous presidential address at the American Economic Association of 1967 (Friedman 1968). The natural rate of unemployment was simply defined as the rate of unemployment at which inflation did not accelerate. Policy makers turned to the output gap, the difference between actual and potential output, when they recognized the difficulties of measuring the right natural rate of unemployment in countries undergoing demographic changes and increasing participation by women in the workforce.

However, it is not obvious how we can readily measure potential output any more easily than we can measure the natural rate of unemployment. Many were caught off guard during the roaring 1990s in the latter part of the Clinton administration, when output growth was much higher than measures of potential output growth and when unemployment was far below commonly accepted measures of the natural rate of unemployment. Mis-reading either the output gap or the difference between the actual and natural rate of unemployment can have a serious downside. If potential output is perceived to be rising or the natural rate of unemployment perceived to be falling, there is the danger that the central bank will overreact and reduce demand when in fact there is no inflationary pressure. Much to his credit, Federal Reserve Chairman Alan Greenspan did not tighten monetary policy during the Clinton expansion.

Swanson (2005) poses the issue as a "signal extraction" problem for a policy maker. In the context of natural rate unemployment, rather than potential output, Swanson takes up the relationship between "diffuse-middle" priors and optimal policy. In his framework, policy makers are uncertain about the natural rate within the interval [4–6] percent, so they are unwilling to revise estimates of the true natural rate within this interval. As observed unemployment moves further away from their prior, they assign less weight to changes in the natural rate, and more weight to cyclical components of unemployment. As a result, Swanson argues, policy makers respond "very cautiously" for small surprises in the realized unemployment rate, between 4 and 6 percent, but respond "very aggressively at the margin as the surprise in unemployment becomes larger" (Swanson 2005, pp. 6–7). The main feature of this type of learning is "policy attenuation for small surprises followed by increasingly aggressive responses at the margin" (Swanson 2005, p. 7).[6]

The aim of this section is more modest. We simply show how to introduce the output gap into our Taylor rule as well as how to apply the projection method to a model with an output gap. We use a direct, specific measure of potential output, namely the level of output that prevails in the absence of sticky price distortions. Intuitively, the output gap is defined as the difference between the level of output in the distorted sticky price environment relative to the level of output that would prevail in a model of perfect wage and price flexibility. Thus the methodology incorporates the output series generated in chapter 2 (flexible prices) into this model with sticky prices.

Our analysis addresses a specific question. It is now well known that interest rates that respond not only to deviations of actual inflation from target but also to the output gap unambiguously improve welfare in closed economy settings with sticky price or wage-setting behavior (see Erceg, Henderson, and Levin 2000). But Razin (2005) has recently noted that as an economy becomes progressively more open to trade in goods and more integrated with world capital markets, the weight for the output gap term in the optimal interest rate rule gets smaller. Does this mean that the gains to welfare for our small open economy from adopting a Taylor rule with an output gap will be small?

3.5.2 Taylor Rule with an Output Gap

The Taylor rule with an output gap is

$$R_t = \phi_2 R_{t-1} + (1 - \phi_2)[R^* + \phi_1(\pi_t - \tilde{\pi}) + \phi_3(y_t - y_t^{flex})],$$

$$\phi_1 > 1, \ \phi_3 > 0, \tag{3.25}$$

where y_t is the log of output $\log(Y_t)$ and y_t^{flex} is the log of output under the flexible price case discussed in chapter 2. The model is re-estimated using this new Taylor rule with an output gap under exactly the same set of shocks as the model that yielded the y_t^{flex} series. We also checked that the Judd-Gaspar statistics and the Den Haan-Marcet test support the accuracy of our results.

Figure 3.7 shows the impulse responses for the case where the Taylor rule includes the output gap (solid line) and the case where it does not include the gap (dashed line). The main result is that the interest rate is more volatile because it has to adjust to another variable, the output gap. Monetary policy has a bigger job to do, so it reacts more often.

Figure 3.8 shows the distribution of welfare under the Taylor rule without an output gap (upper panel) and the distribution of welfare with ouput gap (lower panel). Using the formula above, we compute that there is a very small gain in consumption (0.0019 percent) when the monetary authority changes from a Taylor rule without the output gap to one with an output gap. Canzoneri, Cumby, and Diba (2004) contend that the welfare gain, measured in terms of consumption compensation needed to make the representative household indifferent be-

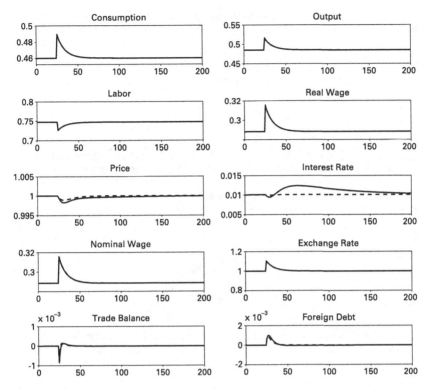

Figure 3.7
Impulse responses: inflation and output gap targeting (*solid line*) and inflation-only targeting (*dashed line*)

tween a sticky price and flexible price environments, is between 1 and 3 percent for most closed economy calibrations. For our open economy model, the welfare gain is even smaller.

3.6   Concluding Remarks

In summary, this chapter introduced price stickiness into the open economy model and showed how to apply the projection method to generate solution paths for the model. As well as exploring the effects of the sticky price mechanism on the dynamics of adjustment of the economy, we have asked the question: Should monetary policy target anything else besides inflation? In particular, we examined whether a Taylor rule that takes into account the deviation of actual inflation from its target as well as the differential between actual output and the

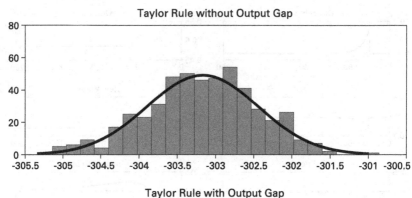

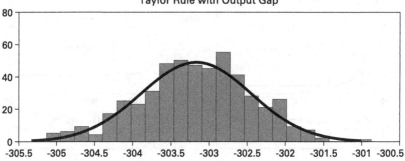

Figure 3.8
Welfare: Case of inflation and output gap targeting compared with case of only targeting inflation

output available under fully flexible prices is able to mitigate the dynamic losses due to the way sticky prices affect the adjustment of key variables. The results of our analysis show that the welfare costs of sticky prices in an open economy, relative to those of flexible prices, are rather small and that the gains from adopting a Taylor rule with an output gap are even smaller.

Computational Exercise: Output in the Taylor Rule

We remind the reader that the measure of output gap applied above is $(y_t - y_t^{flex})$, the difference between the logarithm of output in the sticky price model (y_t) less the logarithm of output in the flexible price model y_t^{flex}. In most operational environments we cannot determine the output in the nondistorted world. Consequently the output gap is often calculated with the help of the Hodrik-Prescott (1980) filter, known more generally as the HP filter.

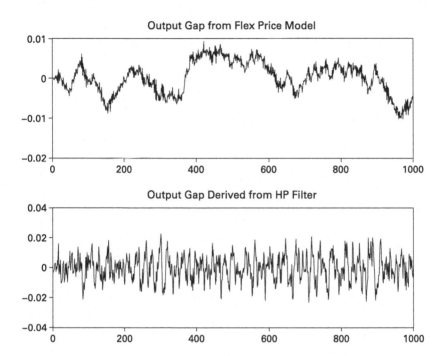

Figure 3.9
Alternative measures of output gap for one simulation

The output gap is now defined simply as $(y_t - y_t^{hp})$, the difference between the logarithm of the output series y_t less the smoothed output series y_t^{hp}. The following equation describes the filter:

$$Min_{y_t^{hp}} \left\{ \sum_{t=1}^{T}(y_t - y_t^{hp}) + \lambda^{hp} \sum_{t=2}^{T}[(y_{t+1}^{hp} - y_t^{hp}) - (y_t^{hp} - y_{t-1}^{hp})]^2 \right\}. \qquad (3.26)$$

The parameter λ^{hp} is the controlling parameter for the smoothness of the trend. It is usually set at 1,600 for quarterly data, at least for the United States and most industrial countries. This smoothing method is between detrending and first differencing of data. The advantage is that it is relatively easy to apply. The drawback is that it is a statistical device that defines cycles by the choice of the smoothing parameter λ^{hp}.7

Based on one realization of the model used in this chapter, figure 3.9 shows the output gap measured as $(y_t - y_t^{flex})$ and the HP-filtered series $(y_t - y_t^{hp})$. We see that the HP filter gap is much more volatile than the gap measured with respect to the flexible price model.

More recently researchers have explored the role of output growth (not output gap) in the Taylor rule. The reasoning is straightforward: the output gap is a difficult concept to measure and the HP-filtered output series could well be purely random variations. An interesting exercise would be to consider a Taylor rule that includes output growth rather than the output gap. What do you think would be the effect of using this revised Taylor rule on the distribution of welfare?

4 Income and Consumption Taxes

4.1 Introduction

This chapter examines alternative fiscal policy regimes in open economies, given an inflation-targeting monetary policy. In the previous chapters we assumed away fiscal deficits and tax rates. In this chapter we introduce fiscal imbalances, domestic government debt, and the further distortions of tax rates on income or consumption. We then examine the effect of alternative tax rules on welfare.

We have ignored fiscal policy so far, not because we do not think it is important for open economy macrodynamics. Nothing could be further from the truth. As Frenkel, Razin, and Yeun (1996) have pointed out, the globalization process has resulted in growing interest in fiscal policies in the integrated world economy. They cite Black Wednesday (standing for the European currency crisis of 1992), the problem of sustainability of current account deficits in the wake of the Mexican crisis of 1994, and the "new map" of Central and Eastern Europe as striking examples bringing fiscal policy to the center stage in macrodynamic models.

In this chapter the monetary rule is the same as in previous chapters: interest rates react to lagged interest rates as well as inflation. However, the addition of fiscal distortions in the model implies that we can no longer benchmark our welfare results with the case of the perfectly flexible price model since flexible prices are no longer the first-best solution. Instead we are in the world of second best. The aim of this chapter is to compare welfare under alternative income and consumption tax regimes, given an inflation targeting regime. In the next chapter we take up current account dynamics and its relation to fiscal balances.

Much of the recent work on monetary and fiscal policy interaction has been in the closed economy framework. For example, Benigno and Woodford (2004) take up targeting rules for the monetary authority and fiscal authority whereby inflation and output gap targets are set for the central bank while tax-smoothing targets are set for the fiscal authority.

Behnabib and Eusepi (2005) argue that in a world of distortionary taxation, monetary policy should respond to output as well as inflation in order to avoid multiple equilibria and costly equilibrium dynamics. On the other hand, Kollmann (2004) argues for monetary rules that just respond to inflation and for a tax rate on household income that responds to public debt. He finds that this monetary/fiscal configuration yields welfare results quite close to more elaborate rules.

Schmidt-Grohé and Uribe (2004) find that further emphasis on inflation by the monetary authority, beyond what is required for determinacy, makes little difference for welfare, while a muted monetary response to output, with passive fiscal rules, with constant tax rates, are best for welfare. Schmidt-Grohé and Uribe (2004) fully incorporate the distortionary steady-state effects of monopolistic competition in their analysis of monetary and fiscal rules.

Another study in the closed economy framework is by Hallet (2005) who examined the interaction of fiscal and monetary coordination with specific objectives for monetary and fiscal policy. He argued for coordinated monetary and fiscal policies, with soft debt targets for the fiscal authority and inflation targeting for the central bank. Under this arrangement, compared to uncoordinated approaches, inflation biases are lower and debt repayments higher, with no loss in output volatility.

As noted previously, Razin (2005) has argued that as economies become more open in trade and capital flows, the optimal monetary policy should put progressively more weight on inflation and less weight (or no weight) on output-gap targets. However, Razin eliminated the steady-state distortion of monopolistic competition by a system of taxes and subsidies, and he did not incorporate distortionary taxes and other forms of fiscal policy in his analysis. In this chapter we fix monetary policy, in order to let alternative fiscal regimes have center stage.

The next section extends the model to allow for alternative fiscal regimes. Section 4.3 derives the Euler equations for this model, and section 4.4 evaluates the impulse-response functions for alternative fiscal policy regimes. The final section compares welfare for alternative tax regimes. The application of the model to understand the interplay of government expenditures and tax regimes is illustrated in the final section.

4.2 Model with Taxes

The main change to the model is the introduction of taxes and endogenous government expenditure. We keep the tax system simple: taxes are levied on wage income and/or on consumption.

4.2.1 Household Euler Equations

The household intertemporal budget constraint is now amended to include tax payments

$$\begin{bmatrix} (1 - \tau_1)W_tL_t + \Pi_t + P_t^kK_t \\ + (1 + R_{t-1})B_{t-1} + S_tF_t \end{bmatrix} = \begin{bmatrix} (1 + \tau_2)P_tC_t + P_t^fI_t + B_t \\ + (1 + R_{t-1}^* + \Phi_t)S_tF_{t-1} \end{bmatrix},$$

where τ_1 is the income tax rate and τ_2 is the consumption tax rate. The Lagrangian problem becomes

$$\mathscr{L} = \sum_{i=0}^{\infty} \beta^i \left\{ U(C_{t+i}, L_{t+i}) - \Lambda_{t+i} \begin{bmatrix} (1 + \tau_2)P_{t+i}C_{t+i} + P_{t+i}^f K_{t+i} \\ + B_{t+i} + (1 + R_{t-1+i}^*)S_{t+i}F_{t-1+i} \\ - (1 - \tau_1)W_{t+i}L_{t+i} - \Pi_{t+i} \\ - P_{t+i}^kK_{t+i} - (1 + R_{t-1+i})B_{t-1+i} \\ - S_{t+i}F_{t+i} \end{bmatrix} \right\}.$$

The first-order conditions are

$$C_t^{-\eta} = \Lambda_t(1 + \tau_2)P_t, \tag{4.1}$$

$$L_t^{\varpi} = \Lambda_t(1 - \tau_1)W_t, \tag{4.2}$$

$$P_t^f = P_t^k, \tag{4.3}$$

$$\Lambda_t = \Lambda_{t+1}\beta(1 + R_t), \tag{4.4}$$

$$\Lambda_t S_t = \Lambda_{t+1}\beta(1 + R_t^* + \Phi_t + \Phi_t'F_t)S_{t+1}, \tag{4.5}$$

where the risk premium is

$$\Phi_t = \text{sign}(F_{t-1}) \cdot \varphi[e^{(|F_{t-1}|-\bar{F})} - 1]. \tag{4.6}$$

For completeness, the two equations describing the demand for imports and its price are

$$K_t = I_t, \tag{4.7}$$

$$P_t^f = P_t^* S_t. \tag{4.8}$$

4.2.2 Firms—Production and Calvo Pricing

The equations describing the behavior of each firm are the same as in chapter 3. The relevant aggregate equations are

$$Y_t = Z_t[(1 - \alpha_1)(L_t)^{\kappa_1} + \alpha_1(K_t)^{\kappa_1}]^{1/\kappa_1}, \tag{4.9}$$

$$\ln(Z_t) = \rho \ln(Z_{t-1}) + (1 - \rho) \ln(\bar{Z}) + \epsilon_t, \qquad \epsilon_t \sim N(0, \sigma_z^2), \tag{4.10}$$

$$Y_t = C_t + G_t + X_t; \tag{4.11}$$

$$A_t^{p1} = Y_t(P_t^d)^\zeta A_t + \beta \xi A_{t+1}^{p1}, \tag{4.12}$$

$$A_t^{p2} = Y_t(P_t^d)^\zeta + \beta \xi A_{t+1}^{p2}, \tag{4.13}$$

$$P_t^a = \frac{A_t^{p1}}{A_t^{p2}}; \tag{4.14}$$

$$A_t = \left\{ \begin{array}{c} (\frac{1}{Z})[(1 - \alpha)(\alpha W)^{\kappa/(\kappa-1)} + \alpha((1 - \alpha)P^k)^{\kappa/(\kappa-1)}]^{-1/\kappa} \\ \times [W(\alpha W)^{1/(\kappa-1)} + P^k((1 - \alpha)P^k)^{1/(\kappa-1)}] \end{array} \right\}, \tag{4.15}$$

$$P_t = [\xi(P_{t-1})^{1-\zeta} + (1 - \xi)(P_t^a)^{1-\zeta}]^{1/(1-\zeta)}. \tag{4.16}$$

4.2.3 Monetary Policy

As in earlier chapters we assume that the central bank follows a very simple Taylor (1993) rule aimed solely at inflation stabilization:

$$R_t = \phi_2 R_{t-1} + (1 - \phi_2)[R^* + \phi_1(\pi_t - \tilde{\pi})], \qquad \phi_1 > 1, \tag{4.17}$$

$$\pi_t = \left(\frac{P_t}{P_{t-1}}\right)^4 - 1.$$

Note that we have simplified the analysis by not considering an output gap in the rule. As mentioned above, since we are comparing monetary and fiscal rules for different distorted economies, it is not clear that the best measure of potential output is the output generated under a fully flexible pricing system.

4.2.4 Taxes and Domestic Debt

Government spending G is assumed to be sensitive to the size of the public debt, B relative to its steady-state value $\bar{B}$:

$$G_t = \bar{G} + \chi_1(B_{t-1} - \bar{B}) \tag{4.18}$$

In other words, government expenditure has an automatic stabilizing property.[1] The Treasury/central bank receives taxes. It borrows to finance government expenditure, and the evolution of the bonds is

$$B_t = (1 + R_{t-1})B_{t-1} + P_tG_t - (\tau_1 W_tL_t + \tau_2 P_tC_t), \tag{4.19}$$

where B is a one-period domestic bond.

4.2.5 Exports and Foreign Debt

Exports is still exogenously determined in this chapter:

$$X_t = \bar{X}. \tag{4.20}$$

The foreign debt evolves as follows:

$$S_tF_t = (1 + R^*_{t-1} + \Phi_{t-1})S_tF_{t-1} + (S_tP^*_tI_t - P_tX_t). \tag{4.21}$$

4.2.6 Calibration

Steady-State Initial Values The calibrated values are the same as in the previous chapter. The monetary policy parameters are $\phi_1 = 1.5$ and $\phi_2 = 0.9$, and the income and consumption tax rates are set respectively as $\tau_1 = 0.2$ and $\tau_2 = 0.1$. Using the same normalization as before ($Z = 1$, $\bar{S} = 1.0$, $\bar{P} = 1.0$), and the same pre-set foreign variables ($P^* = 1.0$, $\bar{R}^* = 0.04$), we solve for the initial steady-state values of the other variables so that the initial values of foreign and domestic debt are zero ($\bar{F} = \bar{B} = 0$) and the Euler equations are satisfied. As before, in the fully stochastic simulations, in which we examine welfare based on consumption and labor, the effect of initialization is mitigated by discarding the first 15 percent of the sample size. We note too that this model is specified and calibrated for the case where the steady-state inflation rate is assumed to be zero. The main point here is that the initial steady-state values will now be dependent on the tax regimes and be different from the steady-state values in chapters 2 and 3.

4.3   Model Solution

4.3.1   Decision Rules

As in chapter 3 we have four decision rules: one for consumption C, one for the exchange rate S, and two for the price (one for the numerator A^{p1} and one for the denominator A^{p2}). But now we have domestic bonds as an additional state variable:

$$\hat{C}_t = \psi^c(\Omega^c; \mathbf{x}_t),$$

$$\hat{S}_t = \psi^s(\Omega^s; \mathbf{x}_t),$$

$$\hat{A}_t^{p1} = \psi^{p1}(\Omega^{p1}; \mathbf{x}_t),$$

$$\hat{A}_t^{p2} = \psi^{p2}(\Omega^{p2}; \mathbf{x}_t),$$

$$\mathbf{x}_t = \{(Z_t - \bar{Z}), (F_{t-1} - \bar{F}), (R_{t-1} - \bar{R}), (B_{t-1} - \bar{B})\}.$$

The approximating functions ψ^c, ψ^s, ψ^{p1}, and ψ^{p2} are again neural net specifications with the following form:

$$\Delta_t^c = \Omega_1^c(Z_t - \bar{Z}) + \Omega_2^c(F_{t-1} - \bar{F}) + \Omega_3^c(R_{t-1} - \bar{R}) + \Omega_4^c(B_{t-1} - \bar{B}),$$

$$\hat{C}_t = \bar{C}\left(\frac{1}{1 + \exp(-\Delta_t^c)} - 0.5\right),$$

$$\Delta_t^s = \Omega_1^s(Z_t - \bar{Z}) + \Omega_2^s(F_{t-1} - \bar{F}) + \Omega_3^s(R_{t-1} - \bar{R}) + \Omega_4^s(B_{t-1} - \bar{B}),$$

$$\hat{S}_t = \bar{S}\left(\frac{1}{1 + \exp(-\Delta_t^s)} - 0.5\right);$$

$$\Delta_t^{p1} = \Omega_1^{p1}(Z_t - \bar{Z}) + \Omega_2^{p1}(F_{t-1} - \bar{F}) + \Omega_3^{p1}(R_{t-1} - \bar{R}) + \Omega_4^{p1}(B_{t-1} - \bar{B}),$$

$$\hat{A}_t^{p1} = \overline{A^{p1}}\left(\frac{1}{1 + \exp(-\Delta_t^{p1})} - 0.5\right);$$

$$\Delta_t^{p2} = \Omega_1^{p2}(Z_t - \bar{Z}) + \Omega_2^{p2}(F_{t-1} - \bar{F}) + \Omega_3^{p2}(R_{t-1} - \bar{R}) + \Omega_4^{p2}(B_{t-1} - \bar{B}),$$

$$\hat{A}_t^{p2} = \overline{A^{p2}}\left(\frac{1}{1 + \exp(-\Delta_t^{p2})} - 0.5\right).$$

4.3.2 Euler Errors

The Euler errors now include the effects of taxation:

$$\epsilon_t^c = \frac{\hat{C}_t^{-\eta}}{(1 + \tau_2)\hat{P}_t}\left[\frac{1}{(1 + R_t)}\right] - \beta\left[\frac{\hat{C}_{t+1}^{-\eta}}{(1 + \tau_2)\hat{P}_{t+1}}\right],$$

$$\epsilon_t^s = \frac{\hat{C}_t^{-\eta}}{P_t}\left[\frac{\hat{S}_t}{(1 + R_t^* + \Phi_t + \Phi_t'F_t^*)}\right] - \beta\left[\hat{S}_{t+1}\frac{\hat{C}_{t+1}^{-\eta}}{P_{t+1}}\right],$$

$$\epsilon_t^P = \frac{\hat{A}_t^{p1}}{\hat{A}_t^{p2}} - \frac{Y_t(P_t)^\zeta A_t + \beta\xi\hat{A}_{t+1}^{p1}}{Y_t(P_t)^\zeta + \beta\xi\hat{A}_{t+1}^{p2}}.$$

4.3.3 Accuracy Checks

Table 4.1 and figure 4.1 show the mean (standard error) of the Judd-Gasper statistics and their corresponding histograms. Table 4.2 shows the rejection probabilities for the Den-Hann Marcet test statistics, and figure 4.2 shows the cumulative density function.

4.4 Stochastic Simulations

4.4.1 Impulse-Response Analysis

To ensure that the calibrated model is stable, and makes economic sense, it is useful to do an impulse-response analysis. As in earlier chapters we set the shock to the log of the productivity index at 0.1, at period 25, and zero thereafter. Figure 4.3 shows the impulse-response paths for the model, which now includes sticky prices, income and consumption taxes, plus an endogenous government expenditure that is sensitive to the deviation of domestic debt from its steady-state value.

Following a productivity shock, we see an increase in consumption, but we note that the steady-state level with taxes is below the steady-state level without taxes. The exchange rate depreciates, labor services fall, and the real wage increases. The trade balance worsens

Table 4.1
Judd-Gaspar statistic ($\times 10^{-2}$)

	$\dfrac{\lvert \epsilon_t^c \rvert}{C_t}$	$\dfrac{\lvert \epsilon_t^s \rvert}{S_t}$	$\dfrac{\lvert \epsilon_t^p \rvert}{P_t}$
Mean	0.2053	0.7921	0.0355
Standard deviation	0.0117	0.0449	0.0021

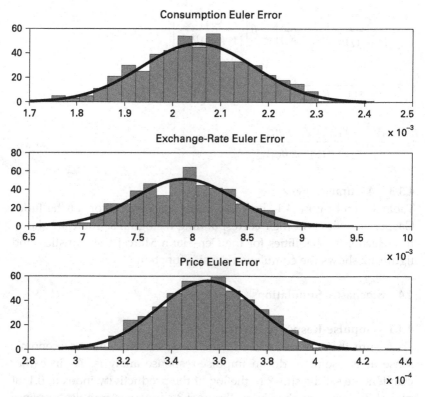

Figure 4.1
Judd-Gasper statistic

Table 4.2
DenHann-Marcet test

	Lag order			
	1	2	3	4
Lower region ($p < 0.05$)	0.046	0.048	0.048	0.050
Upper region ($p > 0.95$)	0.058	0.030	0.044	0.048

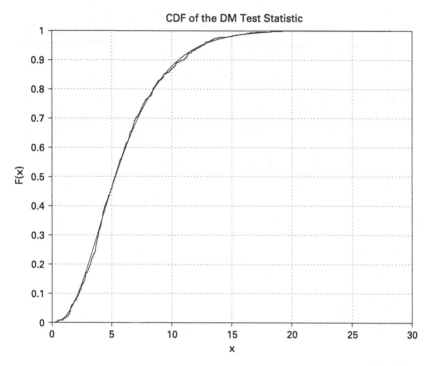

Figure 4.2
DenHann-Marcet test for accuracy

(because nominal import payments rise with the exchange rate), and the fiscal balance improves (because both labor income and nominal consumption increase). Note, however, that price (and hence interest rate) rises relative to the system without taxes. The price rise occurs to equate the supply of output with the increased demand from households (due to higher consumption) and the government (whose expenditure increased in this model with the fall in domestic debt).

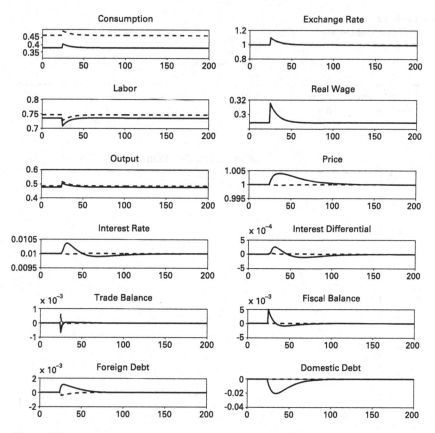

Figure 4.3
Impulse responses following a productivity shock: with (*solid line*) and without (*dashed line*) taxes and endogenous government expenditure

4.4.2   Welfare Comparisons

Welfare under a tax regime will be unambiguously lower than welfare in a no-tax regime. But what about the correlations? Figure 4.4 shows the correlations of productivity with price, exchange rate and output in an economy with sticky prices, and without and with taxes. The most significant result is the change in correlation of productivity and price from being negative (without taxes) to positive (with taxes).

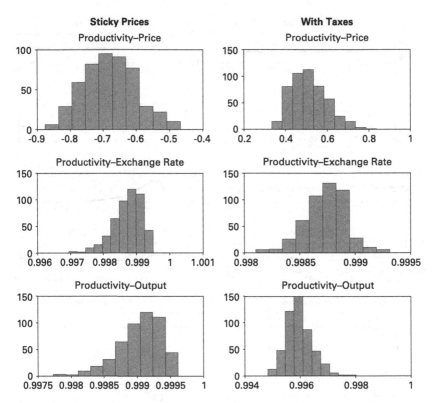

Figure 4.4
Correlations

4.5   Scenario Analysis

4.5.1   Alternative Fiscal Policy Regimes
Taxes can be levied either on labor income or on consumption:

$$Tax_t = \tau_0 + \tau_1 W_t L_t + \tau_2 P_t C_t, \tag{4.22}$$

where τ_0 is a lump-sum tax while τ_1 and τ_2 are the respective tax rates on labor income (pay-as-you-earn system) and consumption. Income taxes distorts the incentive to work while consumption taxes affect the prices of goods purchased.

In the section above we examined a system where households are taxed more on their wage income than on the goods they buy, $\tau_1 > \tau_2$. In this scenario we examine the case where the income tax is less than the consumption tax, $\tau_1 < \tau_2$. Since the tax system affects the first-order

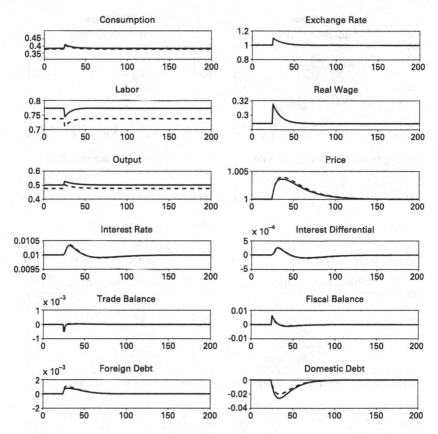

Figure 4.5
Impulse response functions: case where income tax is less than the consumption tax (*solid line*) and case where income is greater than the consumption tax (*dashed line*)

conditions differently, the steady-state values of the key variables appear in table 4.3 for the two tax regimes studied. Note how the higher consumption tax encourages more production (which is supported by more labor), while the lower income tax is associated with higher labor.

4.5.2 Impulse-Responses

Figure 4.5 shows the response paths across tax regimes under a common set of assumptions for monetary policy. Following a productivity shock, we see an increase in consumption, a depreciation of the exchange rate, and increases in both the price and interest rate. The trade

Table 4.3
Steady-state values for different tax regimes

Variables	$\tau_1 = 0.2, \tau_2 = 0.1$	$\tau_1 = 0.1, \tau_2 = 0.2$
$\bar{C}$	0.3713	0.3759
$\bar{Y}$	0.4777	0.5015
$\bar{K}$	0.0268	0.0282
$\bar{L}$	0.7357	0.7725

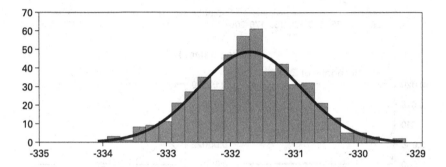

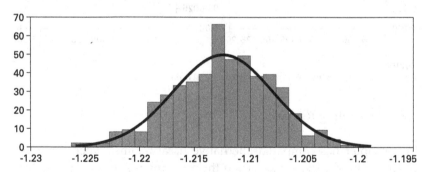

Figure 4.6
Welfare differences

balance worsens (because imports increase) and the fiscal balance falls (because taxes rises).

But what about the welfare? The top panel in figure 4.6 shows the welfare for the case when consumption taxes dominate, and the bottom panel shows the differences between the two system (welfare consumption minus welfare income). The negative numbers show that welfare under a tax regime with higher consumption taxes dominates welfare under a tax regime with higher income taxes.

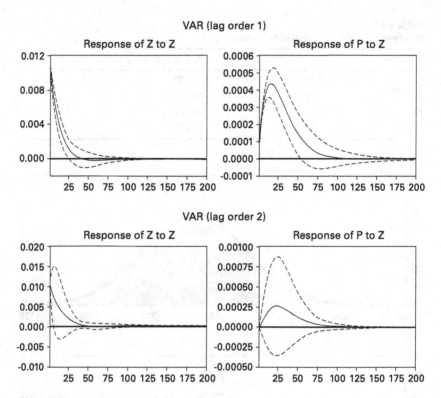

Figure 4.7
Impulse response from VAR model with artificial data

4.6   Concluding Remarks

This chapter has compared alternative fiscal regimes when there are recurring productivity shocks and the economy is subject to the distortions of monopolistic competition. Our aim was to show that the methodology can be applied to an economy with distortion from taxes. Further distortions coming from pricing to market and incomplete pass-through and sticky wage settings, as well as inertia in spending due to habit persistence, will come to play as we move through the chapters.

From a welfare point of view, we see that consumption taxes yield better outcomes than taxes on labor income. This is a well-known result in the field of public finance. Labor income taxes, of course, are more common. One reason is that it is politically more difficult to switch to consumption taxes once labor income taxes are in place. But the more obvious reason is that labor income taxes are much easier to collect (at payroll time), and more predictable, than consumption taxes.

Computational Exercise: Model Validation with VARs

The vector autoregressive (VAR) model is a popular macroeconometric tool for studying the interactions between key economic variables. Sims's seminal paper, "Macroeconomics and Reality," argued that these methods can also be used to evaluate macroeconomic models. Put simply, we can apply a VAR to actual observed data and a VAR to the model-generated data, and compare their respective impulse-response paths. If the impulse-response paths estimated from the model-generated data falls within the confidence bands of the impulse-response paths based on observed data, then we have some evidence to suggest that the DSGE model bears some semblance to the real world.

An interesting alternative exercise is to generate some "artificial" data from our nonlinear DSGE model, estimate a linear VAR, generate impulse-response paths, and then see if they are similar to the impulse-response paths from the underlying nonlinear model. In this exercise we estimate a bivariate VAR for our model-generated data: productivity and price. Figure 4.7 shows that the VAR model with one lag yields estimated impulse-response paths that are consistent with the "theoretical" or model-simulated impulse response path in figure 4.3. In this path the price level rises following a one standard deviation shock to productivity. Compare this result with those generated from a VAR model with two lags. What would you conclude about the behavior of price to a productivity shock from this analysis?

This exercise illustrates a point made by Chari, Kehoe, and McGratten (2005): there can be large differences between the VAR-generated impulse-response and the theoretical impulse-response. Indeed one should not be too surprised that multivariate linear VAR models can produce divergent results from nonlinear model-generated impulse-responses.

5   Current Account Dynamics

5.1   Introduction

This chapter takes up the relationship between current account and fiscal balances in the context of an economy that imports capital and consumption goods. In this framework we examine the behavior of fiscal and current account balances under two scenarios: shocks to productivity and shocks to government expenditure.

The motivation for the scenario analysis comes from comments by Bradford De Long and former Undersecretary of the Treasury John Taylor about the US experience of "twin" current account and fiscal deficits. In his Weblog De Long (2004) notes that "we have a large trade deficit now and did not back in 1997, because the federal budget deficit is much larger now than it was then." In contrast, Taylor (2004) argues that the US trade deficit simply reflects the growth of US productivity, leading to capital formation growing faster than US saving.

Martin Feldstein and Charles Horioka (1980) have argued that for a highly open economy, savings–investment correlations should be low or insignificant when there is perfect capital mobility. In this context, since a government deficit represents negative government saving, the fiscal deficit would be mirrored by a current account deficit, since it lowers economywide saving relative to investment. For their part, Feldstein and Horioka reported positive savings–investment correlations, thereby challenging the assumption of perfect capital mobility, at least for the United States.

However, the Feldstein-Horioka thesis is not without controversy. The strongly positive twin deficit relationship assumes the absence of Ricardian equivalence, that is, that taxpayers will not discount the expected future tax liabilities of government dissaving and thus raise personal savings to offset the fiscal deficit effects on the current account. Furthermore, as Mendoza (1991) has pointed out, theoretical work has cast doubt on the inference of Feldstein and Horioka relating positive savings–investment correlations to limited or imperfect capital mobility.

Obstfeld (1986) has shown that a dynamic general equilibrium model subject to recurring productivity shocks can produce high savings–investment correlations even with perfect capital mobility. Similarly Finn (1990) has shown that a two-country general equilibrium model can generate any kind of savings–investment correlation depending on the stochastic structure of the technological disturbances. The empirical literature also gives divergent estimates about the effects of fiscal deficits on trade deficits (see in particular recent econometric time-series studies of several European countries by Bussière, Fratzscher, and Müller 2005).

Section 5.2 follows Erceg, Guerrieri, and Gust (2004) in using a dynamic stochastic general equilibrium modeling approach to examine the correlations of fiscal and trade balances under recurring productivity and government expenditure shocks. Like Erceg, Guerrieri, and Gust, the model used here includes sticky prices and incorporates the distortionary effects of monopolistic competition. However, our model also includes features crucial to an analysis of current account and budget deficits. The model incorporates an export demand function that responds to the real exchange rate, endogenous risk premia that depend on the foreign debt, and a distortionary income and consumption tax system.[1] As usual, we pay special attention to the accuracy of the approximations before we assess the economic implications from stochastic simulations. This is contained in section 5.3. In section 5.4 we examine the impulse-response functions for alternative export demand regimes, one with relatively high and one with relatively low elasticity with respect to the real exchange rate.

5.2 Model with Endogenous Exports

The model in chapter 4 with Calvo pricing and taxes is now modified to allow for more international interactions. Households now import consumption goods as well as capital-type goods. Exports are also no longer fixed but are endogenously determined. They now respond to changes in the real exchange rate.

5.2.1 Households—Consumption and Labor

The five equations that characterize household consumption, labor, and financial decisions carry over from chapter 4:

$$C_t^{-\eta} = \Lambda_t(1 + \tau_2)P_t, \tag{5.1}$$

$$L_t^\varpi = \Lambda_t(1 - \tau_1)W_t, \tag{5.2}$$

$$P_t^f = P_t^k, \tag{5.3}$$

$$\Lambda_t = \Lambda_{t+1}\beta(1 + R_t), \tag{5.4}$$

$$\Lambda_t S_t = \Lambda_{t+1}\beta(1 + R_t^* + \Phi_t + \Phi_t' F_t^*)S_{t+1}, \tag{5.5}$$

$$\Phi_t = \text{sign}(F_{t-1}^*) \cdot \varphi[e^{(|F_{t-1}^*| - \bar{F}^*)} - 1]. \tag{5.6}$$

However, the household now demands domestic C_t^d and imported goods C_t^f such that composite consumption C_t is given (using the Dixit-Stiglitz aggregators) by the following expression:

$$C_t = [(1 - \gamma_1)^{1/\theta_1}(C_t^d)^{(\theta_1-1)/\theta_1} + (\gamma_1)^{1/\theta_1}(C_t^f)^{(\theta_1-1)/\theta_1}]^{\theta_1/(\theta_1-1)}.$$

The parameter $\theta_1 > 0$ is the intratemporal elasticity of substitution between domestically produced goods C_t^d and internationally produced goods C_t^f; the parameter γ_1 represents the share of foreign goods in total consumption. Minimizing expenditures gives the demand for domestic and imported goods as

$$C_t^d = (1 - \gamma_1)\left(\frac{P_t^d}{P_t}\right)^{-\theta_1} C_t, \tag{5.7}$$

$$C_t^f = \gamma_1\left(\frac{P_t^f}{P_t}\right)^{-\theta_1} C_t. \tag{5.8}$$

Each composite good is a bundle of differentiated goods j using a Dixit-Stiglitz aggregator

$$C_t^d = \left[\int_0^1 (C_{j,t}^d)^{(\zeta-1)/\zeta} dj\right]^{\zeta/(\zeta-1)},$$

$$C_t^f = \left[\int_0^1 (C_{j,t}^f)^{(\zeta-1)/\zeta} \, dj \right]^{\zeta/(\zeta-1)},$$

where j denotes the domestic goods and the elasticity of substitution among differentiated goods is given by $\zeta > 1$. Standard cost minimization yields the demand for each differentiated goods as

$$C_{j,t}^d = \left(\frac{P_{j,t}^d}{P_t^d} \right)^{-\zeta} C_t^d,$$

$$C_{j,t}^f = \left(\frac{P_{j,t}^f}{P_t^f} \right)^{-\zeta} C_t^f,$$

where $P_{j,t}^d$, $P_{j,t}^f$ are the prices of each differentiated domestic and imported good, and P_t^d and P_t^f, are given by

$$P_t^d = \left[\int_0^1 (P_{j,t}^d)^{1-\zeta} \, dj \right]^{1/(1-\zeta)},$$

$$P_t^f = \left[\int_0^1 (P_{j,t}^f)^{1-\zeta} \, dj \right]^{1/(1-\zeta)}.$$

The consumer price index P_t is given by the following formula:

$$P_t = [(1 - \gamma_1)(P_t^d)^{1-\theta_1} + \gamma_1 (P_t^f)^{1-\theta_1}]^{1/(1-\theta_1)}. \tag{5.9}$$

Recall that the household sector also includes entrepreneurs who own capital stock K_t and hold shares in all the firms in the economy. Thus far we have assumed that there is no capital accumulation or depreciation and that all capital is imported:

$$K_t = I_t, \tag{5.10}$$

where I is imported investment goods. The entrepreneurs now buy import goods Y_t^f at the price $S_t P_t^*$ and rebundle them for consumption C_t^f and investment I_t:

$$Y_t^f = I_t + C_t^f, \tag{5.11}$$

$$P_t^f = S_t P_t^*. \tag{5.12}$$

The importer sells these goods at a domestic currency price P^f, which is set to cover costs. Note that since all capital is imported $(K = I)$, the rental price of capital P_t^k is also equal to the price of the intermediate goods P_t^f.

5.2.2 Firms—One-Sector Production and Pricing

The equations describing the behavior of firms is the same as in chapter 3. The relevant aggregate equations are

$$Y_t = Z_t[(1 - \alpha_1)(L_t)^{\kappa_1} + \alpha_1(K_t)^{\kappa_1}]^{1/\kappa_1}, \tag{5.13}$$

$$\ln(Z_t) = \rho \ln(Z_{t-1}) + (1 - \rho) \ln(\bar{Z}) + \epsilon_t, \qquad \epsilon_t \sim N(0, \sigma_z^2), \tag{5.14}$$

$$Y_t^d = C_t^d + G_t + X_t;$$

$$A_t^{p1} = Y_t(P_t^d)^\zeta A_t + \beta\xi A_{t+1}^{p1}, \tag{5.15}$$

$$A_t^{p2} = Y_t(P_t^d)^\zeta + \beta\xi A_{t+1}^{p2}, \tag{5.16}$$

$$P_t^a = \frac{A_t^{p1}}{A_t^{p2}}; \tag{5.17}$$

$$A_t = \left\{ \left(\frac{1}{Z}\right) \left[\begin{array}{c} (1 - \alpha)(\alpha W)^{\kappa/(\kappa-1)} \\ + \alpha((1 - \alpha)P^k)^{\kappa/(\kappa-1)} \end{array} \right]^{-1/\kappa} \left[\begin{array}{c} W(\alpha W)^{1/(\kappa-1)} \\ + P^k((1 - \alpha)P^k)^{1/(\kappa-1)} \end{array} \right] \right\},$$

$$P_t^d = [\xi(P_{t-1}^d)^{1-\zeta} + (1 - \xi)(P_t^a)^{1-\zeta}]^{1/(1-\zeta)}. \tag{5.18}$$

5.2.3 Monetary and Fiscal Authorities

Monetary Policy The central bank is assumed to adopt a Taylor rule, where the actual interest rate follows a partial adjustment mechanism

$$R_t = \phi_2 R_{t-1} + (1 - \phi_2)[R^* + \phi_1(\pi_t - \tilde{\pi})], \qquad \phi_1 > 1, \tag{5.19}$$

$$\pi_t = \left(\frac{P_t}{P_{t-1}}\right)^4 - 1.$$

Taxes and Domestic Debt   As in chapter 4, government spending G is assumed to be sensitive to the size of the public debt B relative to its steady-state value $\bar{B}$:

$$G_t = \bar{G} + \chi_1(B_{t-1} - \bar{B}). \tag{5.20}$$

The one-period domestic bond evolves as

$$B_t = (1 + R_{t-1})B_{t-1} + P_tG_t - (\tau_1 W_t L_t + \tau_2 P_t C_t). \tag{5.21}$$

The fiscal balance is defined as ($+$ is a surplus)

$$-(B_t - B_{t-1}) = (\tau_1 W_t L_t + \tau_2 P_t C_t) - P_t G_t - R_{t-1}B_{t-1}.$$

5.2.4   Exports and Foreign Debt

Exports depend on the lagged real exchange (S_{t-1}/P_{t-1}) relative to its steady-state value $(\overline{S/P})$:[2]

$$\ln(X_t) = \ln(\bar{X}) + \chi_2\left[\ln\left(\frac{S_{t-1}}{P_{t-1}}\right) - \ln\left(\frac{\bar{S}}{\bar{P}}\right)\right]. \tag{5.22}$$

The foreign debt evolves as follows:

$$S_t F_t = (1 + R^*_{t-1} + \Phi_{t-1})S_t F_{t-1} + S_t P^*_t Y^f_t - P^d_t X_t. \tag{5.23}$$

The current account balance is given by the following expression:

$$-S_t(F^*_t - F^*_{t-1}) = P^d_t X_t - S_t P^*_t Y^f_t - (R^*_{t-1} + \Phi_{t-1})S_t F^*_{t-1}.$$

5.3   Computational Analysis

5.3.1   Decision Rules and Euler Errors

The four decision rules, one for consumption C, one for the exchange rate S, and two for the price (one for the numerator A^{p1} and one for the denominator A^{p2}) are the same as those in chapter 4:

$$\hat{C}_t = \psi^c(\Omega^c; \mathbf{x}_t),$$

$$\hat{S}_t = \psi^s(\Omega^s; \mathbf{x}_t),$$

$$\hat{A}^{p1}_t = \psi^{p1}(\Omega^{p1}; \mathbf{x}_t),$$

$$\hat{A}^{p2}_t = \psi^{p2}(\Omega^{p2}; \mathbf{x}_t),$$

$\mathbf{x}_t = \{(Z_t - \bar{Z}), (F_{t-1} - \bar{F}), (R_{t-1} - \bar{R}), (B_{t-1} - \bar{B})\}.$

The Euler errors are also the same as those in chapter 3:

$$\epsilon_t^c = \frac{\hat{C}_t^{-\eta}}{(1 + \tau_2)\hat{P}_t}\left[\frac{1}{(1 + R_t)}\right] - \beta\left[\frac{\hat{C}_{t+1}^{-\eta}}{(1 + \tau_2)\hat{P}_{t+1}}\right],$$

$$\epsilon_t^s = \frac{\hat{C}_t^{-\eta}}{P_t}\left[\frac{\hat{S}_t}{(1 + R_t^* + \Phi_t + \Phi_t'F_t^*)}\right] - \beta\left[\hat{S}_{t+1}\frac{\hat{C}_{t+1}^{-\eta}}{P_{t+1}}\right],$$

$$\epsilon_t^p = \frac{\hat{A}_t^{p1}}{\hat{A}_t^{p2}} - \frac{Y_t(P_t)^\zeta A_t + \beta\xi\hat{A}_{t+1}^{p1}}{Y_t(P_t)^\zeta + \beta\xi\hat{A}_{t+1}^{p2}}.$$

The coefficients of the decision rules are based on minimization of the sum of squared Euler equation errors.

5.3.2 Accuracy Checks
Table 5.1 and figure 5.1 shows the results from an examination of the Judd-Gaspar error measures. We see that the errors do not differ by much and represent less than 1 percent of their respective decision-rule variables.

Table 5.2 and figure 5.2 shows the results from an examination of the DenHann-Marcet test statistics. These results suggest that the approximations are robust.

5.4 Productivity Shocks

5.4.1 Impulse-Response Analysis
Figure 5.3 shows the impulse-responses following a productivity shock for a model with sticky prices, taxes, and endogenous government expenditure and now endogenous exports sensitive to the real exchange rate. The results show that a temporary increase in the productivity index leads to an increase in consumption, a fall in labor services, an increase in real wages and a depreciation of the exchange rate. These results are not qualitatively different from the case discussed in chapter 4. However, export demand now reacts to the depreciation and the foreign debt actually improves after an initial deterioration. The boost to the economy yields a larger fiscal surplus. Note that the adjustment in prices (and hence interest rate) are larger in this case to accommodate the increased demand from exports.

Table 5.1
Judd-Gaspar statistic ($\times 10^{-2}$)

	$\dfrac{|\epsilon_t^c|}{C_t}$	$\dfrac{|\epsilon_t^s|}{S_t}$	$\dfrac{|\epsilon_t^p|}{P_t}$
Mean	0.2918	0.6051	0.5910
Standard deviation	0.0174	0.0369	0.0355

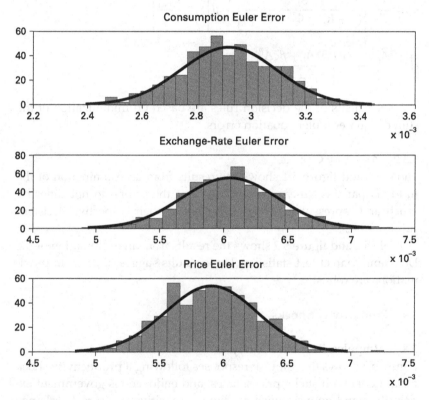

Figure 5.1
Judd-Gasper statistic

Table 5.2
DenHann-Marcet test

	Lag order			
	1	2	3	4
Lower region ($p < 0.05$)	0.040	0.042	0.036	0.058
Upper region ($p > 0.95$)	0.036	0.038	0.036	0.044

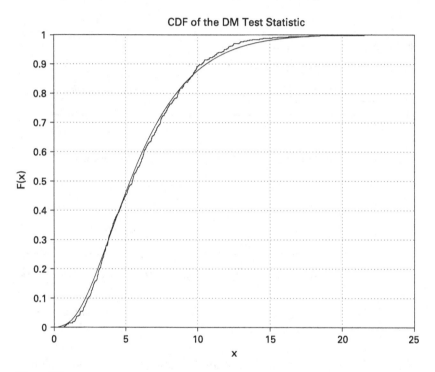

Figure 5.2
DenHann-Marcet test of accuracy

5.4.2 Stochastic Simulations

Figure 5.4 presents selected correlations. We see that the positive price–output correlations are stronger for the case where exports respond to changes in the real exchange rate. However, given the lagged response of exports to real exchange-rate depreciations, the correlations between the per period deterioration in the trade balance and changes in the exchange rate are negative. Note, these correlations become positive as the lag increases. This result is an example of the J-curve phenomenon

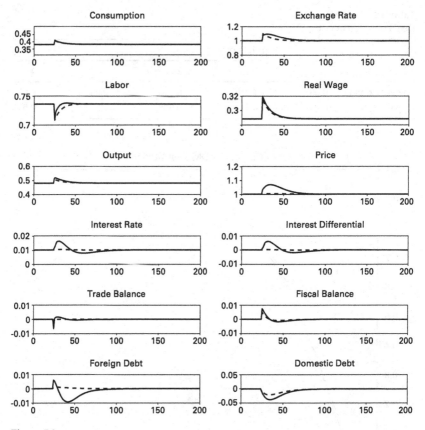

Figure 5.3
Impulse responses following a productivity shock: with (*solid line*) and without (*dashed line*) endogenous exports

where, following a depreciation of the exchange rate, the trade balance initially worsens and then improves over time.

5.5 Scenario Analysis

5.5.1 Low Export Elasticity
In this scenario we examine the sensitivity of results to alternative parameter values. This is suggested by the study of Senhadji and Montenegro (1999) who found that export elasticities of countries vary quite a bit, with Asian countries having the highest elasticities with respect to prices and African countries the lowest. In this scenario we compare the results derived thus far with a relatively high export price elasticity

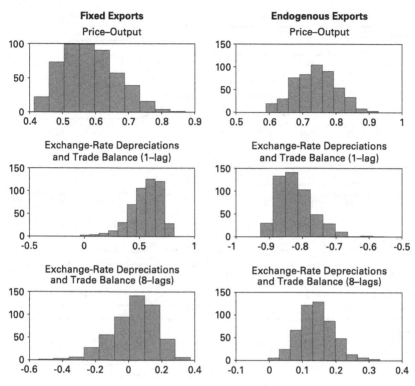

Figure 5.4
Macroeconomic correlations

($\chi = 1.0$) with the case of low elasticity ($\chi = 0.1$). As before, we check the accuracy of the estimation by examining the Judd-Gaspar error measures and the Den-Hann Marcet statistics.

Figure 5.5 shows the impulse-responses following a productivity shock of 0.1, for both high and low elasticity of exports with respect to the real exchange rate. The results show that a temporary increase in productivity leads to an improvement in the fiscal balance, as expected. Consumption rises in both cases of high and low export elasticity. However, the current account worsens under low elasticity as the increased demand for imports dominates the effect of favorable export responses.

How do the correlations between key macroeconomic variables change with the value of the export price elasticity? Figure 5.6 shows that the correlations between productivity and consumption are hardly affected, but the strong positive relationship between price

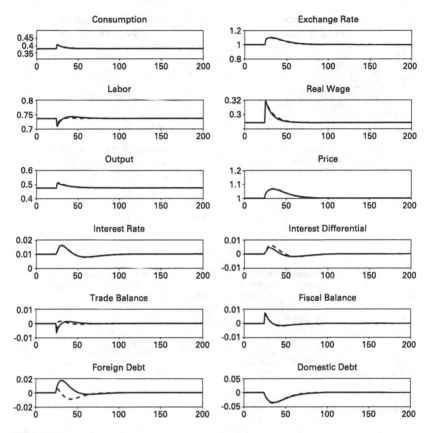

Figure 5.5
Impulse responses: high (*dashed line*) and low (*solid line*) elasticity of export demand

and output (which allows for a strong export response) is lost when the export elasticity is low. More interesting, the correlations between the fiscal–current account balances change signs—they are weakly negative under high elasticity and strongly positive under low export elasticity. The effect of the lower export elasticity with respect to the real exchange rate is to shift the histogram of the correlations to the right, to such a degree that the correlations become unambiguously positive.

5.5.2 Government Expenditure
The next scenario we consider is the effect of shocks to government expenditure on the real exchange rate and on the current account. In

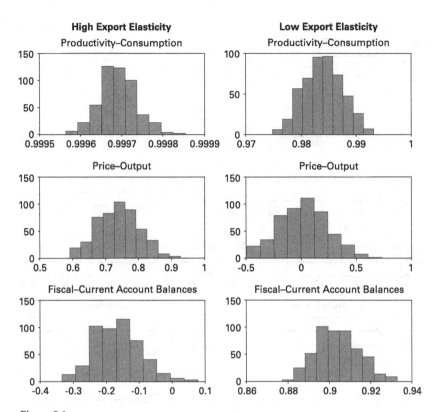

Figure 5.6
Correlations

particular, we would like to know whether there is a positive correlation between the fiscal and current account deficits.

The equation describing the behavior of G is altered in two ways. First, the response of G to the size of the debt is halved to allow the fiscal authority to be less concerned (but not completely independently of) the size of the domestic debt. Second, a shock term is added:

$$G_t = \bar{G} + 0.5\chi_1(B_{t-1} - \bar{B}) + \epsilon_t, \qquad \epsilon_t \sim N(0, \sigma_g^2).$$

Figure 5.7 compares the impulses from a shock to government expenditure with the impulses from a shock to productivity. Output increases by less and consumption falls. Domestic debt soars, as expected.

Figure 5.8 shows selected correlations. Note the positive correlations of productivity shocks and consumption and the negative correlations

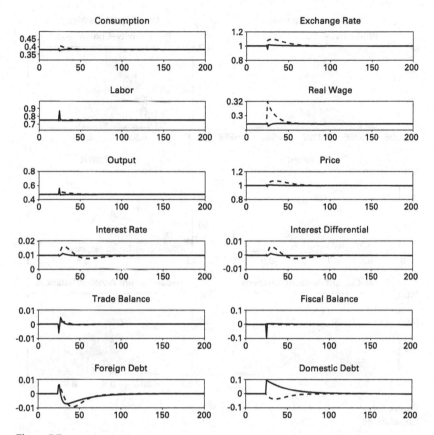

Figure 5.7
Impulse responses following a shock to government expenditure (*solid line*) and productivity (*dashed line*)

of government shocks and consumption. As shown in the middle panel,
the real exchange rate depreciates following productivity shocks and
appreciates following government shocks as expected. Note too the
strong positive correlation between the two deficits.

5.6   Concluding Remarks

Why are some current account and budget deficits positively and some
negatively related? The simulations in this chapter suggest that the
type of shock matters. Positive correlations result from productivity
shocks because both the fiscal and current account balances *improve*;

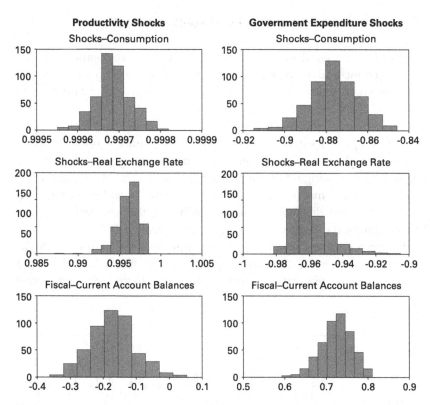

Figure 5.8
Correlations between key variables

positive correlations can also result from government expenditure shocks because both the fiscal and current account balances *deteriorate*. However, more interesting, the elasticity of exports can influence the sign of the correlation. The simulations in this chapter show that in the presence of continuing productivity shocks, the fiscal and trade balances are "twins," or positively correlated, under a relatively high export elasticity and negatively correlated under a relatively low export elasticity.

The model we used in this chapter incorporates many of the distortions and stickiness popular in the new neoclassical synthesis or new open economy macroeconomics, such as monopolistic competition, sticky price-setting behavior for prices, and distortionary taxes. In the next chapter we introduce capital and real frictions in the form of adjustment costs for investment.

Computational Exercise: Real Exchange-Rate Volatility

In this chapter we drew attention to the changing correlations of current account and fiscal balances. A related issue in open economy models characterized by sticky prices is the degree of real exchange rate volatility.

Chari, Kehoe, and McGrattan (2002) have argued that new Keynesian sticky price models for open economies require a relatively high coefficient of relative risk aversion to match the observed volatility of the real exchange rate found in the data for most industrialized countries. They measure the real exchange-rate volatility as the ratio of the standard deviation of the logarithm of the real exchange rate to the standard deviation of the logarithm of real GDP.

Figure 5.9 shows the real exchange rate and real output, in logarithms, for one realization, of sample size 1,000, from our model. The real exchange-rate volatility, measured relative to the volatility of real

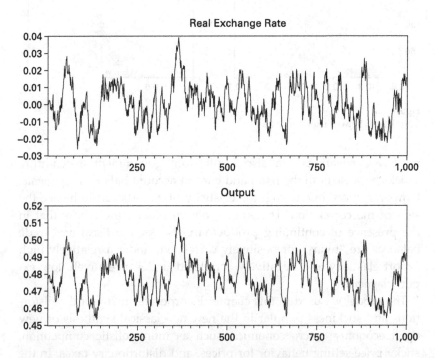

Figure 5.9
Logarithms of real exchange rates and output: simulated data

output, is about 1. Chari, Kehoe, and McGrattan (2002) report measured real exchange volatility ratios of 7 or more.

The reason why the standard deviation of the real exchange rate, relative to the standard deviation of GDP, is so small, of course, is that we assume a value of 1.5 for the coefficient of relative risk aversion, represented by the parameter η, in the model simulations of this chapter. Chari, Kehoe, and McGratten (2002, p. 534), for their model, report that setting $\eta = 5$ reproduces real exchange-rate volatility (relative to GDP volatility) that is found in the data. A useful exercise for readers is to change the specification of η to higher values and examine how the volatility of the real exchange-rate changes.

6   Capital and Tobin's Q

6.1   Introduction

Until now we have assumed full depreciation of the capital stock so that investment goods simply mean intermediate goods in production. We now relax this assumption and allow the capital stock to depreciate slowly. We also assume that there are adjustment costs for investment. The model has now become more complex to accommodate production technology and more realistic investment dynamics. It also throws light on the Q variable and its role in the dynamics of capital accumulation.

As in the earlier chapter, we will present results for the case of a shock to productivity. However, the experiment we are particularly interested in is the role of the Q variable, introduced by Tobin (1969), as an extra target of monetary policy.

The focus on Q is influenced by Brainard and Tobin (1977), who argued that Q plays an important role in the transmission of monetary policy both directly via the capital investment decision of enterprises and indirectly via consumption decisions. Thus volatility of Q has implications for inflation and growth. Large swings in Q can lead to systematic overinvestment, and in the open economy context, overborrowing and serious capital account deficits.

This chapter is concerned with the thought experiment: What happens to consumption, inflation, and welfare if the central bank also monitors Q? In particular, we will generate the welfare implications of adopting a stance of monetary policy that includes targeting consumer price inflation as well as changes in Q.

The idea of using Q is motivated by the observation that many economies experience asset price volatility (e.g., in the form of exchange-rate instability in Australia or share-market bubbles in the United States). The practice of controlling changes in goods prices is taken for granted by many central banks, but there is no consensus about the management of asset-price inflation, except in the sense that it is not desirable for asset prices to be too high or too volatile. At the World Economic Forum in Davos in 2003, Lawrence Summers suggested that policy makers should use other tools, such as margin lending requirements or public jawboning, to combat asset-price inflation. He compared raising interest rates to combat asset-price inflation to a preemptive attack, and stated "it takes enormous hubris to know when the right moment has come to start a war" (Summers 2003, p. 1).

Recent research shows that central bankers should not target asset prices (e.g., for a closed economy study, see Bernanke and Gertler 1999, 2001; Gilchrist and Leahy 2002). However, Cecchetti, Genberg, and Wadhwani (2002) have argued that central banks should react to asset price misalignments. In essence, they show that when disturbances are nominal, reacting to close misalignment gaps significantly improves macroeconomic performance. Smets (1997) has also stressed that the proper response of monetary policy to asset-price inflation depends on the source of the asset-price movements. If productivity changes are the driving force, accommodation is called for, and real interest rates should remain unchanged. However, if the source is due to nonfundamental shocks in the equity market, in the form of bullish predictions about productivity, then monetary policy should raise interest rates.

The model in this chapter does not include an explicit financial sector and consequently we are not in a position to address the issue of asset price inflation. However, we can begin to think about the issue indirectly by understanding the behavior of Q. In particular, we will consider the rate of growth of Tobin's Q as a potential target variable for monetary policy. Our reasoning is that Q growth would be small when the growth in the market valuation of capital assets corresponds roughly with the growth of replacement costs. Since asset prices (in the market value) are a lot less sticky than good prices (in the replacement cost), the presence of high Q growth would be indicative of misalignment of market value and replacement cost, in other words, an indication of an "excessive" change in the share price. Thus monitoring and targeting Q growth may be viewed as a proxy policy for monitoring and targeting asset-price inflation, but with the advantage that the asset price is evaluated relative to a benchmark (the replacement cost).

The chapter is organized as follows. The model is described in section 6.2, and the solution algorithm is presented in section 6.3. Section 6.4 contains the simulation results for the alternative policy frameworks.

6.2 Model with Capital Accumulation

The main change to the model is to expand the behavior of the private sector to allow for capital accumulation. The behavior patterns of the other agents are unaffected.

6.2.1 Householders and Entrepreneurs

The household sector includes entrepreneurs who own the capital stock and hold shares in all the firms in the economy. The accumulation equation for capital is now

$$K_t = I_t + (1 - \delta)K_{t-1} - \frac{\Psi}{2} \frac{(I_t - \delta K_{t-1})^2}{K_{t-1}}, \tag{6.1}$$

where I is imported investment goods and δ is depreciation. We also assume that the creation of capital occurs with an adjustment cost. The adjustment term $\Psi(I_t - \delta K_{t-1})^2/2K_{t-1}$ picks up the quadratic adjustment costs, which rise with the level of investment or disinvestment (in excess of that required to replace capital) relative to the size of the capital stock. The parameter Ψ is the adjustment cost weight. This specification of adjustment costs is the form described in Canzoneri, Cumby, and Diba (2005). These costs are introduced to induce some sluggishness in the dynamics of investment and capital accumulation. See, for example, Smets and Wouter (2003) for other specifications of adjustment costs.

As in earlier chapters, without an explicit financial sector, the household lends directly to the domestic government and accumulates bonds B that pay the nominal interest rate R. They can also borrow internationally and accumulate international debt F^* at the rate $R^* + \Phi$, where Φ is the currency premium.

The Lagrangian problem becomes

$$\mathscr{L} = \sum_{t=0}^{\infty} \beta^t$$

$$\times \left\{ U(C_{t+i}, L_{t+i}) - \Lambda_{t+i} \begin{bmatrix} (1+\tau_2)P_{t+i}C_{t+i} + P_{t+i}^f I_{t+i} + B_{t+i} \\ + (1 + R_{t-1+i}^* + \Phi_{t+i})S_{t+i}F_{t-1+i}^* \\ + (\tau_1 - 1)W_{t+i}L_{t+i} - \Pi_{t+i} - P_{t+i}^k K_{t+i} \\ - (1 + R_{t-1+i})B_{t-1+i} - S_{t+i}F_{t+i}^* \end{bmatrix} \right.$$
$$\left. - Q_{t+i}\left[K_{t+i} - I_{t+i} - (1-\delta)K_{t-1+i} + \frac{\Psi}{2}\frac{(I_{t+i} - \delta K_{t-1+i})^2}{K_{t-1+i}} \right] \right\},$$

where Φ_t has the following symmetric functional form:

$$\Phi_t = \text{sign}(F_{t-1}^*) \cdot \varphi[e^{(|F_{t-1}^*| - \bar{F}^*)} - 1], \tag{6.2}$$

where $\bar{F}^*$ represents the steady-state value of the international asset. The variable Λ is the familiar Lagrangian multiplier representing the marginal utility of wealth. The terms Q known as Tobin's Q, represent the Lagrange multiplier for the evolution of capital—they are the shadow prices for new capital.[1] Maximizing the Lagrangian with respect to C_t, L_t, B_t, F_t^*, K_t, and I_t yields the first-order conditions

$$\frac{\partial \mathscr{L}}{\partial C_t} = C_t^{-\eta} - \Lambda_t(1 + \tau_2)P_t = 0,$$

$$\frac{\partial \mathscr{L}}{\partial L_t} = -L_t^{\omega} - \Lambda_t(\tau_1 - 1)W_t = 0,$$

$$\frac{\partial \mathscr{L}}{\partial B_t} = -\Lambda_t + \Lambda_{t+1}\beta(1 + R_t) = 0,$$

$$\frac{\partial \mathscr{L}}{\partial F_t^*} = -\Lambda_{t+1}\beta(1 + R_t^* + \Phi_t + \Phi_t'F_t^*)S_{t+1} + \Lambda_t S_t = 0,$$

$$\frac{\partial \mathscr{L}}{\partial K_t} = \Lambda_t P_t^k - Q_t + \beta Q_{t+1}(1 - \delta) - \beta Q_{t+1}\frac{\Psi}{2}\begin{bmatrix} \dfrac{-2(I_{t+1} - \delta K_t)\delta}{K_t} \\ - \dfrac{(I_{t+1} - \delta K_t)^2}{K_t^2} \end{bmatrix} = 0,$$

$$\frac{\partial \mathscr{L}}{\partial I_t} = -\Lambda_t P_t^f + Q_t - Q_t \frac{\Psi}{2} \frac{2(I_t - \delta K_{t-1})}{K_{t-1}} = 0.$$

Again, these conditions are identical across all households, and they hold in the aggregate:

$$C_t^{-\eta} = \Lambda_t(1 + \tau_2)P_t, \tag{6.3}$$

$$L_t^{\varpi} = \Lambda_t(1 - \tau_1)W_t, \tag{6.4}$$

$$\Lambda_t = \Lambda_{t+1}\beta(1 + R_t), \tag{6.5}$$

$$\Lambda_t S_t = \Lambda_{t+1}\beta(1 + R_t^* + \Phi_t + \Phi_t' F_t^*)S_{t+1}, \tag{6.6}$$

$$Q_t = \Lambda_t P_t^k + \beta Q_{t+1}\left[(1 - \delta) + \frac{\Psi(I_{t+1} - \delta K_t)\delta}{K_t} + \frac{\Psi(I_{t+1} - \delta K_t)^2}{2K_t^2}\right], \tag{6.7}$$

$$\Lambda_t P_t^f = Q_t - Q_t \Psi \frac{(I_t - \delta K_{t-1})}{K_{t-1}}. \tag{6.8}$$

Compared to the earlier chapters, the model now includes two extra equations which contain the forward looking variable Q. Equations (6.7) and (6.8) show that the solutions for Q_t, which determine investment and the evolution of capital, come from forward-looking stochastic Euler equations. The shadow price of capital includes the contribution from the discounted value of adjustment costs due to new capital stock and the effect of depreciation.

Again, for completeness, the other equations describing household behavior are

$$C_t = [(1 - \gamma_1)^{1/\theta_1}(C_t^d)^{(\theta_1-1)/\theta_1} + (\gamma_1)^{1/\theta_1}(C_t^f)^{(\theta_1-1)/\theta_1}]^{\theta_1/(\theta_1-1)},$$

$$C_t^d = (1 - \gamma_1)\left(\frac{P_t^d}{P_t}\right)^{-\theta_1}C_t, \tag{6.9}$$

$$C_t^f = \gamma_1\left(\frac{P_t^f}{P_t}\right)^{-\theta_1}C_t. \tag{6.10}$$

The consumer price index P_t is given by the following formula:

$$P_t = [(1 - \gamma_1)(P_t^d)^{1-\theta_1} + \gamma_1(P_t^f)^{1-\theta_1}]^{1/(1-\theta_1)}. \tag{6.11}$$

As in chapter 5 the entrepreneurs buy import goods Y_t^f at the price $S_t P_t^*$ and rebundle them for consumption (C_t^f) and investment (I_t):

$$Y_t^f = C_t^f + I_t, \tag{6.12}$$

$$P_t^f = P_t^* S_t, \tag{6.13}$$

where S is the exchange rate and P^{f*} is the internationally determined price, in foreign currency, of these imported goods. The importer sells these goods at a domestic currency price P^f that is set to cover costs. Note that while the price of the imported investment is P_t^f, the rental price of capital is P_t^k.

6.2.2 One-Sector Production

We are still in a one-good world. Hence, as in previous chapters, each firm j produces differentiated goods using a constant elasticity of substitution production function and the aggregate product Y is demanded by households C^d, by the government sector G, and by foreigners (exports X). The aggregate equations are

$$Y_t = Z_t [(1 - \alpha_1)(L_t)^{\kappa_1} + \alpha_1 (K_t)^{\kappa_1}]^{1/\kappa_1} \tag{6.14}$$

$$\ln(Z_t) = \rho \ln(Z_{t-1}) + (1 - \rho) \ln(\bar{Z}) + \epsilon_t; \qquad \epsilon_t \sim N(0, \sigma_z^2), \tag{6.15}$$

$$Y_t = C_t^d + G_t + X_t. \tag{6.16}$$

We assume that firms set prices according to the Calvo (1983) staggered price system, and the equations are

$$A_t^{p1} = Y_t (P_t^d)^\zeta A_t + \beta \xi A_{t+1}^{p1}, \tag{6.17}$$

$$A_t^{p2} = Y_t (P_t^d)^\zeta + \beta \xi A_{t+1}^{p2}, \tag{6.18}$$

$$P_t^a = \frac{A_t^{p1}}{A_t^{p2}}; \tag{6.19}$$

$$A_t = \left\{ \begin{array}{c} \left(\frac{1}{Z}\right)[(1 - \alpha)(\alpha W)^{\kappa/(\kappa-1)} + \alpha((1 - \alpha)P^k)^{\kappa/(\kappa-1)}]^{-1/\kappa} \\ \times [W(\alpha W)^{1/(\kappa-1)} + P^k((1 - \alpha)P^k)^{1/(\kappa-1)}] \end{array} \right\}, \tag{6.20}$$

$$P_t^d = [\xi(P_{t-1}^d)^{1-\zeta} + (1 - \xi)(P_t^a)^{1-\zeta}]^{1/(1-\zeta)}. \tag{6.21}$$

There are still only two input costs: the price of labor and the price of capital. The dividends distributed to households are still

$$\Pi_t = P_t^d Y_t - P_t^k K_t - W_t L_t.$$

6.2.3 Monetary and Fiscal Authorities

Monetary Policy In the base case the central bank is assumed to be concerned with goods price inflation only. The central bank adopts a Taylor rule with smoothing:

$$R_t = \phi_2 R_{t-1} + (1 - \phi_2)[R^* + \phi_1(\pi_t - \tilde{\pi})], \qquad \phi_1 > 1 \tag{6.22}$$

$$\pi_t = \left(\frac{P_t}{P_{t-1}}\right)^4 - 1.$$

Taxes and Domestic Debt The equations describing government spending G and evolution of the bonds B_t are

$$G_t = \bar{G} + \chi_1(B_{t-1} - \bar{B}), \tag{6.23}$$

$$B_t = (1 + R_{t-1})B_{t-1} + P_t G_t - (\tau_1 W_t L_t + \tau_2 P_t C_t). \tag{6.24}$$

6.2.4 Exports and Foreign Debt
The equations describing exports and the evolution of foreign debt are

$$\ln(X_t) = \ln(\bar{X}) + \chi_2 \left[\ln\left(\frac{S_{t-1}}{P_{t-1}}\right) - \ln\left(\frac{\bar{S}}{\bar{P}}\right) \right], \tag{6.25}$$

$$S_t F_t^* = (1 + R_{t-1}^* + \Phi_{t-1})S_t F_{t-1}^* + S_t P_t^* Y_t^f - P_t^d X_t. \tag{6.26}$$

6.3 Solution Algorithm

6.3.1 Approximating Equations
The introduction of capital accumulation in this chapter adds an extra decision rule, namely Q_t, and an extra state variable K_t to the system in chapter 5:

$$\hat{C}_t = \psi^c(\Omega^c; \mathbf{x}_t),$$

$$\hat{S}_t = \psi^s(\Omega^s; \mathbf{x}_t),$$

$$\hat{A}_t^{p1} = \psi^{p1}(\Omega^{p1}; \mathbf{x}_t),$$

$$\hat{A}_t^{p2} = \psi^{p2}(\Omega^{p2}; \mathbf{x}_t),$$

$$\hat{I}_t = \psi^I(\Omega^I; \mathbf{x}_t),$$

$$\mathbf{x}_t = \{(Z_t - \bar{Z}), (F_{t-1} - \bar{F}), (R_{t-1} - \bar{R}), (B_{t-1} - \bar{B}), (K_{t-1} - \bar{K})\}.$$

Note that to ensure nonnegativity of I_t, we have specified decision rules for investment and we then solve for the implied value of Q as follows:

$$\hat{K}_t = \hat{I}_t + (1 - \delta)K_{t-1} - \frac{\Psi}{2}\frac{(\hat{I}_t - \delta K_{t-1})^2}{K_{t-1}},$$

$$\hat{\Lambda}_t = \frac{\hat{C}_t^{-\eta}\hat{A}_t^{p2}}{(1 + \tau_2)\hat{A}_t^{p1}},$$

$$\hat{\Lambda}_t P_t^* \hat{S}_t = Q_t\left[1 - \Psi\frac{(\hat{I}_t - \delta\hat{K}_t)}{\hat{K}_t}\right].$$

There are now four Euler errors:

$$\epsilon_t^c = \frac{\hat{C}_t^{-\eta}}{(1 + \tau_2)\hat{P}_t}\left[\frac{1}{(1 + R_t)}\right] - \beta\left[\frac{\hat{C}_{t+1}^{-\eta}}{(1 + \tau_2)\hat{P}_{t+1}}\right],$$

$$\epsilon_t^s = \frac{\hat{C}_t^{-\eta}}{P_t}\left[\frac{\hat{S}_t}{(1 + R_t^* + \Phi_t + \Phi_t' F_t^*)}\right] - \beta\left[\hat{S}_{t+1}\frac{\hat{C}_{t+1}^{-\eta}}{P_{t+1}}\right],$$

$$\epsilon_t^P = \frac{\hat{A}_t^{p1}}{\hat{A}_t^{p2}} - \frac{Y_t(P_t)^\zeta A_t + \beta\xi\hat{A}_{t+1}^{p1}}{Y_t(P_t)^\zeta + \beta\xi\hat{A}_{t+1}^{p2}},$$

$$\epsilon_t^q = \frac{(\hat{Q}_t - \Lambda_t P_t^k)}{\left[(1 - \delta) + \frac{\Psi(I_t - \delta K_t)\delta}{K_t} + \frac{\Psi(I_t - \delta K_t)^2}{2K_t^2}\right]} - \beta\hat{Q}_{t+1}.$$

Table 6.1
Judd-Gaspar statistic ($\times 10^{-2}$)

	$\dfrac{\lvert \epsilon_t^c \rvert}{C_t}$	$\dfrac{\lvert \epsilon_t^s \rvert}{S_t}$	$\dfrac{\lvert \epsilon_t^p \rvert}{P_t}$	$\dfrac{\lvert \epsilon_t^q \rvert}{Q_t}$
Mean	0.3757	0.4553	1.4495	0.3312
Standard deviation	0.0236	0.0852	0.0843	0.0191

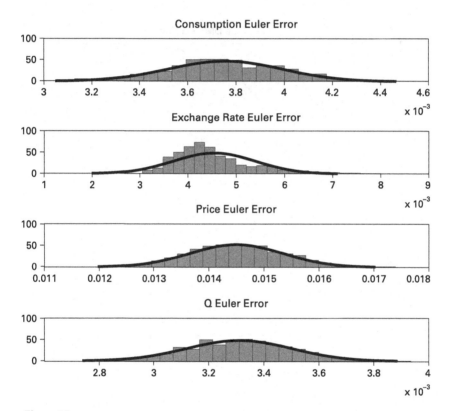

Figure 6.1
Judd-Gasper statistic

Table 6.2
DenHann-Marcet test

	Lag order			
	1	2	3	4
Lower region ($p < 0.05$)	0.050	0.040	0.036	0.044
Upper region ($p > 0.95$)	0.056	0.050	0.040	0.056

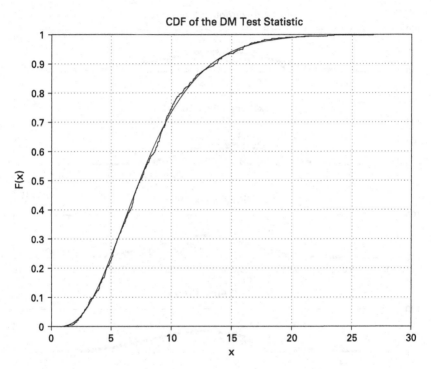

Figure 6.2
DenHann-Marcet test of accuracy

As is usual, the parameters of these decision rules are selected to minimize the squared Euler equation errors.

6.3.2 Accuracy Tests

The Judd-Gaspar and DenHann Marcet test statistics are as shown in table 6.1, table 6.2, figure 6.1, and figure 6.2. These results do not give us cause for concern about the accuracy of the approximations.

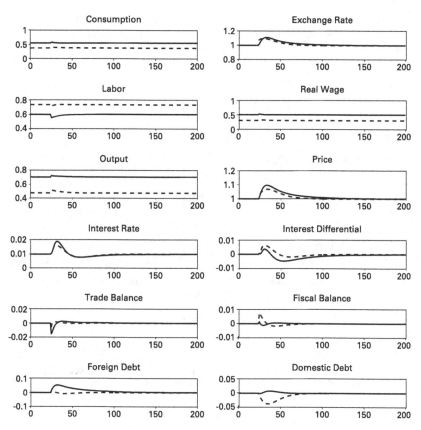

Figure 6.3
Impulse responses following a productivity shock: with (*solid line*) and without (*dashed line*) capital accumulation and real adjustment costs

6.4 Stochastic Dynamic Simulations

6.4.1 Impulse-Response Functions

The impulse-responses for a model with capital accumulation as well as sticky prices, taxes, endogenous government expenditure, and exports are shown in figure 6.3. Compared to the results in chapter 5, we see that the steady-state levels of consumption are higher when there is capital accumulation. The behavior of consumption, the exchange rate, labor, and the real wage are as expected. The response of price and the interest rate are further exacerbated with real rigidities. Positive productivity worsens both domestic and foreign debt positions. The

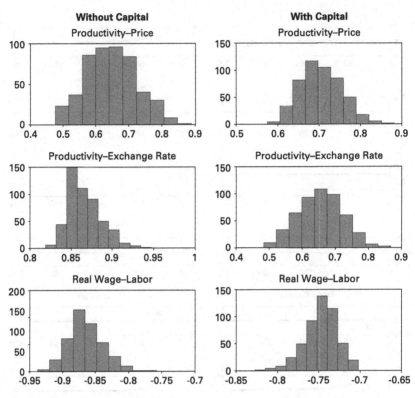

Figure 6.4
Correlations

former worsens because the increase in price discourages the demand by foreigners, and the later worsens with the fall in labor income.

6.4.2 Macroeconomic Correlations

The main implication of introducing capital accumulation into the model as seen in figure 6.4 seems to be the weakening of correlations among the key real variables. This should not be surprising since we have now introduced another form of stickiness—that of real adjustment costs.

6.5 Scenario Analysis—Q Targeting

The Taylor rule with annualized price inflation targeting (π) and Q growth targeting (π, q) is

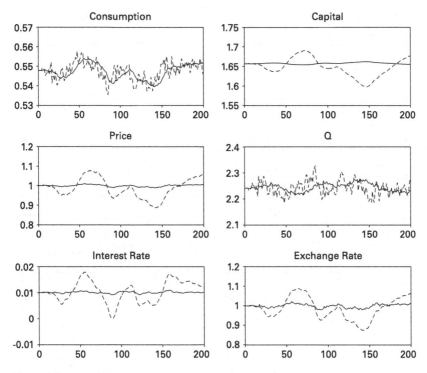

Figure 6.5
Simulated date under recurring productivity shocks: Taylor rule with inflation and Q growth targeting (*solid line*) and Taylor rule with only inflation targeting (*dashed line*)

$$R_t = \phi_2 R_{t-1} + (1 - \phi_2)[R^* + \phi_1(\pi_t - \tilde{\pi}) + \phi_3(q_t - \tilde{q})],$$

where $q_t = ((Q_t/Q_{t-4}) - 1)$ represent an annualized rate of Q growth and $\tilde{q}$ represents the target for this rate of growth that is set to zero. The Taylor coefficients are predetermined at $\phi_2 = 0.9$, $\phi_1 = 1.5$, and $\phi_3 = 0.5$.

6.5.1 Productivity Shocks

Figure 6.5 shows the simulated data for one realization of recurring productivity shocks. The simulations show, not surprisingly, the fall in the volatility of Q, when we change from an inflation only to an inflation–Q growth regime. The implications of this is for a less volatile capital accumulation and consumption. Prices now hardly vary and given the nature of the rule, the interest rate and exchange rate are also less variable.

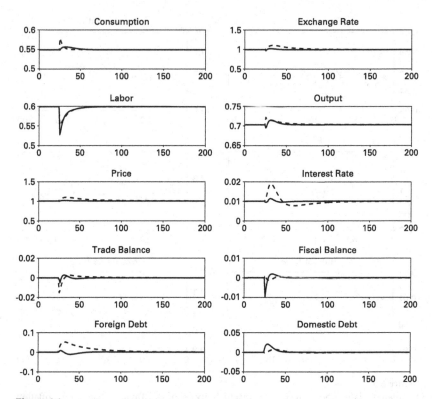

Figure 6.6
Impulse responses following a shock to productivity: inflation and Q growth targeting
(*solid line*) and inflation targeting only (*dashed line*)

Figure 6.6 shows the impulse-responses for the two cases. The main point to note is that consumption increases by less and labor falls by more in an environment with Q growth targeting. On balance, the welfare differences are negligible (see figure 6.7). As in chapter 3, we compute the average consumption compensation necessary for a household to be as well off in the reference regime (inflation targeting only) compared to the alternative (inflation and Q growth targeting). Positive values indicate what households can give up to be as well off in the alternative regime compared to the reference regime; negative values indicate the consumption compensation necessary for households to be as well off. The results here is −0.0007 percent, meaning that the rule with Q growth is, on average, welfare-reducing albeit negligible.

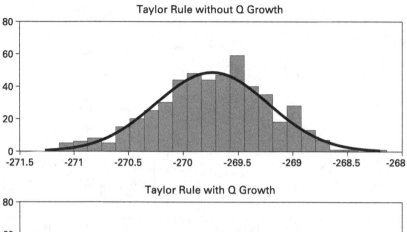

Figure 6.7
Welfare under different policy regimes

6.5.2   Export Shocks

As in chapter 2 we will now examine the case of demand shocks, but this time the export demands are highly volatile:

$$\ln(X_t) = 0.1 \ln(X_{t-1}) + 0.9 \ln(\overline{X}) + \epsilon_t, \qquad \epsilon_t \sim N(0, \sigma_z^2).$$

Figure 6.8 shows the results of one simulated run of recurring export shocks. Compared to figure 6.5, the base runs for the variables in an only inflation targeting regime are highly volatile. Again, the introduction of Q growth greatly reduced the volatility in the variables, but again there is negligible effect on welfare.

6.6   Concluding Remarks

In summary, this chapter has introduced real rigidities in the form of adjustment costs to capital formation and drawn attention to the forward-looking Tobin's Q.[2] We have also examined the effect of

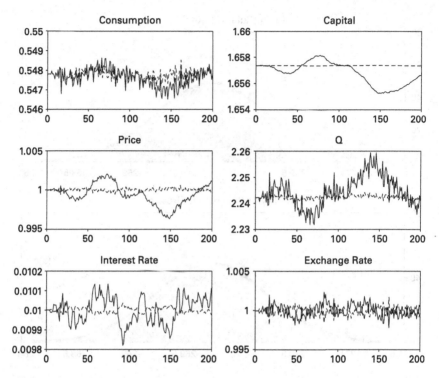

Figure 6.8
Simulated data under recurring export shocks: Taylor rule with inflation and Q growth targeting (*solid line*) and Taylor rule with only inflation targeting (*dashed line*)

incorporating the rate of growth of Tobin's Q as an additional target to inflation for monetary policy. Our simulation results show that adding Q growth in addition to goods price inflation is, on average, welfare-reducing, albeit negligible.[3]

However, more important, the results of this chapter show how changes in monetary policy affect the volatility of real and nominal variables. Since volatility is a key measure of risk, we have thus illustrated a fundamental link between changes in the conduct of monetary policy and risk. Specifically we have shown the reduction in volatility when the Taylor rule includes a Q growth target.

While issues about the financing of investment are not explicit in this model, we echo a comment of Cochrane (2006), namely, "What makes the relationship between macroeconomics and finance so interesting is that risk and related risk premia are not at all 'second order'" (Cochrane 2006, p. 62).

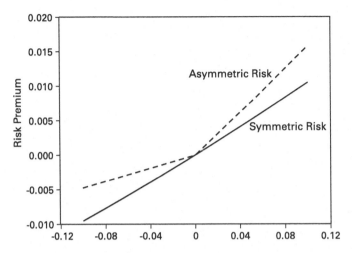

Figure 6.9
Alternative specifications for the risk premium

Computational Exercise: Risk and Q Growth

There is an extensive literature on the behavior of asset prices and excess returns. Specifically, are intertemporal optimizing models able to replicate key features of asset prices and excess returns observed in the real world? One example is the well-known equity premium puzzle first noted by Mehra and Prescott (1985). They found an equity premium or excess return, at annualized rates, of about 6 percent. Despite an extensive literature there is still no widely accepted explanation for the premium except in the most general terms: higher returns are needed to compensate for higher risk.

Risk appears in three ways in this model: in the volatility in the shock process (σ_z), in the coefficient of relative risk aversion in the utility function (η), and in the determination of the risk premia as a function of foreign debt (Φ_t). In previous exercises we suggested changing the stochastic process to allow for time-varying risk as well as changing the coefficient of risk aversion to higher values. Here we suggest changing the determination of the risk premium from the symmetric form used in the book to an asymmetric form. Figure 6.9 shows the changing nature of the risk for different values of the foreign debt. As commented earlier, the projection method is capable of handling such asymmetric behavior. What is the effect of this alternative asymmetric form of risk on Q growth?

7 Economy with Natural Resources

7.1 Introduction

Many small open economies are endowed with rich natural resources but the price of the goods is determined in international markets. What then are the implications of a terms of trade boom for such an economy? The resource boom is hypothesized, in the first instance, to cause a shift in production toward further exploitation of the natural resources. However, theory suggests that an increase in revenue from natural resources will de-industrialize a nation's economy because the ensuing appreciation of the exchange rate will cause the manufacturing sector to be less competitive.

This phenomenon has been studied by many economists and is often called the Dutch disease. The term was coined in 1977 by *The Economist* to describe the decline of the manufacturing sector in the Netherlands after the discovery of natural gas in the 1960s. The classic economic model describing Dutch disease was developed by the economists W. Max Corden and J. Peter Neary in 1982.

Another interesting hypothesis about sectoral differences is associated with the Harrod-Balassa-Samuelson effect. Harrod (1933), Balassa (1964), and Samuelson (1964) drew attention to the phenomenon of how rising productivity-led growth in the traded goods sector led to rising nontraded goods inflation, and real exchange-rate appreciation.

These sort of phenomena can be studied by simulating a multisector DSGE model. The aim of this chapter is to do just that—expand our one-sector model to a two-sector model and simulate the model to compare and contrast the dynamic effects associated with productivity shocks and with terms of trade shock. In reality, open economies are subject to both types of shocks simultaneously and a challenge for emerging market economies is to ensure that the gains associated with the booming resource sectors (due to terms of trade effects) is also translated to economywide improvements in productivity.

The economy we now study has an export sector and an imported manufactured goods sector. The terms of trade are driven by movements in the commodity export price relative to the price of manufactured goods. In this chapter we evaluate monetary policy in a small open economy framework, and in particular, we are concerned with investment in a resource-rich small open economy subjected to the vagaries of international terms of trade shocks.

7.2   Two-Sector Model

The main change to the model studied thus far is the expansion of the production sector to allow for two types of goods: a traded goods sector that "produces" a natural resource (superscript o) and a nontraded sector that produces manufactured goods (superscript h). The natural resource good is consumed domestically as well as exported, and the price is set internationally. The nontraded good is consumed domestically, and the price is set according to the Calvo pricing system. The monetary authority sets the interest rate using a simple linear Taylor rule, and the fiscal authority sets the income tax rate. There is also a range of differentiated products.

7.2.1   Householders and Entrepreneurs

The economy has two types of capital. For simplicity, we assume that the capital stock for the natural resource sector is a fixed endowment:

$$K_t^o = \bar{K}. \tag{7.1}$$

The other capital (manufacturing) is owned by the entrepreneurs who hold shares in all the firms in the economy. The accumulation equation for capital in the manufacturing sector is

$$K_t^h = I_t + (1 - \delta)K_{t-1}^h - \frac{\Psi}{2} \frac{(I_t - \delta K_{t-1}^h)^2}{K_{t-1}^h}, \tag{7.2}$$

where I is imported investment goods and δ is depreciation. These capital equations will not change the first-order conditions in chapter 6, which are

$$C_t^{-\eta} = \Lambda_t(1 + \tau_2)P_t, \tag{7.3}$$

$$L_t^{\varpi} = \Lambda_t(1 - \tau_1)W_t, \tag{7.4}$$

$$\Lambda_t = \Lambda_{t+1}\beta(1 + R_t), \tag{7.5}$$

$$\Lambda_t S_t = \Lambda_{t+1}\beta(1 + R_t^* + \Phi_t + \Phi_t' F_t^*)S_{t+1}, \tag{7.6}$$

$$Q_t = \Lambda_t P_t^k + \beta Q_{t+1}\left[(1 - \delta) + \frac{\Psi(I_{t+1} - \delta K_t^h)\delta}{K_t^h} + \frac{\Psi(I_{t+1} - \delta K_t^h)^2}{2(K_t^h)^2}\right], \tag{7.7}$$

$$\Lambda_t P_t^f = Q_t - Q_t\Psi\frac{(I_t - \delta K_{t-1}^h)}{K_{t-1}^h}, \tag{7.8}$$

$$\Phi_t = \text{sign}(F_{t-1}^*) \cdot \varphi[e^{(|F_{t-1}^*|-\bar{F}^*)} - 1]. \tag{7.9}$$

However, the equations describing the allocation of consumption between the different types of goods needs to be expanded. We start with the household demanding domestic C_t^d and imported goods C_t^f such that composite consumption C_t is given (using the Dixit-Stiglitz aggregators) by the following expression:

$$C_t = [(1 - \gamma_1)^{1/\theta_1}(C_t^d)^{(\theta_1-1)/\theta_1} + (\gamma_1)^{1/\theta_1}(C_t^f)^{(\theta_1-1)/\theta_1}]^{\theta_1/(\theta_1-1)}.$$

The parameter $\theta_1 > 0$ is the intratemporal elasticity of substitution between domestically produced goods C_t^d and internationally produced goods C_t^f, and the parameter γ_1 represents the share of foreign goods in total consumption. Minimizing expenditures gives the demand for domestic and imported goods as

$$C_t^d = (1 - \gamma_1)\left(\frac{P_t^d}{P_t}\right)^{-\theta_1}C_t, \tag{7.10}$$

$$C_t^f = \gamma_1\left(\frac{P_t^f}{P_t}\right)^{-\theta_1}C_t. \tag{7.11}$$

Each composite good is a bundle of differentiated goods j using a Dixit-Stiglitz aggregator

$$C_t^d = \left[\int_0^1 (C_{j,t}^d)^{(\zeta-1)/\zeta}\,dj\right]^{\zeta/(\zeta-1)},$$

$$C_t^f = \left[\int_0^1 (C_{j,t}^f)^{(\zeta-1)/\zeta} \, dj \right]^{\zeta/(\zeta-1)},$$

where j denotes the domestic goods and the elasticity of substitution between differentiated goods is given by $\zeta > 1$. The consumer price index P_t is given by the following formula:

$$P_t = [(1 - \gamma_1)(P_t^d)^{1-\theta_1} + \gamma_1 (P_t^f)^{1-\theta_1}]^{1/(1-\theta_1)}. \tag{7.12}$$

The consumption of domestically-produced goods is, in turn, a composite of nontraded home goods C_t^h and internationally exported goods C_t^o:

$$C_t^d = [(1 - \gamma_2)^{1/\theta_2}(C_t^h)^{(\theta_2-1)/\theta_2} + (\gamma_2)^{1/\theta_2}(C_t^o)^{(\theta_2-1)/\theta_2}]^{\theta_2/(\theta_2-1)}.$$

The parameter θ_2 is the intratemporal elasticity of substitution between domestically produced nontraded home goods C_t^h and domestically produced export goods C_t^o, and the parameter γ_2 represents the share of export goods in the consumption of domestically produced goods. Minimizing expenditures gives the demand for nontraded home goods and traded export goods as

$$C_t^h = (1 - \gamma_2) \left(\frac{P_t^h}{P_t^d} \right)^{-\theta_2} C_t^d, \tag{7.13}$$

$$C_t^o = \gamma_2 \left(\frac{P_t^o}{P_t^d} \right)^{-\theta_2} C_t^d. \tag{7.14}$$

The domestic goods price index P_t^d is given by the following formula:

$$P_t^d = [(1 - \gamma_2)(P_t^h)^{1-\theta_2} + \gamma_2 (P_t^o)^{1-\theta_2}]^{1/(1-\theta_2)}. \tag{7.15}$$

The entrepreneurs also act as importers. We assume that they purchase imported goods Y_t^f at price $S_t P_t^{o*}$. The goods are then rebundled for consumption C_t^f and investment I_t, and sold at a domestic currency price P^f, which is set to cover costs

$$Y_t^f = I_t + C_t^f, \tag{7.16}$$

$$P_t^f = S_t P_t^*. \tag{7.17}$$

Note that this implies that the effects of changes in the exchange rate are fully *passed-through* to the domestic prices of imported goods. There is no stickiness in the price-setting behavior.

7.2.2 Two-Sector Production and Pricing

Production Decisions There are two sectors: a nontraded (home) goods sector (superscript h) and a traded goods (export) sector (superscript o). Both sectors produce differentiated goods via the constant elasticity of substitution production function. Using the artifice of a "bundler" we obtain the following aggregate equations:

$$Y_t^h = Z_t[(1 - \alpha_1)(L_t^h)^{\kappa_1} + \alpha_1(K_t^h)^{\kappa_1}]^{1/\kappa_1}, \tag{7.18}$$

$$Y_t^o = Z_t[(1 - \alpha_2)(L_t^o)^{\kappa_2} + \alpha_2(K_t^o)^{\kappa_2}]^{1/\kappa_2}. \tag{7.19}$$

The export sector is more capital intensive; hence $\alpha_2 > \alpha_1$. For productivity, we assume that the economywide productivity index follows an autoregressive process (in log terms):

$$\ln(Z_t) = \rho \ln(Z_{t-1}) + (1 - \rho) \ln(\bar{Z}) + \epsilon_t, \qquad \epsilon_t \sim N(0, \sigma_z^2). \tag{7.20}$$

The market-clearing conditions becomes

$$Y_t^h = C_t^h + G_t, \tag{7.21}$$

$$Y_t^o = C_t^o + X_t. \tag{7.22}$$

Pricing Decisions The firm producing export goods Y_t^o combines labor L_t^o and capital K_t^o, and sells at a world price P_t^{o*} that is determined overseas. The firm producing nontraded home goods Y_t^h combines labor (L_t^h) and capital K_t^h and sells at a domestic price P_t^h that is determined according to the Calvo pricing system. We assume that the same nominal wage rate W_t holds across both the export producing and nontraded goods producing sectors. The total dividends from firms passed on to households is the sum of the dividends from the export and nontraded goods producing firms:

$$\Pi_t = \Pi_t^o + \Pi_t^h,$$

$$\Pi_t^o = P_t^o Y_t^o - W_t L_t^o,$$

$$\Pi_t = P_t^d Y_t - P_t^k K_t^h - W_t L_t^h.$$

Price of the Export   We assume that the price of exports is determined in the world markets; hence

$$P_t^o = S_t P_t^{o*}. \tag{7.23}$$

Calvo Price Setting for Domestic Goods   We assume that firms set the price of the manufacturing good according to the Calvo (1983) staggered price system. The equations are

$$A_t^{p1} = Y_t^h (P_t^h)^\zeta A_t + \beta \xi A_{t+1}^{p1}, \tag{7.24}$$

$$A_t^{p2} = Y_t^h (P_t^h)^\zeta + \beta \xi A_{t+1}^{p2}, \tag{7.25}$$

$$P_t^a = \frac{A_t^{p1}}{A_t^{p2}}; \tag{7.26}$$

$$A_t = \left\{ \begin{array}{c} \left(\frac{1}{Z}\right)[(1-\alpha)(\alpha W)^{\kappa/(\kappa-1)} + \alpha((1-\alpha)P^k)^{\kappa/(\kappa-1)}]^{-1/\kappa} \\ \times [W(\alpha W)^{1/(\kappa-1)} + P^k((1-\alpha)P^k)^{1/(\kappa-1)}] \end{array} \right\},$$

$$P_t^h = [\xi(P_{t-1}^h)^{1-\zeta} + (1-\xi)(P_t^a)^{1-\zeta}]^{1/(1-\zeta)}. \tag{7.27}$$

7.2.3   Monetary and Fiscal Authorities

Monetary Policy   The domestic interest rate R_t is assumed to follow a partial adjustment mechanism for inflation targeting:

$$R_t = \phi_2 R_{t-1} + (1-\phi_2)[R^* + \phi_1(\pi_t - \tilde{\pi})], \qquad \phi_1 > 1, \tag{7.28}$$

$$\pi_t = \left(\frac{P_t}{P_{t-1}}\right)^4 - 1,$$

where $\bar{R}$ is the long-run steady-state interest rate, π_t is the actual inflation rate, and $\tilde{\pi}$ is the target inflation rate. The parameter ϕ_2 reflects the fact that the monetary authority engages in interest-rate smoothing, while the restriction $\phi_1 > 1$ respects the Taylor principle.

Taxes and Domestic Debt   The income and consumption tax rates are fixed, but government spending G_t is assumed to be sensitive to the size of the public debt B_t relative to the steady-state value $\bar{B}$:

$$G_t = \bar{G} + \chi_1(B_{t-1} - \bar{B}). \tag{7.29}$$

The Treasury receives taxes and borrows to finance government expenditure so that the evolution of the bonds becomes

$$B_t = (1 + R_{t-1})B_{t-1} + P_tG_t - (\tau_1 W_t L_t + \tau_2 P_t C_t), \tag{7.30}$$

where B is a one-period domestic bond.

7.2.4   Exports and Foreign Debt

Exports depend on the lagged real exchange rate (S_{t-1}/P_{t-1}) relative to its steady-state value $\overline{S/P}$:

$$\ln(X_t) = \ln(\bar{X}) + \chi_2\left[\ln\left(\frac{S_{t-1}}{P_{t-1}}\right) - \ln\left(\frac{\bar{S}}{\bar{P}}\right)\right]. \tag{7.31}$$

The foreign debt evolves as follows:

$$S_tF_t^* = (1 + R_{t-1}^* + \Phi_{t-1})S_tF_{t-1}^* + S_tP_t^*Y_t^f - P_t^oX_t. \tag{7.32}$$

7.3   Solution Algorithm

Overall, we seek to determine decision rules for consumption C_t, the exchange rate S_t, the numerator and denominator of the forward-looking Calvo prices for the nontraded domestic goods A_t^{p1}, A_t^{p1}, as well as decision rule for investment I_t from which we back out Q_t. The decision rules are specified as nonlinear neural network functional forms of state variables. The state variables used as arguments for these decision rules are the current shocks to productivity Z_t, foreign debt F_{t-1}, the interest rate R_{t-1}, government bonds, B_{t-1} and the capital stock K_{t-1}^h.

$$\hat{C}_t = \psi^c(\Omega^c; \mathbf{x}_t),$$

$$\hat{S}_t = \psi^s(\Omega^s; \mathbf{x}_t),$$

$$\hat{A}_t^{p1} = \psi^{p1}(\Omega^{p1}; \mathbf{x}_t),$$

$$\hat{A}_t^{p2} = \psi^{p2}(\Omega^{p2}; \mathbf{x}_t),$$

$$\hat{I}_t = \psi^I(\Omega^I; \mathbf{x}_t),$$

$$\mathbf{x}_t = \{(Z_t - \bar{Z}), (F_{t-1} - \bar{F}), (R_{t-1} - \bar{R}), (B_{t-1} - \bar{B}), (K^h_{t-1} - \overline{K^h})\}.$$

7.3.1 Euler Errors

The Euler errors are the same as those in chapter 6, except that it is P^h that is subjected to price stickiness and K^h that is subjected to investment dynamics:

$$\epsilon^c_t = \frac{\hat{C}^{-\eta}_t}{(1 + \tau_2)\hat{P}_t}\left[\frac{1}{(1 + R_t)}\right] - \beta\left[\frac{\hat{C}^{-\eta}_{t+1}}{(1 + \tau_2)\hat{P}_{t+1}}\right],$$

$$\epsilon^s_t = \frac{\hat{C}^{-\eta}_t}{P_t}\left[\frac{\hat{S}_t}{(1 + R^*_t + \Phi_t + \Phi'_t F^*_t)}\right] - \beta\left[\hat{S}_{t+1}\frac{\hat{C}^{-\eta}_{t+1}}{P_{t+1}}\right],$$

$$\epsilon^{P^h}_t = \frac{\hat{A}^{p1}_t}{\hat{A}^{p2}_t} - \frac{Y_t(P^h_t)^\zeta A_t + \beta\xi\hat{A}^{p1}_{t+1}}{Y_t(P^h_t)^\zeta + \beta\xi\hat{A}^{p2}_{t+1}},$$

$$\epsilon^q_t = \frac{(\hat{Q}_t - \Lambda_t P^k_t)}{\left[(1 - \delta) + \frac{\Psi(I_t - \delta K^h_t)\delta}{K^h_t} + \frac{\Psi(I_t - \delta K^h_t)^2}{2(K^h_t)^2}\right]} - \beta\hat{Q}_{t+1}.$$

The coefficients of the decision rules are obtained from stochastic simulations based on minimization of the sum of squared Euler equation errors.

7.3.2 Accuracy Checks

Descriptive statistics of the Judd-Gaspar statistics (the absolute Euler equation errors relative to their respective forward-looking variable) are shown in table 7.1. Figure 7.1 shows that the distribution of the Judd-Gaspar statistics. They are all relatively small.

The robustness of the approximations is corroborated by the DenHann-Marcet test statistics shown in table 7.2 and figure 7.2.

7.4 Simulation Analysis

7.4.1 Impulse-Response Paths

To recap, we are working with a two-sector model: a resource-rich sector with fixed capital and variable labor costs, and a manufacturing

Table 7.1
Judd-Gaspar statistic ($\times 10^{-2}$)

	$\dfrac{\|\epsilon_t^c\|}{C_t}$	$\dfrac{\|\epsilon_t^s\|}{S_t}$	$\dfrac{\|\epsilon_t^p\|}{P_t^h}$	$\dfrac{\|\epsilon_t^q\|}{Q_t}$
Mean	0.3733	0.3852	1.3899	0.3094
Standard deviation	0.0236	0.0728	0.0800	0.0176

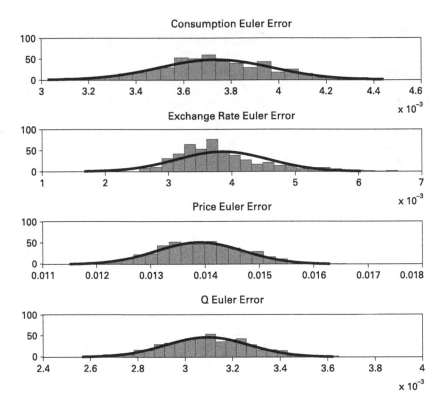

Figure 7.1
Judd-Gasper statistic

Table 7.2
DenHann-Marcet test

	Lag order			
	1	2	3	4
Lower region ($p < 0.05$)	0.046	0.036	0.034	0.048
Upper region ($p > 0.95$)	0.056	0.052	0.034	0.056

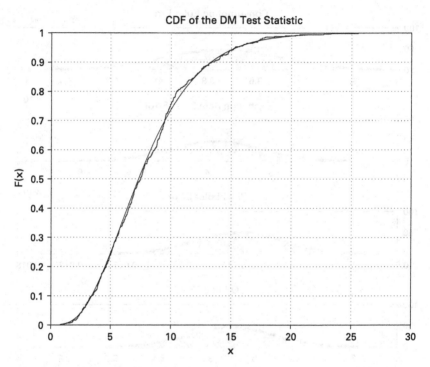

Figure 7.2
DenHann-Marcet test of accuracy

sector with variable capital and labor costs. The productivity shock is an economywide shock. Following a once-only shock in the productivity index, figure 7.3 shows that the impulse-response paths for aggregate consumption, the exchange rate, the real wage and the interest rate are similar to those we have already seen.

In this scenario, while output in both sectors increases, the output in the manufacturing sector is relatively higher than output in the natural resource (export) sector. Prices in the home goods manufacturing

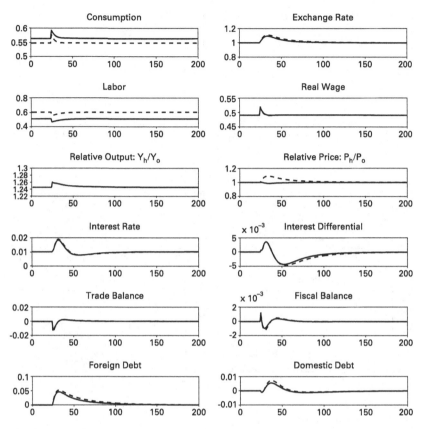

Figure 7.3
Impulse responses following a productivity shock: with (*solid line*) and without (*dashed line*) natural resources sector

sector fall by more, which in turn encourages more consumption of home goods. The foreign debt worsens because imports for consumption and investment exceed the exports of the traded (natural resource) good (recall that the terms of trade, P^o/P^f, is fixed in this scenario).

7.4.2 Stochastic Simulations

We have come a long way from the flexible price no frictions model discussed in chapter 2. It might be useful at this point to consider how frictions affect the time-series behavior of the forward-looking variables: consumption, exchange rate, and price. Figure 7.4 shows the distribution of the first-order autocorrelations for the case with no

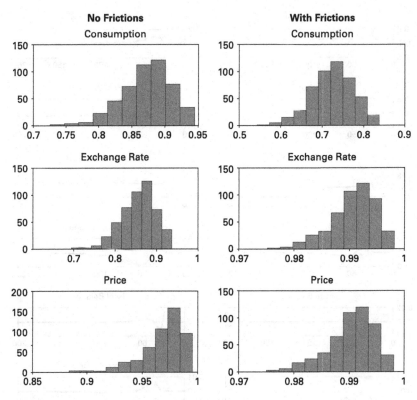

Figure 7.4
First-order autocorrelations

frictions and the case with frictions. As expected, allowing for stickiness in the setting of prices increases the levels of the first-order autocorrelations. However, frictions, in general, lower consumption, which in turn lower the size of the autocorrelations. The exchange rate becomes even more persistent in its behavior. Intuitively this is because more factors now react less fully to a shock—the past plays a bigger role.

7.5 Terms-of-Trade Shocks

The two-sector model allows us to explore the macroeconomic implications of terms of trade shocks for an open economy with a natural resource sector and a home sector. Specifically,

$$\ln(P_t^{x*}) = \rho \ln(P_{t-1}^{x*}) + (1 - \rho) \ln(\overline{P_t^{x*}}) + \epsilon_t, \qquad \epsilon_t \sim N(0, \sigma_z^2).$$

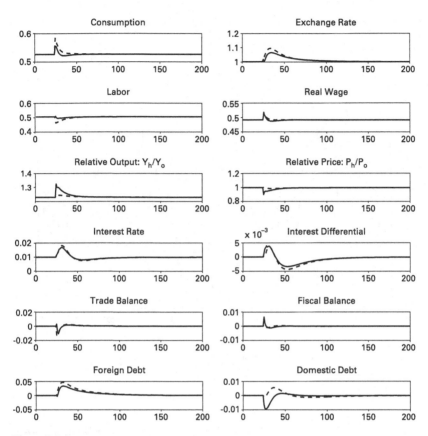

Figure 7.5
Impulse responses: Terms-of-trade shock (*solid line*) and productivity shock (*dashed line*)

The evolution of the price mimics actual data generating processes, with a normally distributed innovation with standard deviation set at 0.01. We assume that the price of the imports P_t^{m*} is constant (normalized at one) so that the stochastic process describes a mean-reverting terms-of-trade process. This is a simulation study about the design of monetary policy for an economy subjected to relative price shocks.

Figure 7.5 shows the impulse-responses—both shocks result in an increase in consumption and a depreciation of the exchange rate. Both shocks also result in a fall in labor and increase in the real wage. However, for a terms-of-trade shock there is a fall in the relative price of home goods, which encourages consumers to shift to home goods. The terms-of-trade shock discourages export. Domestic debt improves in

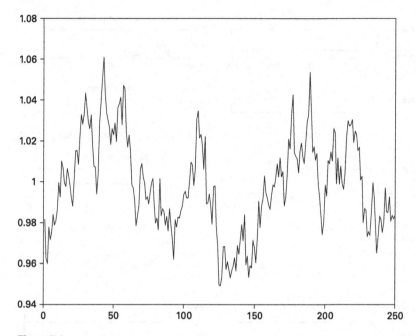

Figure 7.6
One realization of the terms-of-trade shocks

this environment, which then supports an increase in government expenditure.

To ensure that the results are robust, we conducted 500 simulations (each containing a time series of 200 realizations of terms-of-trade shocks). Figure 7.6 shows the simulated paths for one time series realization of the exogenous terms of trade index.

The correlations in figure 7.7 show the positive relationship between fiscal and current account balances for a productivity shock, and the negative relationship between fiscal and current account balances for a terms-of-trade shock. The former traces the supply implications of the shock while the latter traces out the demand implications.

7.6 Concluding Remarks

This chapter has expanded the production side to allow for a manufacturing sector with capital accumulation and a natural resource sector with fixed endowments of capital. We compared the dynamic effects of two types of shocks: an economywide technology shock

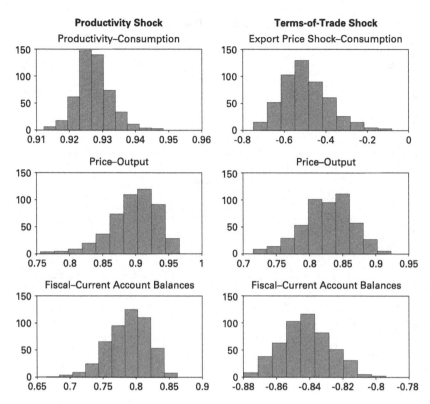

Figure 7.7
Correlations

and a terms-of-trade shock for the price of export goods. Obviously economies are subject to changes in productivity as well as to changes in their terms of trade. In fact favorable terms-of-trade shocks are opportunities for countries to enhance underlying economywide productivity growth, and understanding the relationship among terms-of-trade movements, productivity, and economic policy design is a challenge for development macroeconomists. We have treated the shocks independently in this chapter simply to highlight their individual effects.

Computational Exercise: Real Exchange Cross-Correlations

In this chapter we examined *contemporaneous* correlation coefficients. However, we also stressed that persistence of exchange rates increases

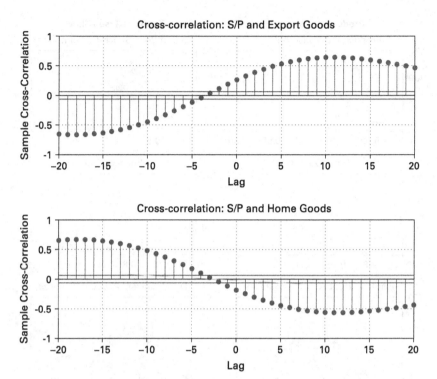

Figure 7.8
Cross-correlations of S/P with Y^o and Y^h. Data are in logarithms and HP filtered.

as we incorporate more frictions into the model. Further insights about behavior can be gleaned by examining the correlations of variables with different lags. For example, how does the production of exports or home goods correlate with lagged as well as current real exchange rates? Since the real exchange rate is an endogenous variable, we can also ask how the real exchange rate correlates with lagged expansion or contraction in home goods and export production?

Figure 7.8 shows the *cross-correlations* for lags and leads of $-20 < \tau_1 < 20$ for the real exchange rate with Y^h and Y^o for the case of recurring terms of trade shocks. Values to the right of zero show the correlations of the output variables with increasing lags of the real exchange rate, while values to the left of zero represent correlations of the real exchange rate with lags of the output variables.

We see persistence in the cross-correlations. A depreciation of the real exchange rate, not surprisingly, is correlated with a sustained increase in Y^o and a fall in Y^h. Similarly a rise in Y^o is correlated with an appreciation of the real exchange rate over many quarters.

An obvious computational exercise is to repeat this exercise for the same variables, for continuing economywide real productivity shocks. Will we obtain the same pattern of cross-correlation coefficients? Why not?

8 Financial Frictions

8.1 Introduction

This chapter introduces a banking sector with limited participation by households. Up to now, we have assumed that there are no financial constraints: the cost of borrowing is the same as the cost of lending, and they are both in turn equal to the risk-free rate. What happens to the dynamics of our economy if we now allow for financial frictions?

In this context we take up the issue of flexible exchange rates for a small open economy. Guillermo Calvo has argued that there are "compelling reasons" for small emerging market countries to stay away from exchange rate flexibility. A hard peg such as dollarization may put a country on a "fast track" toward monetary and financial stability, which otherwise may take years to achieve (Calvo 2005, p. 404). At the same time, inflation targeting is gaining ground among policy makers around the world. Calvo notes that inflation targeting, while having a flexbile exchange rate, differs from the classical pure flexible system originally described by Mundell (1961) and summarized by De Grauwe (1994). The advantage of inflation targeting is that it prevents deflation of the basket of goods, which, of course, include nontradeables (Calvo 2005, p. 418).

Faia (2005) has examined the choice of exchange rate regime in a two-country framework. She finds that the stabilization property of a flexible exchange rate system is enhanced in the presence of financial frictions, whether or not the monetary or productivity shocks of the two countries are correlated. Lahiri, Singh, and Végh (2005) have examined the choice of exchange rate regimes in the context of financial frictions but without sticky prices. They found that fixed rates dominate flexible rates under productivity shocks, whereas flexible rates dominate under monetary shocks. This result is in stark contrast to the Mundell (1961) result, which, of course, assumes complete price rigidity.

In this chapter we examine the issue of inflation targeting versus fixed exchange rates in the context of a small open economy with limited participation, endogenous risk premia, investment dynamics in traded and nontraded goods sectors, as well as sticky prices and distortionary taxes. We only examine an economywide productivity shock, in a one-country model, but with two sectors.

8.2   DSGE Model with Banking

In this chapter we allow for an explicit financial sector. Households now lend to the banks (in the form of deposits); firms borrow from the banks to finance their production activity. The banks in turn accept deposits from households and borrow from foreignors and lend to firms and the government sector. They also comply with the reserve ratio requirement.

8.2.1   Household Sector: Consumption and Saving

The main change is that householders now invest their savings as bank deposits. The household budget equation can be written as

$$W_t L_t + (1 + R_{t-1}^m) M_{t-1} + \Pi_t + P_t^k K_t^h$$

$$= P_t C_t + M_t + \tau_1 W_t L_t + \tau_2 P_t C_t + P_t^f I_t,$$

where W is the wage rate, M is deposits with the banking sector, R^m is the interest rate on deposits, Π is distributed profits, τ_1 is the income tax rate, and τ_2 is the consumption tax rate. The financial asset is state-contingent with one period maturity. The amount deposited in the banking sector, M_t, can be obtained from the following law of motion:

$$M_t = [(1 - \tau_1) W_t L_t + \Pi_t + P_t^k K_t^h] + (1 + R_{t-1}^m) M_{t-1}$$

$$- (1 + \tau_2) P_t C_t - P_t^f I_t. \tag{8.1}$$

As in chapter 7, we assume that one of the capital stock is fixed (given endowment/resources) while the other type of capital evolves as follows:

$$K_t^o = \bar{K}, \tag{8.2}$$

$$K_t^h = I_t + (1 - \delta)K_{t-1}^h - \frac{\Psi}{2} \frac{(I_t - \delta K_{t-1}^h)^2}{K_{t-1}^h}. \tag{8.3}$$

The household takes the wage as given and chooses consumption, labor, money holdings, capital, and investment to maximize utility subject to the budget constraint. We assume that each household chooses nontrivial solutions in that $C_t > 0$, $L_t > 0$, $M_t > 0$, $K_t^h > 0$, and $I_t > 0$. The Lagrangean problem becomes

$$\mathcal{L} = \sum_{t=0}^{\infty} \beta^t \left\{ \begin{array}{l} U(C_{t+t}, L_{t+t}) - \Lambda_{t+t} \left[\begin{array}{l} (1 + \tau_2)P_{t+t}C_{t+t} + M_{t+t} + P_{t+t}^f I_{t+i} \\ + (\tau_1 - 1)W_{t+t}L_{t+t} - \Pi_{t+t} \\ - (1 + R_{t-1+t}^m)M_{t-1+t} - P_{t+t}^k K_{t+i}^h \end{array} \right] \\ - Q_{t+i} \left[K_{t+i}^h - I_{t+i} - (1 - \delta)K_{t-1+i}^h + \frac{\Psi}{2} \frac{(I_{t+i} - \delta K_{t-1+i}^h)^2}{K_{t-1+i}^h} \right] \end{array} \right\},$$

and the first order conditions are

$$\frac{\partial \mathcal{L}}{\partial C_t} = C_t^{-\eta} - \Lambda_t(1 + \tau_2)P_t = 0,$$

$$\frac{\partial \mathcal{L}}{\partial L_t} = -L_t^{\varpi} - \Lambda_t(\tau_1 - 1)W_t = 0,$$

$$\frac{\partial \mathcal{L}}{\partial M_t} = -\Lambda_t + \beta\Lambda_{t+1}(1 + R_t^m) = 0,$$

$$\frac{\partial \mathcal{L}}{\partial K_t^h} = \Lambda_t P_t^k - Q_t + \beta Q_{t+1}(1 - \delta) - \beta Q_{t+1}\frac{\Psi}{2} \left[\begin{array}{l} \dfrac{-2(I_{t+1} - \delta K_t^h)\delta}{K_t^h} \\ - \dfrac{(I_{t+1} - \delta K_t^h)^2}{(K_t^h)^2} \end{array} \right] = 0,$$

$$\frac{\partial \mathcal{L}}{\partial I_t} = -\Lambda_t P_t^f + Q_t - Q_t\Psi\frac{(I_t - \delta K_t^h)}{K_t^h} = 0.$$

The behavioral equations with savings as deposits now become

$$C_t^{-\eta} = \Lambda_t(1 + \tau_2)P_t, \tag{8.4}$$

$$L_t^{\varpi} = \Lambda_t(1 - \tau_1)W_t, \tag{8.5}$$

$$\Lambda_t = \Lambda_{t+1}\beta(1 + R_t^m), \tag{8.6}$$

$$Q_t = \Lambda_t P_t^k + \beta Q_{t+1}\left[(1 - \delta) + \frac{\Psi(I_{t+1} - \delta K_t^h)\delta}{K_t^h} + \frac{\Psi(I_{t+1} - \delta K_t^h)^2}{2(K_t^h)^2}\right], \tag{8.7}$$

$$\Lambda_t P_t^f = Q_t - Q_t \Psi \frac{(I_t - \delta K_{t-1}^h)}{K_{t-1}^h}. \tag{8.8}$$

The other consumption equations are

$$C_t^d = (1 - \gamma_1)\left(\frac{P_t^d}{P_t}\right)^{-\theta_1} C_t, \tag{8.9}$$

$$C_t^f = \gamma_1\left(\frac{P_t^f}{P_t}\right)^{-\theta_1} C_t, \tag{8.10}$$

$$C_t^h = (1 - \gamma_2)\left(\frac{P_t^h}{P_t^d}\right)^{-\theta_2} C_t^d, \tag{8.11}$$

$$C_t^o = \gamma_2\left(\frac{P_t^o}{P_t^d}\right)^{-\theta_2} C_t^d; \tag{8.12}$$

$$P_t = [(1 - \gamma_1)(P_t^d)^{1-\theta_1} + \gamma_1(P_t^f)^{1-\theta_1}]^{1/(1-\theta_1)}, \tag{8.13}$$

$$P_t^d = [(1 - \gamma_2)(P_t^h)^{1-\theta} + \gamma_2(P_t^o)^{1-\theta_2}]^{1/(1-\theta_2)}. \tag{8.14}$$

The importers buy goods Y_t^f at the price $S_t P_t^*$ and rebundle the goods for consumption C_t^f and investment I_t:

$$Y_t^f = C_t^f + I_t. \tag{8.15}$$

We now assume that they borrow a fraction μ_1 of the funds necessary for their purchases from the banks. The importer sells these goods at a domestic currency price P^f, which is set to cover the costs of buying the imports $S_t P_t^* Y_t^f$ plus the inputed costs of the loan $R_{t-1}^n N_t^f$:

$$N_t^f = \mu_1(S_t P_t^* Y_t^f), \tag{8.16}$$

$$P_t^f Y_t^f = S_t P_t^* Y_t^f + R_{t-1}^n N_t^f,$$

$$P_t^f = (1 + \mu_1 R_{t-1}^n)(S_t P_t^*). \tag{8.17}$$

This implies that the effect of changes in the exchange rate on the domestic price of imported goods P_t^f, have a time-varying pass-through effect.

8.2.2 Firms—Production, Pricing, and Borrowing

The production and market-clearing equations carry over from chapter 7:

$$Y_t^h = Z_t[(1 - \alpha_1)(L_t^h)^{\kappa_1} + \alpha_1(K_t^h)^{\kappa_1}]^{1/\kappa_1}, \tag{8.18}$$

$$Y_t^o = Z_t[(1 - \alpha_2)(L_t^o)^{\kappa_2} + \alpha_2(K_t^o)^{\kappa_2}]^{1/\kappa_2}; \tag{8.19}$$

$$\ln(Z_t) = \rho \ln(Z_{t-1}) + (1 - \rho) \ln(\bar{Z}) + \epsilon_t, \qquad \epsilon_t \sim N(0, \sigma_z^2); \tag{8.20}$$

$$Y_t^h = C_t^h + G_t, \tag{8.21}$$

$$Y_t^o = C_t^o + X_t. \tag{8.22}$$

The firm producing export goods Y_t^o combines labor L_t^o and capital K_t^o and sells at a price P_t^o, which is determined overseas. Thus the pass-through effect for exports is unitary:

$$P_t^o = S_t P_t^{o*} \tag{8.23}$$

The firm producing nontraded home goods Y_t^h combines labor L_t^h and capital K_t^h and sells at a price P_t^h, which is determined according to the Calvo pricing system. There are two input costs: the price of labor and the price of capital. The wage rate is determined competitively, and we assume that the same nominal wage rate W_t holds across both the export and nontraded goods producing sectors.

We now assume that firms have an overdraft arrangement with the banks. They borrow bank loans N_t at rate R_t^n. The amount borrowed is a certain fraction, μ_2, of their wage bill, $W_t L_t^h$, for which they impute the interest cost at the prevailing rate R_{t-1}^n (there are no loans in the export goods sector). In other words, the demand for loans N_t^h by the manufacturing firms is given by the following equation:

$$N_t^h = \mu_2 W_t L_t^h \tag{8.24}$$

Thus, overall, total dividends firms passed on to households is the sum of the dividends from the export and nontraded goods producing firms:

$$\Pi_t = \Pi_t^o + \Pi_t^h,$$

$$\Pi_t^o = P_t^o Y_t^o - W_t L_t^o,$$

$$\Pi_t^h = P_t^h Y_t^h - P_t^k K_t^h - (1 + \mu_2 R_{t-1}^n) W_t L_t^h.$$

Assuming then that firms set the price of each manufacturing good according to the Calvo (1983) staggered price system yields the equations

$$A_t^h = \left\{ \left(\frac{1}{Z}\right) \left[\begin{array}{c} (1-\alpha)(\alpha(1+\mu_2 R_{t-1}^n)W_t)^{\kappa/(\kappa-1)} \\ + \alpha((1-\alpha)P_t^k)^{\kappa/(\kappa-1)} \end{array} \right]^{-1/\kappa} \times \left[\begin{array}{c} (1+\mu_2 R_{t-1}^n)W_t(\alpha(1+\mu_2 R_{t-1}^n)W_t)^{1/(\kappa-1)} \\ + P_t^k((1-\alpha)P_t^k)^{1/(\kappa-1)} \end{array} \right] \right\}, \qquad (8.25)$$

$$A_t^{p1} = Y_t^h(P_t^h)^\zeta A_t^h + \beta \xi A_{t+1}^n, \qquad (8.26)$$

$$A_t^{p2} = Y_t^h(P_t^h)^\zeta + \beta \xi A_{t+1}^d, \qquad (8.27)$$

$$P_t^a = \frac{A_t^{p1}}{A_t^{p2}}, \qquad (8.28)$$

$$P_t^h = [\xi(P_{t-1}^h)^{1-\zeta} + (1-\xi)(P_t^a)^{1-\zeta}]^{1/(1-\zeta)}. \qquad (8.29)$$

8.2.3   Monetary and Fiscal Authorities

Monetary Policy   The central bank is assumed to adopt a Taylor rule with smoothing:

$$R_t = \phi_2 R_{t-1} + (1-\phi_2)[R^* + \phi_1(\pi_t - \tilde{\pi})], \qquad \phi_1 > 1, \qquad (8.30)$$

$$\pi_t = \left(\frac{P_t}{P_{t-1}}\right)^4 - 1.$$

Taxes and Domestic Debt The income and consumption tax rates are fixed, but government spending G_t is assumed to be sensitive to the size of the public debt B_t relative to the steady-state value $\bar{B}$:

$$G_t = \bar{G} + \chi_1(B_{t-1} - \bar{B}). \tag{8.31}$$

The central bank manages the finances of the Treasury. Hence it receives taxes and borrows by issuing one period bonds B to finance the government expenditure. Also, in a model with financial frictions (inputed interest costs and reserve requirements), the central bank has to manage the amount of liquidity LQ in the system to support its monetary policy (intuitively it has to ensure that the demand and supply of funds clears at the policy interest rate). We assume that liquidity is managed via open market operations so that the evolution of bonds becomes

$$B_t = (1 + R_{t-1})B_{t-1} + P_t^h G_t - (\tau_1 W_t L_t + \tau_2 P_t C_t) + LQ_t. \tag{8.32}$$

The required liquidity to support this policy regime is

$$LQ_t = (1 + R_{t-1}^n)[(1 - \psi_2)N_{t-1} - N_t] - \psi_1 M_t, \tag{8.33}$$

$$N_t = N_t^f + N_t^h, \tag{8.34}$$

where ψ_1 is the reserve requirement ratio and ψ_2 is the default loan rate. As we can see from the equation, LQ_t bridges the gap caused by imputed and actual interest costs as well as the cost of loan defaults and the cost of maintaining reserves.

8.2.4 Exports and Foreign Debt

Exports depend on the lagged real exchange (S_{t-1}/P_{t-1}) relative to its steady-state value $(\overline{S/P})$:

$$\ln(X_t) = \ln(\bar{X}) + \chi_2\left[\ln\left(\frac{S_{t-1}}{P_{t-1}}\right) - \ln\left(\frac{\bar{S}}{\bar{P}}\right)\right]. \tag{8.35}$$

As in earlier chapters, we introduce a risk premium term Φ_t:

$$\Phi_t = \text{sign}(F_{t-1}) \cdot \varphi[e^{(|F_{t-1}| - \bar{F})} - 1]. \tag{8.36}$$

The foreign debt evolves as follows:

$$S_t F_t^* = (1 + R_{t-1}^* + \Phi_{t-1})S_t F_{t-1}^* + S_t P_t^* Y_t^f - P_t^o X_t \tag{8.37}$$

8.2.5 Financial Sector

Banks accept deposits from households (M_t), pay a rate R_t^m, and hold reserves as a fixed proportion of deposits, ψ_1 given by the expression $\psi_1 M_t$. They lend to firms (N_t), but we assume that ψ_2 of total loans default. They also lend to the government (in the form of bonds B_t) and receive a risk-free rate on government bonds given by R_t. Finally, banks can borrow internationally (F_t). But while the international return on foreign assets is given by R_t^*, we also assume an asset-elastic foreign interest-rate risk premium. The Lagrangian problem is

$$\mathcal{L} = \sum_{t=0}^{\infty} \beta^t \left\{ \begin{array}{l} (1 + R_{t-1+t})B_{t-1+t} + (1 + R_{t-1+t}^n)(1 - \psi_2)N_{t-1+t} \\ - (1 + R_{t-1+t}^* + \Phi_{t-1+t})F_{t-1+t}^* S_{t+t} - (1 + R_{t-1+t}^m)M_{t-1+t} \\ - \Upsilon_{t+t}(B_{t+t} + N_{t+t} + \psi_1 M_{t+t} - M_{t+t} - S_{t+t}F_{t+t}^*) \end{array} \right\}.$$

This expressions tells us that the cash flow of the bank comes from its gross returns from bonds and loans plus new deposits and foreign borrowings, less gross interest on deposits and foreign loans as well as the costs associated with loans and reserve deposits. The first-order conditions are

$$\frac{\partial \mathcal{L}}{\partial B_t} = -\Upsilon_t + \beta(1 + R_t),$$

$$\frac{\partial \mathcal{L}}{\partial F_t^*} = \Upsilon_t S_t - \beta(1 + R_t^* + \Phi_t + \Phi_t' F_t^*)S_{t+1},$$

$$\frac{\partial \mathcal{L}}{\partial M_t} = \Upsilon_t(1 - \psi_1) - \beta(1 + R_t^m),$$

$$\frac{\partial \mathcal{L}}{\partial N_t} = -\Upsilon_t + \beta(1 + R_t^n)(1 - \psi_2).$$

Substituting out Υ_t yields

$$(1 + R_t)S_t = (1 + R_t^* + \Phi_t + \Phi_t' F_t^*)S_{t+1}, \tag{8.38}$$

$$(1 + R_t)(1 - \psi_1) = (1 + R_t^m), \tag{8.39}$$

$$\frac{(1 + R_t)}{(1 - \psi_2)} = (1 + R_t^n). \tag{8.40}$$

We see that the deposit rate is always below the risk-free government bond rate while the lending rate is always above the risk-free rate.

8.3 Solution Algorithm

The decision variables are as in chapter 7, but we now have an extra state variables, deposits M_{t-1}:

$$\hat{C}_t = \psi^c(\Omega^c; x_t),$$

$$\hat{S}_t = \psi^s(\Omega^s; x_t),$$

$$\hat{A}_t^{p1} = \psi^{p1}(\Omega^{p1}; x_t),$$

$$\hat{A}_t^{p2} = \psi^{p2}(\Omega^{p2}; x_t),$$

$$\hat{I}_t = \psi^I(\Omega^I; x_t),$$

$$x_t = \left\{ \begin{array}{l} (Z_t - \bar{Z}), (F_{t-1} - \bar{F}), (R_{t-1} - \bar{R}), \\ (B_{t-1} - \bar{B}), (K_{t-1}^h - \bar{K^h}), (M_{t-1} - \bar{M}) \end{array} \right\}.$$

The Euler errors must also be adjusted to reflect the fact that we have introduced different interest rates:

$$\epsilon_t^c = \frac{\hat{C}_t^{-\eta}}{(1+\tau_2)\hat{P}_t} \left[\frac{1}{(1+R_t^m)} \right] - \beta \left[\frac{\hat{C}_{t+1}^{-\eta}}{(1+\tau_2)\hat{P}_{t+1}} \right],$$

$$\epsilon_t^s = \frac{\hat{C}_t^{-\eta}}{P_t} \left[\frac{\hat{S}_t}{(1+R_t^* + \Phi_t + \Phi_t' F_t^*)} \right] - \beta \left[\hat{S}_{t+1} \frac{\hat{C}_{t+1}^{-\eta}}{P_{t+1}} \right],$$

$$\epsilon_t^p = \frac{\hat{A}_t^{p1}}{\hat{A}_t^{p2}} - \frac{Y_t(P_t)^\zeta A_t^h + \beta\xi\hat{A}_{t+1}^{p1}}{Y_t(P_t)^\zeta + \beta\xi\hat{A}_{t+1}^{p2}},$$

$$\epsilon_t^q = \frac{(\hat{Q}_t - \Lambda_t P_t^k)}{\left[(1-\delta) + \frac{\Psi(I_t - \delta K_t^h)\delta}{K_t^h} + \frac{\Psi(I_t - \delta K_t^h)^2}{2(K_t^h)^2} \right]} - \beta\hat{Q}_{t+1}.$$

The Judd-Gaspar statistics in table 8.1 and figure 8.1 and the DenHann-Marcet test are shown in table 8.2 and figure 8.2, confirm the accuracy of the approximations.

Table 8.1
Judd-Gaspar statistic

	$\dfrac{\|\epsilon_t^c\|}{C_t}$	$\dfrac{\|\epsilon_t^s\|}{S_t}$	$\dfrac{\|\epsilon_t^p\|}{P_t}$	$\dfrac{\|\epsilon_t^q\|}{Q_t}$
Mean	0.3966	0.3442	1.2742	0.2959
Standard deviation	0.0232	0.0408	0.0747	0.0175

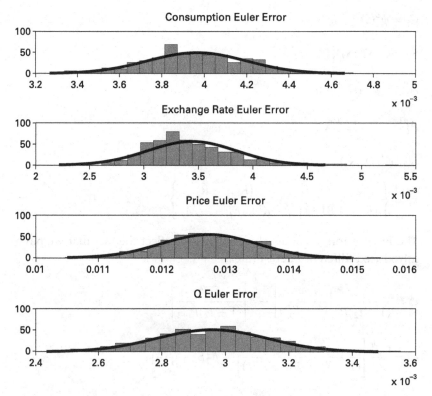

Figure 8.1
Judd-Gasper statistic

Table 8.2
DenHann-Marcet test

	Lag order			
	1	2	3	4
Lower region ($p < 0.05$)	0.050	0.042	0.042	0.050
Upper region ($p > 0.95$)	0.038	0.048	0.050	0.042

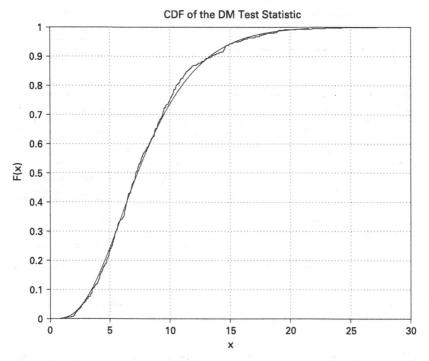

Figure 8.2
DenHann-Marcet test of accuracy

8.4 Simulation Analysis

8.4.1 Impulse-Response Paths
Figure 8.3 shows the impulse-response paths of key macroeconomic indicators for a small open economy following a once-only shock in the productivity index. The model now includes sticky prices, taxes, capital accumulation and financial frictions. In this environment the cost of financial intermediation and the linking of loans to the wage

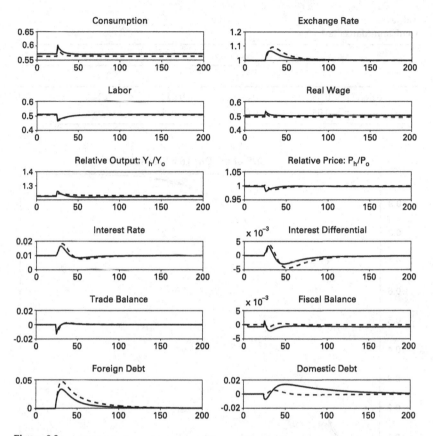

Figure 8.3
Impulse responses following a productivity shock: with (*solid line*) and without (*dashed line*) financial frictions

bill have pushed up the cost of production. Hence the main insight here is that compared to chapter 7, we see that introducing financial frictions affects the behavior of foreign and domestic debt. The deterioration of the foreign debt is less because fewer imports are demanded. The behavior of the domestic debt now reflects the need to engage in open market operations to support the interest-rate policy (via the liquidity variable).

8.4.2 Macroeconomic Correlations

Do financial frictions matter? A priori, frictions can "tighten" or "loosen" relationships observed in a flexible economy, in other words,

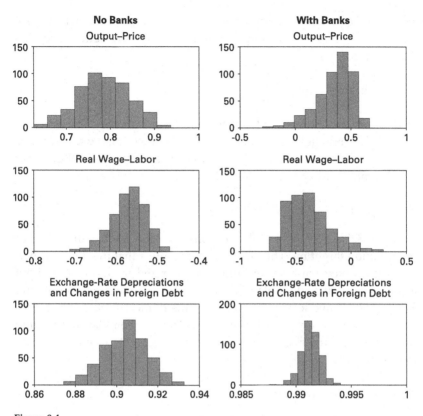

Figure 8.4
Correlations

increase or decrease the correlations between variables. For example, price stickiness implies that adjustments have to take place via other mechanisms—this has the effect of loosening relationships. Figure 8.4 shows that relative to an economy without financial frictions, the introduction of yet another form of rigidity lowers the correlations between output and price as well as between real wage and labor.

Frictions can also "tighten" relationships and increase the covariation between variables. For example, the relationship between exchange-rate depreciations and changes in foreign debt becomes stronger. In this case, it is because the particular friction (i.e., the "wedge") between the price of imports at the docks and the price sold for consumption and investment, $P_t^f = (1 + \mu_1 R_{t-1}^n)(S_t P_t^*)$, raises the cost of production. Hence a change in the exchange rate is translated into a larger change in the domestic currency price, which in turn reduces the demand for imports and consequently reduces foreign debt even further.

8.5   Scenario Analysis

In this scenario we assumed that the monetary authority abandons the Taylor rule and allows the domestic interest rate to follow the overseas rate. Effectively it is keeping the exchange-rate constant, so all the other behavioral equations are unaffected:

$$R_t = R_t^* + \Phi_t.$$

Figure 8.5 shows the impulse-responses for the cases with and without inflation targeting. The most notable result is that the dynamic patterns of the key variables are more exaggerated for the case without inflation targeting; the volatilities of the real variables, domestic and foreign debt, have increased. Note that the domestic interest rate rises by more in the pegging case than in the Taylor-rule inflation targeting case, following the rise in the risk premium generated by the increase in foreign debt.

8.6   Concluding Remarks

This chapter has embedded financial frictions into an open economy model with price stickiness (as well as investment adjustment costs) and explored the differences for the cases with and without Taylor rule inflation targeting. The differences between the two regimes are quite substantial, in terms of volatility of real variables and domestic and foreign debt. These results lend support to the current practice of adopting Taylor-rule inflation targeting to moderate volatility. Is this one cause of the "great moderation"?

In all of our analysis we did not take up the moral hazard issue facing the central bank as a lender of last resort to the banking sector. In the event that the central bank provides large liquidity to the banking sector to avert a financial panic, the government faces a further credibility question about its inflation-targeting program (in the case of flexible rates) or its sustainability of the exchange rate (in a fixed rate system). Banking sector fragility is frequently a source and propagator of volatility in the transmission of international business cycles.

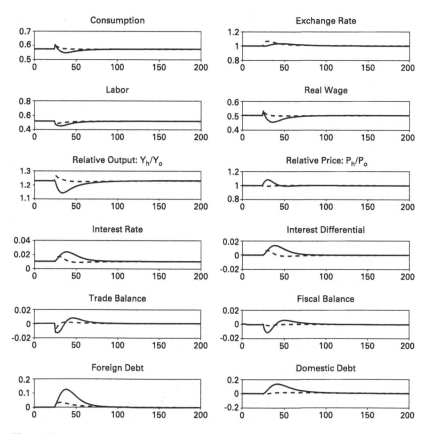

Figure 8.5
Impulse responses without inflation targeting (*solid line*) with inflation targeting (*dashed line*)

As Cochrane (2007) notes, for too long, monetary frictions have been missing ingredients in financial analysis of risk and risk premia. We raise these frictions in the general equilibrium framework, but we realize that this is only scratching the surface of an important research agenda.

Computational Exercise: The "Great Moderation"

Industrialized countries, particularly the United States, over the past twenty years, have experienced a marked fall in business-cycle volatility. For the United States, this fall in real GDP volatility has been called the "great moderation" by Ben Bernanke (2004). Fogli and Perri (2005)

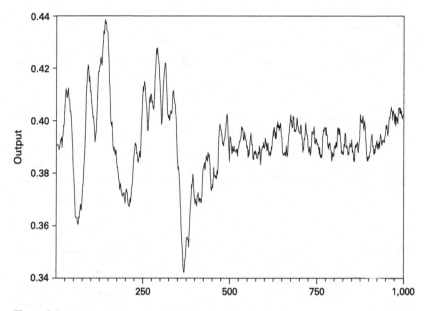

Figure 8.6
Simulated output: without inflation targeting (observations 1–500) and with inflation targeting (observations 501–1,000)

document that the percentage standard deviation in the growth rate of the US GDP has moved from a value of 1.08 in the 1960.1 to 1983.4 period to a value of 0.50 for the period 1984.1 to 2005.4.

There are many explanations for the onset of the great moderation. Summers (2005) offers three: better policy, better inventory management, and simply good luck.

The policy explanation runs as follows: Improvements in the conduct of monetary policy has resulted in low inflation, which has translated into low expected inflation. With lower expected inflation, there is lower volatility in expected real interest rates and overall uncertainty, which then translates into more stable investment and output.

Regarding the structural change in inventory management—with improved forecasting, firms accumulate less inventory, so production and employment become more stable. In other words, keeping inventory levels to a minimum avoids the need for cyclical layoffs when inventories reach unacceptably high thresholds. With better information technology there is also a more streamlined connection between production, distribution, and final sales within industries and across industries.

According to the good luck hypothesis, the volatility of the exogenous shocks affecting the United States simply decreased over the past several decades. The United States simply did not have the large adverse external or domestic shocks it experienced in past decades.

Figure 8.6 shows the simulated path of output with a policy switch to adopting a Taylor rule half way through the simulation period. As shown, the volatility in the output dropped from a standard deviation of 0.0203 (observations 1–500) to 0.0048 (observations 501–1000).

An interesting exercise for the reader is to modify the fractions μ_1 and μ_2 (proportion of costs borrowed) and see its effect on the volatility of output. Does it fall when entrepreneurs and firms lower their need to borrow operational funds?

9 Wage Rigidities

9.1 Introduction

So far we have examined stickiness in price setting for home goods. We assumed that wages were completely flexible, which, of course, is not a realistic assumption. If prices are sticky for domestically produced goods, wages setting surely would be sticky as well. After all, wages are set in contracts that last at least a year. Such contracts are usually staggered for the workforce, with a percentage of the workforce at any time setting their wage for the coming year, while the other workers remain locked in to the wages set in previous contracts. John Taylor (1979) wrote one of the first papers to incorporate staggered wage contracts into a macroeconomic model with rational expectations. Joanna Gray (1978) examined the role of indexation in a model with staggered contracts. However, these models were not DSGE models.

Sticky price-setting behavior has been explored for the pricing of imported goods. Smets and Wouters (2002), for example, allow Calvo-type pricing for both the domestically produced goods and the local-currency price of the imported goods. They conclude that having two sticky prices makes it impossible for a Taylor rule to replicate the welfare of a flexible price economy, or remove the distortions due to stickiness in both domestic and imported goods prices. Smets and Wouters conclude that exclusive focus on stabilizing the prices of domestically produced goods is no longer optimal when we have both forms of stickiness.

In this chapter we incorporate wage as well as domestic-price stickiness. As our model becomes more realistic and thus larger and more complex, more questions arise. A natural question comes to center stage. If wages and domestic prices are sticky, should the central bank target wage inflation as well as domestic-price inflation? Or even use wage inflation as an alternative to domestic-price inflation?

Erceg, Henderson, and Levin (2000) developed a closed economy model, without capital, with Calvo pricing for both domestic prices and wages. They find that sticky wage inflation targeting outperforms sticky domestic price inflation targeting for every combination of structural parameters in their model. The better rule is a hybrid one that incorporates output gaps as well as wage and price inflation.

Canzoneri, Cumby, and Diba (2005) extend the model of Erceg, Henderson, and Levin by including capital into their model. They find that it is important to include capital, and that a very tight form of wage inflation targeting dominates the hybrid rules advocated by Erceg, Henderson, and Levin.

Finally, Schmitt-Grohe and Uribe (2006) compare two variations of the Calvo model for wage stickiness: one where each household is the monopolistic supplier of a differentiated type of labor input, and another where each household supplies a homogeneous labor input that is transformed by monopolistically competitive labor unions into a differentiated labor input. They embed each model into a more extensive medium-scale model with distortionary taxes and habit persistence. They find, in contrast to Erceg, Henderson, and Levin (2000) and Canzoneri, Cumby and Diba (2005), that an operational interest-rate rule based on strict inflation targeting (with a large coefficient on price inflation and a mute response to wage inflation and output growth) dominates the rules incorporating wage inflation. Note that Schmitt-Grohe and Uribe make use of an "operational rule" for monetary policy, where operational means that the interest rate is set as a function of a small number of easily observable macro variables, is a result of a locally determinate competitive equilibrium and is above the zero lower bound.

9.2 Model with Sticky Wages

9.2.1 Household Sector

The main change is to allow for Calvo-type wage setting. The equations describing the behavior of household consumption are the same as in chapter 8:

$$C_t = [(1 - \gamma_1)^{1/\theta_1} (C_t^d)^{(\theta_1 - 1)/\theta_1} + (\gamma_1)^{1/\theta_1} (C_t^f)^{(\theta_1 - 1)/\theta_1}]^{\theta_1/(\theta_1 - 1)},$$

$$C_t^d = (1 - \gamma_1) \left(\frac{P_t^d}{P_t}\right)^{-\theta_1} C_t, \tag{9.1}$$

$$C_t^f = \gamma_1 \left(\frac{P_t^f}{P_t}\right)^{-\theta_1} C_t, \tag{9.2}$$

$$C_t^d = [(1 - \gamma_2)^{1/\theta_2} (C_t^h)^{(\theta_2-1)/\theta_2} + (\gamma_2)^{1/\theta_2} (C_t^o)^{(\theta_2-1)/\theta_2}]^{\theta_2/(\theta_2-1)},$$

$$C_t^h = (1 - \gamma_2) \left(\frac{P_t^h}{P_t^d}\right)^{-\theta_2} C_t^d, \tag{9.3}$$

$$C_t^o = \gamma_2 \left(\frac{P_t^o}{P_t^d}\right)^{-\theta_2} C_t^d. \tag{9.4}$$

The consumer price index P_t and the aggregate domestic price index are

$$P_t = [(1 - \gamma_1)(P_t^d)^{1-\theta_1} + \gamma_1 (P_t^f)^{1-\theta_1}]^{1/(1-\theta_1)}, \tag{9.5}$$

$$P_t^d = [(1 - \gamma_2)(P_t^h)^{1-\theta_2} + \gamma_2 (P_t^o)^{1-\theta_2}]^{1/(1-\theta_2)}. \tag{9.6}$$

As in chapter 8 there are two types of capital stock: one is a fixed natural resource while the other is capital in the manufacturing sector:

$$K_t^o = \bar{K}, \tag{9.7}$$

$$K_t^h = I_t + (1 - \delta)K_{t-1}^h - \frac{\Psi}{2} \frac{(I_t - \delta K_{t-1}^h)^2}{K_{t-1}^h}. \tag{9.8}$$

The entrepreneurs buy goods at the price $S_t P_t^*$ and rebundle them for consumption C_t^f and investment I_t; they borrow a fraction μ_1 of the funds necessary for their purchases from the banks and sell these goods at a domestic currency price P^f that is set to cover costs:

$$Y_t^f = C_t^f + I_t, \tag{9.9}$$

$$N_t^f = \mu_1 (S_t P_t^* Y_t^f), \tag{9.10}$$

$$P_t^f = (1 + \mu_1 R_{t-1}^n)(S_t P_t^*). \tag{9.11}$$

This implies that changes in the exchange rate are only partially *passed-through* to the domestic prices of imported goods.

Staggered Wage Setting   In this case we assume that wages are set as staggered contracts. A fraction $(1 - \xi)$ of households re-negotiates their contracts each period. Each household chooses the optimal wage W_t^a by maximizing the expected discounted utility subject to the demand for its labor:

$$L_t = \left(\frac{W_t^a}{W_t}\right)^{-\zeta} L_t.$$

The household budget equation can be written as

$$\left[\begin{array}{l} (1 - \tau_1)W_t^a(1 + \varkappa)\left(\frac{W_t^a}{W_t}\right)^{-\zeta}L_t \\ + (1 + R_{t-1}^m)M_{t-1} + \Pi_t + P_t^k K_t^h \end{array}\right] = \left(\begin{array}{l} P_t C_t + M_t + \tau_2 P_t C_t \\ + \tau_1 W_t L_t + P_t^f I_t + TAX \end{array}\right),$$

where W is the wage rate, M is deposits with the banking sector, R^m is the interest rate on deposits, Π is distributed profits, τ_1 is the income tax rate, and τ_2 is the consumption tax rate. The financial asset is state contingent, with one-period maturity, and $\varkappa$ is a subsidy. We also assume that there is a lump-sum TAX that acts to ensure that the budget deficit is revenue neutral (i.e., the cost of the subsidy is negated).

Taking a derivative with respect to W_t^a yields the first-order condition

$$E_t \sum_{i=0}^{\infty} \left\{ \begin{array}{l} \xi^i \beta^i (-L_{t+i}^\varpi)(W_{t+i})^\zeta L_{t+i}[-\zeta(W_{t+i}^a)^{-\zeta-1}] \\ + \Lambda_{t+i}(1 - \tau_1)(1 + \varkappa)(W_{t+i})^\zeta L_{t+i}[(-\zeta + 1)(W_{t+i}^a)^{-\zeta}] \end{array} \right\} = 0,$$

which can be rearranged as

$$(W_t^a)^{1+\zeta\varpi} = \frac{\zeta}{(\zeta - 1)} \frac{1}{(1 + \varkappa)} \frac{\sum_{t=0}^{\infty} \xi^t \beta^t (W_t)^{\zeta+\zeta\varpi}(L_t^{1+\varpi})}{\sum_{t=0}^{\infty} \xi^t \beta^t \Lambda_t (1 - \tau_1)(W_t)^\zeta L_t}.$$

We adopt the standard assumption that there is a subsidy to eliminate the markup effects. The wage equation can be rewritten using auxiliary equations as

$$(W_t^a)^{1+\zeta\varpi} = \frac{A_t^{w1}}{A_t^{w2}} = \frac{(W_t)^{\zeta+\zeta\varpi}(L_t^{1+\varpi}) + \xi\beta A_{t+1}^{w1}}{\Lambda_t (1 - \tau_1)(W_t)^\zeta L_t + \xi\beta A_{t+1}^{w2}}. \tag{9.12}$$

Note that in the steady state (or when $\xi = 0$) this collapses to the same condition as the competitive case:

$$(W)^{1+\zeta\varpi} = \frac{(W)^{\zeta\varpi}(L^\varpi)}{\Lambda(1-\tau_1)},$$

$$W = \frac{(L^\varpi)}{\Lambda(1-\tau_1)}.$$

The aggregate wage equation is

$$W_t = [\xi(W_{t-1})^{1-\zeta} + (1-\xi)(W_t^a)^{1-\zeta}]^{1/(1-\zeta)}. \tag{9.13}$$

In the case where wages are set by the households, each household chooses consumption, money holdings, capital, and investment to maximize its utility subject to a budget constraint. The main change to the Euler conditions is to take account of the habit persistence:

$$(C_t - \varrho C_{t-1})^{-\eta} = \Lambda_t(1+\tau_2)P_t + \beta\varrho(C_{t+1} - \varrho C_t)^{-\eta}, \tag{9.14}$$

$$\Lambda_t = \Lambda_{t+1}\beta(1+R_t^m), \tag{9.15}$$

$$Q_t = \Lambda_t P_t^k + \beta Q_{t+1}\left[(1-\delta) + \frac{\Psi(I_{t+1} - \delta K_t^h)\delta}{K_t^h} + \frac{\Psi(I_{t+1} - \delta K_t^h)^2}{2(K_t^h)^2}\right], \tag{9.16}$$

$$\Lambda_t P_t^f = Q_t - Q_t\Psi\frac{(I_t - \delta K_{t-1}^h)}{K_{t-1}^h}. \tag{9.17}$$

9.2.2 Firms—Production, Pricing, and Loans

The production and market-clearing equations carry over from chapter 7:

$$Y_t^h = Z_t[(1-\alpha_1)(L_t^h)^{\kappa_1} + \alpha_1(K_t^h)^{\kappa_1}]^{1/\kappa_1}, \tag{9.18}$$

$$Y_t^o = Z_t[(1-\alpha_2)(L_t^o)^{\kappa_2} + \alpha_2(K_t^o)^{\kappa_2}]^{1/\kappa_2}; \tag{9.19}$$

$$\ln(Z_t) = \rho\ln(Z_{t-1}) + (1-\rho)\ln(\bar{Z}) + \epsilon_t, \qquad \epsilon_t \sim N(0, \sigma_z^2); \tag{9.20}$$

$$Y_t^h = C_t^h + G_t, \tag{9.21}$$

$$Y_t^o = C_t^o + X_t. \tag{9.22}$$

The total dividends firms pass on to households is the sum of the dividends from the export and nontraded goods producing firms:

$$\Pi_t = \Pi_t^o + \Pi_t^h,$$

$$\Pi_t^o = P_t^o Y_t^o - W_t L_t^o,$$

$$\Pi_t^h = P_t^h Y_t^h - P_t^k K_t^h - [1 + \mu_2 R_{t-1}^n] W_t L_t^h.$$

The price of exports in the two sector is determined in the world markets:

$$P_t^o = S_t P_t^{o*}, \tag{9.23}$$

where P^{o*} describes the world price.

As in chapter 8, the firms in the manufacturing sector borrow from the central bank and set the price of the manufacturing good according to the Calvo (1983) staggered pricing system. The equations are

$$N_t^h = \mu_2 W_t L_t^h; \tag{9.24}$$

$$A_t^h = \left\{ \left(\frac{1}{Z}\right) \left[\begin{array}{c} (1-\alpha)(\alpha(1+\mu_2 R_{t-1}^n)W_t)^{\kappa/(\kappa-1)} \\ + \alpha((1-\alpha)P_t^k)^{\kappa/(\kappa-1)} \end{array} \right]^{-1/\kappa} \times \left[\begin{array}{c} (1+\mu_2 R_{t-1}^n)W_t(\alpha(1+\mu_2 R_{t-1}^n)W_t)^{1/(\kappa-1)} \\ + P_t^k((1-\alpha)P_t^k)^{1/(\kappa-1)} \end{array} \right] \right\}, \tag{9.25}$$

$$A_t^{p1} = Y_t^h (P_t^h)^\zeta A_t + \beta \xi A_{t+1}^{p1}, \tag{9.26}$$

$$A_t^{p2} = Y_t^h (P_t^h)^\zeta + \beta \xi A_{t+1}^{p2}, \tag{9.27}$$

$$P_t^a = \frac{A_t^{p1}}{A_t^{p2}}; \tag{9.28}$$

$$P_t^h = [\xi (P_{t-1}^h)^{1-\zeta} + (1-\xi)(P_t^a)^{1-\zeta}]^{1/(1-\zeta)} \tag{9.29}$$

9.2.3 Monetary Policy
The central bank is assumed to adopt a Taylor rule with smoothing:

$$R_t = \phi_2 R_{t-1} + (1 - \phi_2)[R^* + \phi_1(\pi_t - \tilde{\pi})], \qquad \phi_1 > 1, \tag{9.30}$$

$$\pi_t = \left(\frac{P_t}{P_{t-1}}\right)^4 - 1.$$

9.2.4 Taxes and Domestic Debt

Government spending G is assumed to be sensitive to the size of the public debt B relative to the steady-state value $\bar{B}$:

$$G_t = \bar{G} + \chi_1(B_{t-1} - \bar{B}). \tag{9.31}$$

The combined Treasury/central bank receives taxes and production costs (levied on imports). It borrows to finance government expenditure. The evolution of the bonds is

$$B_t = (1 + R_{t-1})B_{t-1} + P_t^h G_t + (\tau_1 W_t L_t + \tau_2 P_t C_t) + LQ_t, \tag{9.32}$$

$$LQ_t = (1 + R_{t-1}^n)[(1 - \psi_2)N_{t-1} - N_t] - \psi_1 M_t, \tag{9.33}$$

$$N_t = N_t^f + N_t^h. \tag{9.34}$$

The term LQ_t represents the amount of high-powered money injected by the central bank to implement monetary policy.

9.2.5 Exports and Foreign Debt

As in chapter 8, the behavioral equations for exports and the evolution of foreign debt are, respectively,

$$\ln(X_t) = \ln(\bar{X}) + \chi_2\left[\ln\left(\frac{S_{t-1}}{P_{t-1}}\right) - \ln\left(\frac{\bar{S}}{\bar{P}}\right)\right], \tag{9.35}$$

$$S_t F_t = (1 + R_{t-1}^* + \Phi_{t-1})S_t F_{t-1} + S_t P_t^* Y_t^f - P_t^o X_t, \tag{9.36}$$

$$\Phi_t = \text{sign}(F_{t-1}) \cdot \varphi[e^{(|F_{t-1}|-\bar{F})} - 1]. \tag{9.37}$$

9.2.6 Financial Sector

The equations linking the interest rates are

$$(1 + R_t)S_t = (1 + R_t^* + \Phi_t + \Phi_t' F_t^*)S_{t+1}, \tag{9.38}$$

$$(1 + R_t)(1 - \psi_1) = (1 + R_t^m), \tag{9.39}$$

$$\frac{(1 + R_t)}{(1 - \psi_2)} = (1 + R_t^n), \tag{9.40}$$

$$\Phi_t' = \varphi[e^{(|F_{t-1}^*|-\bar{F}^*)}].$$

The calibration values for the parameters and the initial conditions for the steady state appear in the appendix at the end of the book.

9.3 Solution Algorithm

9.3.1 Approximating Functions

There are now seven forward-looking variables: consumption C_t, the exchange rate S_t, the numerator and denominator of the forward-looking Calvo prices for the nontraded domestic goods A_t^{p1} and A_t^{p2}, the variable Q_t that determines investment in the manufacturing sector, and the numerator and denominator of the forward-looking wage, A_t^{w1} and A_t^{w2}. The decision rules are specified as nonlinear neural network functional forms of state variables. The state variables used as arguments for these decision rules are the current shocks to productivity Z_t, foreign debt F_{t-1}, the interest rate R_{t-1}, government bonds B_{t-1}, the capital stock K_{t-1}^h, and deposits M_{t-1}. Recalling that we parametrize investment and back out Q gives the set of approximations below:

$$\hat{C}_t = \psi^c(\Omega^c; \mathbf{x}_t),$$

$$\hat{S}_t = \psi^s(\Omega^s; \mathbf{x}_t),$$

$$\hat{A}_t^{p1} = \psi^{p1}(\Omega^{p1}; \mathbf{x}_t),$$

$$\hat{A}_t^{p2} = \psi^{p2}(\Omega^{p2}; \mathbf{x}_t);$$

$$\hat{I}_t = \psi^I(\Omega^I; \mathbf{x}_t);$$

$$\hat{A}_t^{w1} = \psi^{w1}(\Omega^{w1}; \mathbf{x}_t),$$

$$\hat{A}_t^{w2} = \psi^{w2}(\Omega^{w2}; \mathbf{x}_t);$$

$$\mathbf{x}_t = \left\{ \begin{array}{c} (Z_t - \bar{Z}), (F_{t-1} - \bar{F}), (R_{t-1} - \bar{R}), \\ (B_{t-1} - \bar{B}), (K_{t-1}^h - \overline{K^h}), (M_{t-1} - \bar{M}) \end{array} \right\}.$$

It is worth remembering that we derive the wage as follows

$$W_t^a = \left(\frac{A_t^{w1}}{A_t^{w2}}\right)^{1/(1+\zeta w)},$$

$$W_t = [\xi(W_{t-1})^{1-\zeta} + (1-\xi)(W_t^a)^{1-\zeta}]^{1/(1-\zeta)}.$$

The set of Euler errors now include the forward-looking wage equation

$$\epsilon_t^c = \frac{\hat{C}_t^{-\eta}}{(1+\tau_2)\hat{P}_t}\left[\frac{1}{(1+R_t^m)}\right] - \beta\left[\frac{\hat{C}_{t+1}^{-\eta}}{(1+\tau_2)\hat{P}_{t+1}}\right],$$

$$\epsilon_t^s = \frac{\hat{C}_t^{-\eta}}{P_t}\left[\frac{\hat{S}_t}{(1+R_t^*+\Phi_t+\Phi_t'F_t^*)}\right] - \beta\left[\hat{S}_{t+1}\frac{\hat{C}_{t+1}^{-\eta}}{P_{t+1}}\right],$$

$$\epsilon_t^P = \frac{\hat{A}_t^{p1}}{\hat{A}_t^{p2}} - \frac{Y_t(P_t)^\zeta A_t + \beta\xi\hat{A}_{t+1}^{p1}}{Y_t(P_t)^\zeta + \beta\xi\hat{A}_{t+1}^{p2}},$$

$$\epsilon_t^q = \frac{(\hat{Q}_t - \Lambda_t P_t^k)}{\left[(1-\delta) + \frac{\Psi(I_t-\delta K_t)\delta}{K_t} + \frac{\Psi(I_t-\delta K_t)^2}{2K_t^2}\right]} - \beta\hat{Q}_{t+1},$$

$$\epsilon_t^w = \frac{A_t^{w1}}{A_t^{w2}} - \frac{(W_t)^{\zeta+\zeta\varpi}(L_t^{1+\varpi}) + \xi\beta A_{t+1}^{w1}}{\Lambda_t(1-\tau_1)(W_t)^\zeta L_t + \xi\beta A_{t+1}^{w2}}.$$

The coefficients of the decision rules are obtained from stochastic simulations based on minimization of the sum of squared Euler equation errors.

9.3.2 Accuracy Checks
The Judd Gaspar statistics (table 9.1 and figure 9.1) and the Den Hann-Marcet statistics (table 9.2 and figure 9.2) provide support for the accuracy of the approximations.

9.4 Simulation Analysis

9.4.1 Impulse-Response Paths
The impulse-response paths of key macroeconomic indicators for a small open economy with sticky prices and wages, taxes, real and financial rigidities, following a once-only shock in the productivity index is shown in figure 9.3. Note how sticky wages slow the speed of adjustment of real wages. However, this has the effect of increasing tax revenues, which contributes to the improvement in the domestic debt.

Table 9.1
Judd-Gaspar statistic ($\times 10^{-2}$)

	$\dfrac{|\epsilon_t^c|}{C_t}$	$\dfrac{|\epsilon_t^s|}{S_t}$	$\dfrac{|\epsilon_t^p|}{P_t}$	$\dfrac{|\epsilon_t^q|}{Q_t}$	$\dfrac{|\epsilon_t^w|}{W_t}$
Mean	0.0506	0.2777	0.4372	0.1004	0.0062
Standard deviation	0.0041	0.0258	0.0250	0.0058	0.0013

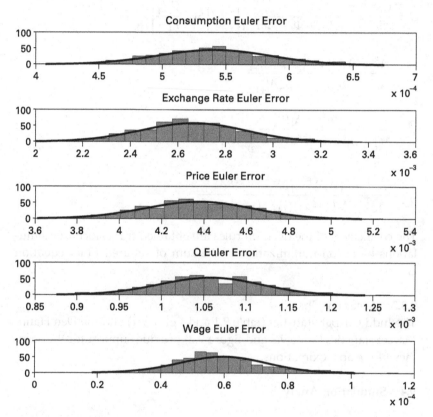

Figure 9.1
Judd-Gasper statistic

Table 9.2
DenHann-Marcet test

	Lag order			
	1	2	3	4
Lower region ($p < 0.05$)	0.054	0.040	0.040	0.034
Upper region ($p > 0.95$)	0.050	0.054	0.048	0.058

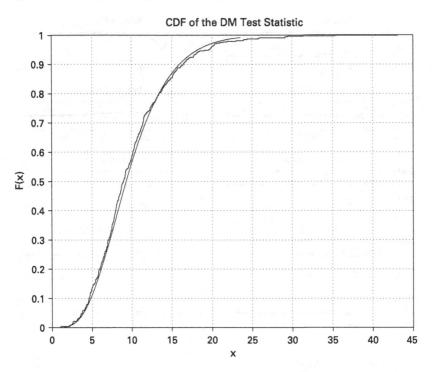

Figure 9.2
DenHann-Marcet test of accuracy

9.4.2 Macroeconomic Correlations

Figure 9.4 shows the distribution of contemporaneous correlations among key macroeconomic variables. They show that an assumption of sticky wages reverses the price–output correlations from positive to negative. A positive productivity shock increases the marginal product of labor, but sticky wages imply that real wages will not increase by the full amount. Consequently output increases by more and prices fall by less than the flexible wage case.

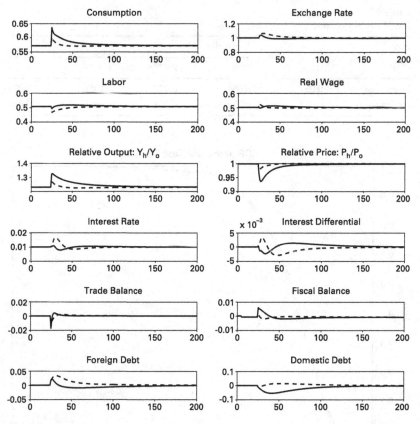

Figure 9.3
Impulse reponses following a productivity shock: with (*solid line*) and without (*dashed line*) sticky wages

9.5   Sensitivity Analysis

Up to now we have explored the workings of the model in a number of ways. We have added new features in each chapter, and we have conducted a number of scenarios. In this section, given our focus on the labor market, we explore the role of ϖ the elasticity of marginal disutility with respect to labor supply. The simulation above has been conducted with $\varpi = 0.25$ in the utility function:

$$U_t(.) = \frac{C_t^{1-\eta}}{1-\eta} - \frac{L_t^{1+\varpi}}{1+\varpi}.$$

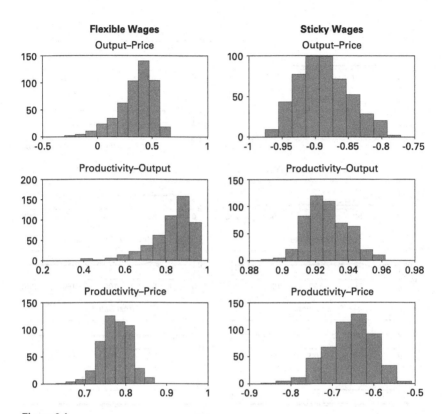

Figure 9.4
Correlations

Here we will set $\varpi = 0.05$, implying that the household derives more disutility from more work.[1] A change in the disutility parameter toward a greater preference for leisure may be an effect of an aging population.

The impulse-response paths for the case of $\varpi = 0.05$ and for the base case $\varpi = 0.25$, appear in figure 9.5, with the solid lines representing $\varpi = 0.05$ and the dashed line representing $\varpi = 0.25$. We see that changing the value of ϖ toward greater disutility (or greater preference for leisure) lowers steady-state consumption and labor. Prices fall to encourage consumption, while the exchange rate appreciates, the trade balance worsens, and domestic debt increases (due to falling wage income).

Figure 9.6 shows the correlations of key macro variables in the two cases of $\varpi = 0.25$ and $\varpi = 0.05$. These results show lower correlations

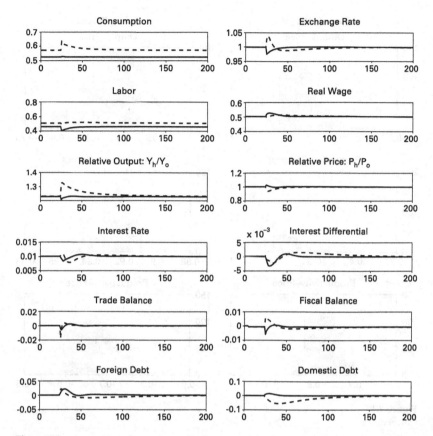

Figure 9.5
Impulse responses: $\varpi = 0.05$ (*solid line*) and $\varpi = 0.25$ (*dashed line*)

between productivity and consumption and price and output for lower ϖ. There is also a stronger positive correlation between the trade and fiscal balances.

9.6 Concluding Remarks

This chapter explored the role of the wage-setting system in DSGE analysis as well as the role of the marginal disutility of labor. A shift in society's preference for more leisure and less work, for example, will lead to greater domestic and foreign debt for a given productivity shock.

We did not take up the case of using wage inflation in the Taylor rule in this chapter. We leave it to the reader to verify the claim of

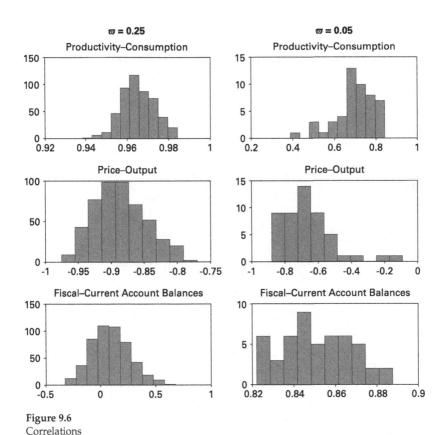

Figure 9.6
Correlations

Schmitt-Grohe and Uribe (2006) with respect to the dominance of pure inflation targeting over wage inflation or other hybrid targeting rules for Taylor rules.

Computational Exercise: Dunlop-Tarshis Puzzle

In his well-know macroeconomics text, Sargent (1987) drew attention to the Dunlop (1938) and Tarshis (1939) puzzle, which shows that real wages and employment are positively correlated. Based on one simulation of the model with $\varpi = 0.25$, and with recurring productivity shocks, we find a positive correlation between real wages and employment (0.79). This is in contrast to the result in chapter 8, which shows a negative correlation between real wages and employment (-0.61).

Has the introduction of wage stickiness caused a significant switch in correlations? Clearly, we cannot base our conclusion on one simulation.

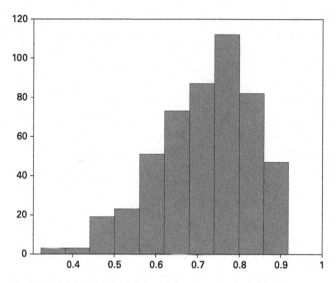

Figure 9.7
Distribution of real wage–employment correlations

In this book we have emphasized the use of many simulations and presented results of key measures in a distributional form.

We can obtain a distribution of the real wages and employment correlations by performing repeated experiments, and we can then check to see if actual real world correlation coefficients falls within, say, a 95 percent interval. For the model described here, the interval is between 0.498 and 0.878 (see figure 9.7). Canova (2007) calls this a "size" test of a given model (and its calibrated values). If a model is a poor approximation, then the actual correlation will be in the tails of the simulated distribution.

The reader might like to generate distributions of first-order autocorrelations of wages from the model and compare them with the AR(1) coefficient estimated from real world data. Can this model capture the persistence in real world wages?

10   Habit Persistence

We have progressed from the flexible price model in chapter 2. Along the way we allowed for sticky prices (chapter 3) and sticky wages (chapter 9). We introduced taxes (chapter 4) and examined different stances of monetary policy—with output gap (chapter 3), with Q targeting (chapter 6), and with no inflation targeting (chapter 8). The production side now includes the dynamics of capital accumulation (chapter 6) as well as different sectors (chapter 7).

We also expanded the external sector to allow a role for international finance via the risk premia and to allow a role for international trade to respond to the real exchange rate (chapter 5). Throughout the book our analysis has focused on the effects of a productivity shock, but we also considered the effects of an export demand shock (chapter 2) and a terms-of-trade shock (chapter 7). Our scenarios tested the sensitivity of results to changes in the tax system (chapter 4), alternative export elasticities (chapter 5), and alternative marginal disutility of labor (chapter 9). Our model was enriched with the introduction of financial intermediaries (chapter 8).

In this chapter we will introduce habit persistence into the behavior of households. The major change is that the utility function includes not only current consumption but also lagged consumption. The utility of current consumption is now relative to recent past consumption. This modification to the utility function is needed to help account for several stylized facts relating to asset pricing, saving behavior and real exchange rate correlations with consumption.

Habit formation has been invoked by Campbell and Cochrane (1999), and by Boldrin, Christiano, and Fischer (1999) to help account for the forecastability of excess returns. On the other hand, Carroll, Overland, and Weil (2000) introduced habit formation into a closed economy real business-cycle model in order to account for the positive effects of productivity growth on saving.

The lagged value of consumption appearing in the utility function can be introduced in a number of ways. It can be introduced as an *external variable*, the average of past consumption that is beyond the control of the individual household. This type of habit formation is called external habit formation. The lagged value of consumption can also be introduced either in a *ratio form*, appearing as the denominator relative to current consumption, or in a *difference form*, as a subtraction (lagged consumption multiplied by a coefficient of habit formation) from current consumption. As noted by Schmidt-Grohé and Uribe (2005), external habit formation simplifies the intertemporal optimization problem of the household. They also point out that the ratio specification of current consumption over lagged consumption (usually raised to a power less than one) is more properly called relative habit persistence.

If the lagged consumption is internalized by the household, the intertemporal optimization becomes more complex. Schmidt-Grohé and Uribe (2005) report that it matters little for the dynamics of the model if the habits are of the internal or external type. However, the distinction becomes important under certain conditions such as when a regime change is expected. For example, consider the effect of an expected abandonment of a currency peg system. Under internal habit formation, consumption will drop before the peg is actually abandoned, but under external habit formation, consumption will stay close to its past value.

We begin with a description of the overall model. As in the preceding chapters we consider the base case of productivity shocks and generate impulse responses and stochastic simulations to obtain insights about the economy we have modeled.

10.1 A DSGE Model with Habit Persistence

The model consists of five sectors: household sector, production sector, government sector, financial sector, and overseas sector.

10.1.1 Household Sector

There is a continuum of infinitely lived households. Each household consumes domestically produced goods C^d and imported (foreign-produced) goods C^f. There are two-types of consumption goods in

$C^d - C^h$ (nontraded home goods) and C^o (traded export goods). The household sector provides labor services L at wage rate W. The household sector are net savers: they lend to banks in the form of deposits, M and receive returns at the deposit rate R^m. Households pay taxes on wage income $\tau_1 WL$ and on consumption $\tau_2 PC$. The household sector also includes entrepreneurs who own the capital stock K. These entrepreneurs import investment goods I to build up the capital stock, but there is a real cost associated with this activity. The entrepreneurs rent the capital to the firms at a rental price P^k and receives profits Π.

A representative household, at period 0, optimizes the intertemporal welfare function

$$V = E_0 \sum_{t=0}^{\infty} \beta^t U_t(C_t, L_t),$$

$$U_t(.) = \frac{(C_t - \varrho C_{t-1})^{1-\eta}}{1-\eta} - \frac{L_t^{1+\varpi}}{1+\varpi},$$

where β is the discount factor, C_t is an index of consumption goods, and $\varrho > 0$ is the coefficient of habit persistence. As before L_t is labor services, η is the coefficient of relative risk aversion, and ϖ is the elasticity of marginal disutility with respect to labor supply. Utility is additively separable in consumption and labour The household's utility depends positively on the level of consumption and negatively on the labor supplied.

The equations describing the household demand for traded export goods C_t^o, nontraded home goods C_t^h, imported goods C_t^f, and the aggregate consumption of domestically produced goods C_t^d and the composite consumption C_t are as follows:

$$C_t = [(1-\gamma_1)^{1/\theta_1}(C_t^d)^{(\theta_1-1)/\theta_1} + (\gamma_1)^{1/\theta_1}(C_t^f)^{(\theta_1-1)/\theta_1}]^{\theta_1/(\theta_1-1)},$$

$$C_t^d = (1-\gamma_1)\left(\frac{P_t^d}{P_t}\right)^{-\theta_1} C_t, \tag{10.1}$$

$$C_t^f = \gamma_1 \left(\frac{P_t^f}{P_t}\right)^{-\theta_1} C_t, \tag{10.2}$$

$$C_t^d = [(1-\gamma_2)^{1/\theta_2}(C_t^h)^{(\theta_2-1)/\theta_2} + (\gamma_2)^{1/\theta_2}(C_t^o)^{(\theta_2-1)/\theta_2}]^{\theta_2/(\theta_2-1)},$$

$$C_t^h = (1 - \gamma_2)\left(\frac{P_t^h}{P_t^d}\right)^{-\theta_2} C_t^d,$$
(10.3)

$$C_t^o = \gamma_2 \left(\frac{P_t^o}{P_t^d}\right)^{-\theta_2} C_t^d.$$
(10.4)

The aggregate domestic price index P_t^d and the consumer price index P_t are given as

$$P_t = [(1 - \gamma_1)(P_t^d)^{1-\theta_1} + \gamma_1(P_t^f)^{1-\theta_1}]^{1/(1-\theta_1)},$$
(10.5)

$$P_t^d = [(1 - \gamma_2)(P_t^h)^{1-\theta_2} + \gamma_2(P_t^o)^{1-\theta_2}]^{1/(1-\theta_2)}.$$
(10.6)

The households provide labor and determine their wages according to

$$(W_t^o)^{1+\zeta\varpi} = \frac{A_t^{w1}}{A_t^{w2}} = \frac{(W_t)^{\zeta+\zeta\varpi}(L_t^{1+\varpi}) + \xi\beta A_{t+1}^{w1}}{\Lambda_t(1 - \tau_1)(W_t)^{\zeta}L_t + \xi\beta A_{t+1}^{w2}},$$
(10.7)

$$W_t = [\xi(W_{t-1})^{1-\zeta} + (1 - \xi)(W_t^a)^{1-\zeta}]^{1/(1-\zeta)}.$$
(10.8)

The household sector also include entrepreneurs who own capital. There are two types of capital stock. One is a fixed natural resource, while the other is capital in the manufacturing sector that is subjected to the capital accumulation equation below:

$$K_t^o = \bar{K},$$
(10.9)

$$K_t^h = I_t + (1 - \delta)K_{t-1}^h - \frac{\Psi}{2}\frac{(I_t - \delta K_{t-1}^h)^2}{K_{t-1}^h}.$$
(10.10)

The entrepreneurs also imports differentiated goods for which the law of one price holds at the dockside. Each importer sets the domestic currency price of imported goods (P^f) according to imperfect pass-through behavior. The capital is imported, and the importers package the imports for capital formation and for consumption according to

$$Y_t^f = C_t^f + I_t,$$
(10.11)

$$N_t^f = \mu_1(S_t P_t^* Y_t^f),$$
(10.12)

$$P^f = (1 + \mu_1 R^n_{t-1})(S_t P^*_t), \tag{10.13}$$

where μ_1 is the proportion of cost financed through borrowing from the financial sector.

Finally, optimizing utility with habit persistence subject to the budget constraint yields the following Euler equations:

$$(C_t - \varrho C_{t-1})^{-\eta} = \Lambda_t (1 + \tau_2) P_t + \beta \varrho (C_{t+1} - \varrho C_t)^{-\eta}, \tag{10.14}$$

$$\Lambda_t = \Lambda_{t+1} \beta (1 + R^m_t), \tag{10.15}$$

$$Q_t = \Lambda_t P^k_t + \beta Q_{t+1} \left[(1 - \delta) + \frac{\Psi(I_{t+1} - \delta K^h_t)\delta}{K^h_t} + \frac{\Psi(I_{t+1} - \delta K^h_t)^2}{2(K^h_t)^2} \right], \tag{10.16}$$

$$\Lambda_t P^f_t = Q_t - Q_t \Psi \frac{(I_t - \delta K^h_{t-1})}{K^h_{t-1}}. \tag{10.17}$$

10.1.2 Production Sector

The economy contains a continuum of firms that operate under monopolistic competition and manufactures two types of goods: non-traded home goods Y^h and exportable goods Y^o. The production function is a constant elasticity of substitution function of labor services L and capital K. The firms sets domestic nontraded prices P^d according to the Calvo pricing system, but the price of exportables P^o is determined overseas as per small open economy assumption. Firms borrow from banks (in the form of loans N) and pay the loan rate R^n.

The production equations are

$$Y^h_t = Z_t[(1 - \alpha_1)(L^h_t)^{\kappa_1} + \alpha_1 (K^h_t)^{\kappa_1}]^{1/\kappa_1}, \tag{10.18}$$

$$Y^o_t = Z_t[(1 - \alpha_2)(L^o_t)^{\kappa_2} + \alpha_2 (K^o_t)^{\kappa_2}]^{1/\kappa_2}, \tag{10.19}$$

$$\ln(Z_t) = \rho \ln(Z_{t-1}) + (1 - \rho) \ln(\bar{Z}) + \epsilon_t, \qquad \epsilon_t \sim N(0, \sigma^2_z). \tag{10.20}$$

The market-clearing equations are

$$Y^h_t = C^h_t + G_t, \tag{10.21}$$

$$Y^o_t = C^o_t + X_t. \tag{10.22}$$

For the export good sector the pricing and profit equations are

$$P_t^o = S_t P_t^{o*},$$

$$\Pi_t^o = P_t^o(C_t^o + X_t) - W_t L_t^o.$$

Since the capital for this good is endowed natural resources, we have abstracted from complications associated with the pricing of natural resources. Instead, we have adopted the approach of assuming that output varies with the labor input given a fixed quantity of capital.

In contrast, the home good sector is a manufacturing sector, and the firm has to pay for the capital it "rents" at the rental price P^k. The firm also borrows a proportion of the wage costs as part of its management of the cost of operations. The profit equation includes an imputed interest cost of borrowing based on the prevailing beginning of period interest rate R_{t-1}^n:

$$N_t = \mu_2 W_t L_t^h,$$

$$\Pi_t^h = P_t^h(C_t^h + G_t) - (1 + \mu_2 R_{t-1}^n)W_t L_t^h - P_t^k K_t^h.$$

The cost and pricing equations are

$$A_t^h = \left\{ \left(\frac{1}{Z}\right)\left[\begin{array}{c}(1-\alpha)(\alpha(1+\mu_2 R_{t-1}^n)W_t)^{\kappa/(\kappa-1)} \\ +\alpha((1-\alpha)P_t^k)^{\kappa/(\kappa-1)}\end{array}\right]^{-1/\kappa} \\ \times \left[\begin{array}{c}(1+\mu_2 R_{t-1}^n)W_t(\alpha(1+\mu_2 R_{t-1}^n)W_t)^{1/(\kappa-1)} \\ +P_t^k((1-\alpha)P_t^k)^{1/(\kappa-1)}\end{array}\right] \right\}, \quad (10.23)$$

$$A_t^{p1} = Y_t^h(P_t^h)^\zeta A_t + \beta\xi A_{t+1}^n, \quad (10.24)$$

$$A_t^{p2} = Y_t^h(P_t^h)^\zeta + \beta\xi A_{t+1}^d, \quad (10.25)$$

$$P_t^a = \frac{A_t^{p1}}{A_t^{p2}}, \quad (10.26)$$

$$P_t^h = [\xi(P_{t-1}^h)^{1-\zeta} + (1-\xi)(P_t^a)^{1-\zeta}]^{1/(1-\zeta)}. \quad (10.27)$$

10.1.3 Government Sector
The monetary authority implements monetary policy by setting the interest rate (R) according to a Taylor rule:

$$R_t = \phi_2 R_{t-1} + (1 - \phi_2)[R^* + \phi_1(\pi_t - \tilde{\pi})], \qquad \phi_1 > 1, \tag{10.28}$$

$$\pi_t = \left(\frac{P_t}{P_{t-1}}\right)^4 - 1.$$

The fiscal authority determines government expenditure (G) as

$$G_t = \bar{G} + \chi_1(B_{t-1} - \bar{B})$$

The Treasury/central bank receives taxes, and borrows from the banks (in the form of bonds B). The government sector determines the level of high-powered money, sets the reserve requirement ratio ψ_1, and engages in open market activity to ensure that there is sufficient liquidity in the system to support its policy:

$$B_t = (1 + R_{t-1})B_{t-1} + P_t^h G_t - (\tau_1 W_t L_t + \tau_2 P_t C_t) + LQ_t, \tag{10.29}$$

$$LQ_t = (1 + R_{t-1}^n)[(1 - \psi_2)N_{t-1} - N_t] - \psi_1 M_t, \tag{10.30}$$

$$N_t = \mu_2(W_t L_t^h) + \mu_1(S_t P_t^* Y_t^f). \tag{10.31}$$

10.1.4 External Sector

The external sector consists of traders and financiers. Foreigners buy domestically produced goods (exports) X. They sell foreign produced goods (imports) for consumption C^f and for production I. International financiers lends to banks F^*:

$$\ln(X_t) = \ln(\bar{X}) + \chi_2\left[\ln\left(\frac{S_{t-1}}{P_{t-1}}\right) - \ln\left(\frac{\bar{S}}{\bar{P}}\right)\right], \tag{10.32}$$

$$\Phi_t = \text{sign}(F_{t-1}) \cdot \varphi[e^{(|F_{t-1}|-\bar{F})} - 1], \tag{10.33}$$

$$S_t F_t = S_t F_{t-1}(1 + R_{t-1}^* + \Phi_{t-1}) + S_t P_t^*(I_t + C_t^f) - (P_t^o X_t). \tag{10.34}$$

10.1.5 Financial Sector

The financial sector consists of financial intermediaries called banks. They borrow from households (in the form of deposits, M) and pay R^m. They also borrow from foreigners (SF^*) and pay $R^* + \psi^f(F^*)$, where $\psi^f(F)$ is the risk premium. The intermediaries lend to business (in the form of loans N) at the loan rate R^n but face a cost of default

$\psi^n(N)$. They lend to the government (in the form of bonds B) and earn the rate R. Banks must comply with reserve requirements $\psi^m(M)$. Optimizing profits yields the equations

$$(1 + R_t)S_t = (1 + R_t^* + \Phi_t + \Phi_t' F_t)S_{t+1}, \tag{10.35}$$

$$\frac{(1 + R_t)}{(1 - \psi_2)} = (1 + R_t^n), \tag{10.36}$$

$$(1 + R_t)(1 - \psi_1) = (1 + R_t^m), \tag{10.37}$$

$$\Phi_t' = \varphi[e^{(|F_{t-1}| - \bar{F})}].$$

These equations show respectively the interest parity relationship and the conditions $R_t^n > R_t$ and $R_t^m < R_t$.

10.2 Solution Algorithm

10.2.1 Approximating Equations
There are still seven forward-looking variables: consumption C_t; the exchange rate S_t; the numerator and denominator of the forward-looking Calvo prices for the nontraded domestic goods A_t^{p1}, A_t^{p2}, the Q variable Q_t, which determines investment in the manufacturing sector; and the numerator and denominator of the forward-looking wage, A_t^{w1}, A_t^{w2}. The decision rules are as in the previous chapter:

$$\hat{C}_t = \psi^c(\Omega^c; x_t),$$

$$\hat{S}_t = \psi^s(\Omega^s; x_t),$$

$$\hat{A}_t^{p1} = \psi^{p1}(\Omega^{p1}; x_t),$$

$$\hat{A}_t^{p2} = \psi^{p2}(\Omega^{p2}; x_t),$$

$$\hat{I}_t = \psi^I(\Omega^I; x_t),$$

$$\hat{A}_t^{w1} = \psi^{w1}(\Omega^{w1}; x_t),$$

$$\hat{A}_t^{w2} = \psi^{w2}(\Omega^{w2}; x_t),$$

$$\mathbf{x}_t = \left\{ \begin{array}{c} (Z_t - \bar{Z}), (F_{t-1} - \bar{F}), (R_{t-1} - \bar{R}), \\ (B_{t-1} - \bar{B}), (K_{t-1}^h - \bar{K^h}), (M_{t-1} - \bar{M}) \end{array} \right\}.$$

10.2.2 Euler Errors

The set of Euler errors is also the same as in chapter 9, but recall that the consumption equation needs to be modified to allow for habit persistence:

$$\epsilon_t^c = \Lambda_t - \Lambda_{t+1}\beta(1 + R_t^m),$$

$$\epsilon_t^s = \left[\frac{\hat{S}_t}{(1 + R_t^* + \Phi_t + \Phi_t' F_t^*)} \right] - \beta[\hat{S}_{t+1}],$$

$$\epsilon_t^P = \frac{\hat{A}_t^{p1}}{\hat{A}_t^{p2}} - \frac{Y_t(P_t^h)^\zeta A_t + \beta\xi\hat{A}_{t+1}^{p1}}{Y_t(P_t^h)^\zeta + \beta\xi\hat{A}_{t+1}^{p2}},$$

$$\epsilon_t^q = (\hat{Q}_t - \Lambda_t P_t^k) - \beta\hat{Q}_{t+1}\left[(1 - \delta) + \frac{\Psi(I_{t+1} - \delta K_t^h)\delta}{K_t^h} + \frac{\Psi(I_{t+1} - \delta K_t^h)^2}{2(K_t^h)^2} \right],$$

$$\epsilon_t^w = \frac{A_t^{w1}}{A_t^{w2}} - \frac{(W_t)^{\zeta+\zeta\varpi}(L_t^{1+\varpi}) + \xi\beta A_{t+1}^{w1}}{\Lambda_t(1 - \tau_1)(W_t)^\zeta L_t + \xi\beta A_{t+1}^{w2}}.$$

10.2.3 Accuracy Checks

The Judd Gaspar statistics are reported in table 10.1 and figure 10.1 while the DenHann-Marcet statistics are reported in table 10.2 and figure 10.2. These statistics show that we may consider the approximations to be accurate.

10.3 Stochastic Simulations

10.3.1 Impulse-Responses to a Productivity Shock

Figure 10.3 shows the impulse-response paths for selected variables. As in previous chapters the solid lines present the paths of the model in this chapter, and the dashed line represent the paths of the model without habit persistence, namely the results of the previous chapter.

The effect of yet another source of stickiness (in this case, the introduction of habit persistence) on the steady state is clearly shown in the higher steady-state level of consumption. As before, productivity

Table 10.1
Judd-Gaspar statistic ($\times 10^{-2}$)

	$\dfrac{|\epsilon_t^c|}{C_t}$	$\dfrac{|\epsilon_t^s|}{S_t}$	$\dfrac{|\epsilon_t^p|}{P_t}$	$\dfrac{|\epsilon_t^q|}{Q_t}$	$\dfrac{|\epsilon_t^w|}{W_t}$
Mean	0.0441	0.2067	0.2782	0.0847	0.6986
Standard deviation	0.0026	0.0116	0.0250	0.0052	0.0370

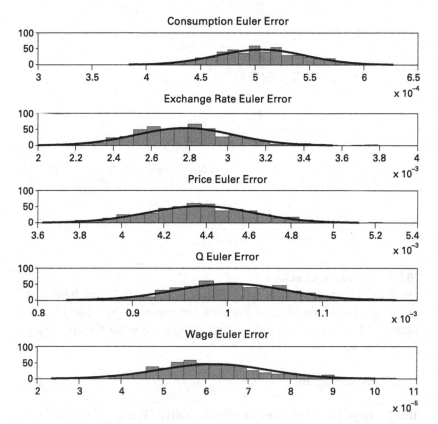

Figure 10.1
Judd-Gasper statistic

Table 10.2
DenHann-Marcet test

	Lag order			
	1	2	3	4
Lower region ($p < 0.05$)	0.060	0.050	0.062	0.050
Upper region ($p > 0.95$)	0.040	0.040	0.060	0.050

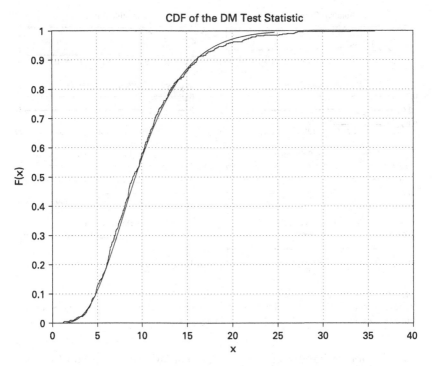

Figure 10.2
DenHann-Marcet statistics

improvements occur in both sectors, but sticky wages discourage production in export-type goods. Thus relative output favors home goods, and the home price has to fall by more to encourage a demand switch away from export-type goods toward home-type goods.

10.3.2 Macroeconomic Correlations
Figure 10.4 shows the histograms of the cross-correlations for key macroeconomic variables. The interesting result here is that the

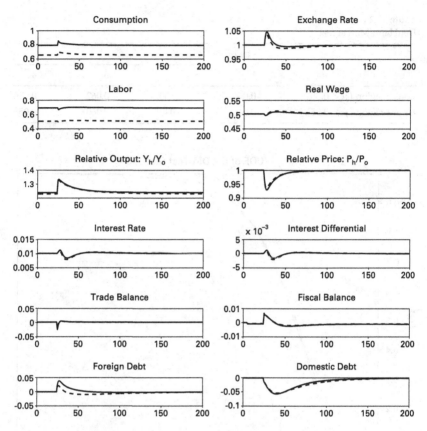

Figure 10.3
Impulse response functions: with habit persistence (*solid line*) and without habit persistence (*dashed line*)

introduction of habit persistence has no significant effects on the contemporaneous correlations of many of the key macroeconomic variables. This result is consistent with a finding by Chari, Kehoe, and McGratten (2002). They found that incorporating habit persistence, in the form we used in this chapter, did not prove to be very promising for lowering the general positive correlations between consumption and real exchange rates generated by these models. Actual data show negative consumption–real exchange rate correlations for the United States and Europe, and for other country pairs it ranges from small and positive values to negative values. They call this inability of model to replicate these empirical correlations the consumption–real exchange rate anomaly.

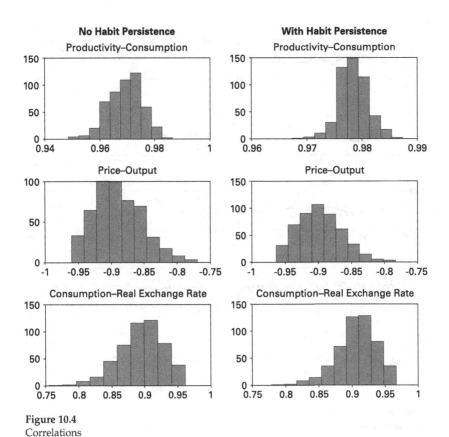

Figure 10.4
Correlations

10.4 Simulating Alternative Scenarios

10.4.1 No-Inflation Targeting

The first scenario we would like to explore is the case without inflation targeting. The monetary authority now implements monetary policy by setting the domestic interest rate R to be equal to the overseas rate plus the risk premium:

$$R_t = R_t^* + \Phi_t.$$

This policy has the effect of keeping the exchange rate relatively constant. Monetary policy in this case is designed not to manage inflation, but rather to keep the exchange rate stable by ensuring that the domestic rate moves with the overseas rate. This policy is equivalent to targeting inflation in imported goods. Figure 10.5 shows the time

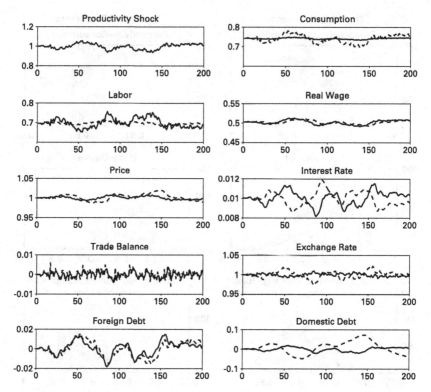

Figure 10.5
Simulated data

paths of key variables for one simulation of productivity shocks. As expected, the exchange rate is relatively constant.

Figure 10.6 compares the impulse responses for the case of no-inflation targeting (solid lines) and with inflation targeting (dashed lines). They show that, following a productivity shock that labor falls by more and consumption increases by less in the no-targeting environment. The interesting result is the increase in domestic debt following the fall in tax revenues. In this environment, since the exchange rate is "not allowed" to depreciate (as in the inflation targeting case), the potential to sell overseas is severely restricted.

10.4.2 International Shocks

Figure 10.7 compares the impulses following a export demand shock with a export price shock. The solid lines represents the paths generated by an export demand shock and the dashed lines represent the

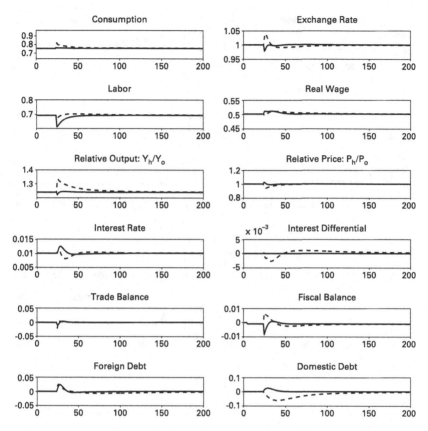

Figure 10.6
Impulse responses: no inflation targeting (*solid line*) and with inflation targeting (*dashed line*)

paths generated by an export price shock, both under the case of inflation targeting. The higher price of exports discourages the demand for the export goods, and the relative price of P^h/P^o falls to shift demand toward domestic nontraded home goods. Contrast this with the export demand shock that stimulates production of the export good.

10.5 Concluding Remarks

This chapter has examined the effects of including habit persistence in a model with sticky prices and wages, financial market frictions, investment dynamics in the production of home goods, and a resource sector. Overall, this additional complexity has the effect of raising the

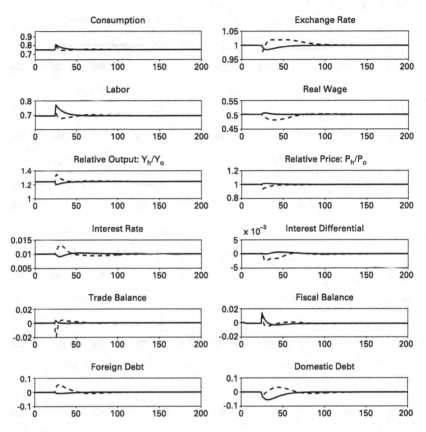

Figure 10.7
Impulse responses following an international export demand shock (*solid line*) and a export price shock (*dashed line*)

level of steady-state consumption and reduce the speed of dynamic adjustments. However, the degree of habit persistence introduced in this chapter is too low to influence the nature of the dynamic adjustments or the correlations among key variables.

Computational Exercise: Output and Interest Rate

Boldrin, Christiano, and Fisher (2001) found that introducing habit persistence (along with limitations on intersectoral mobility of factors of production) for a closed economy helped to explain effects such as the inverse leading indicator property of high interest rates on future output. In other words, future output is a function of current interest rate. We can test this effect using a Granger causality test.

Table 10.3
Granger causality tests (4 lags)

Hypothesis	F statistics	p value
Output does not Granger cause interest rate	47.414	(0.000)
Interest rate does not Granger cause output	1.105	(0.353)

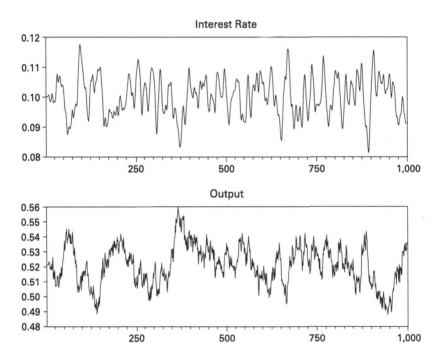

Figure 10.8
Simulated data: interest rate and output

Figure 10.8 shows the time-series plots of the simulated data, and table 10.3 presents the Granger causality tests for lags of order 4. The results are robust across other lag orders. The test shows that lagged outputs are significant determinants of interest rates while lagged interest rates are not significant determinants of output. This is inconsistent with the finding of Boldrin, Christiano, and Fisher.

In this open economy model the degree of habit persistence is quite low ($\varrho = 0.6$). A useful exercise would be to change the degree of habit persistence. Can we obtain the leading indicator property of the rate of interest by changing the degree of habit persistence?

11   International Capital Flows and Adjustment

Thus far we have compared the dynamic responses of key macroeconomic variables either to a once-only shock or to recurring shocks. We have put aside uncertainty about changes in parameters (e.g., in the risk premium coefficient), or to sudden changes in exogenous variables (e.g., "sudden stops" in capital inflows/outflows, or unexpected changes to the collateral constraints on the amount of foreign borrowings). We have kept the stochastic setting simple so that we could check both the accuracy and intuitive plausibility of the results of the model as we progressed from relatively simple to more complex extensions. Obviously policy makers have to formulate their responses in more complex global stochastic settings, facing multivariate shocks that, at times, piggyback on one another (when it rains it pours!).

In this final chapter we use the model of chapter 10, with sticky prices and wages, financial frictions, adjustment costs, and habit persistence, to simulate scenarios similar to sudden changes in capital flows. Our aim is to show how the models we have developed—after they have been solved, checked for accuracy and analyzed for coherence and convergence with stochastic simulations—may be put to work to analyze the response of the macroeconomy to a wider variety of shocks and exogenous developments.

We will consider two scenarios. The first asks the question: What happens if there is a sudden exogenous rise in the currency risk premium that has little or nothing to do with a country's fundamentals and that then severely curtailed the country's ability to borrow? The second scenario asks the opposite question: What happens if there is an unexpected exogenously determined fall in the currency risk premium caused by an unprecedented exogenous inflow of capital into the country? To be sure, we do not intend to capture all of the features of "sudden stop" or, for that matter, the issue of global imbalances. A more complete approach to these issues, related to global imbalances and continuing real exchange rate changes, require multicountry models (e.g., see Caballero, Farhi, and Gourinchas 2007).

Our choice of scenarios is motivated by a general interest in international capital flows because they can have a variety of effects. They can be beneficial in facilitating growth in emerging countries; they can be disastrous in speading contagious financial crises, and they can generate intergenerational issues when they stimulate consumption rather than investment.

The scenarios also illustrate the appeal and practicality of solving DSGE models with nonlinear projection methods. Arellano and Mendoza (2002) point out that sudden stops are a property of equilibrium that occurs in a region of the state space where negative shocks make borrowing constraints bind. The resulting nonlinear effects, they emphasize, require nonlinear solution methods. However, they acknowledge that research in this area is at an early stage and their survey, like this book, aims to stimulate further work.

11.1 Capital Reversals

11.1.1 Sudden Stops and Contagion Effects

Calvo (2005) drew attention to the role of sudden stops, meaning abrupt declines or stops in capital flows, and the ensuing large drops in outputs of recipient countries. What accounts for these sudden stops? Calvo (2005) cites herding behavior, which is a consequence of the extreme sensitivity of foreign investors to news and which may or may not be related to changes in the fundamentals driving asset returns or growth in a country. He points out that high risk assessment costs make herding more likely and emerging markets are especially vulnerable because, according to Calvo (2005, p. 139), these countries have narrow production bases for tradable goods, short track records in international capital markets, and political systems prone to polarization.

More important, the information costs associated with risk assessments are high because entry costs are high, and because informational value decays quickly. Thus information gathering is subject to large-scale economies, and this is likely to lead to the formation of specialist fund management clusters that encompass regions of emerging markets. Given the formation of such clusters, Calvo emphasizes that emerging markets, far from being sources of shocks, can be victims of contagious effects either as innocent bystanders or as victims of country-specific rumors.

In his book Calvo discusses the issue of sudden stops more broadly, but he observes that capital reversals signify a serious blow to an economy in that they cause falls in output. Chari, Kehoe, and McGrattan (2005b) offer an insight into this observation. They show that sudden stops, generated by an abrupt tightening of a country's collateral constraint on foreign borrowing, do not lead to deceases in output in a standard general equilibrium model. Instead, to generate an output drop, the model must include frictions that generate negative effects that swamp the positive effects of the sudden stop. The type of frictions documented by these authors are similar to the financial frictions we discussed in preceding chapters. Without these frictions, the sudden stop would actually trigger an increase in labor and an expansion of output.

Chari, Kehoe, and McGrattan (2005b) argue that the frictions that generate output drops in the wake of sudden stops are subtle ones for which there is little direct evidence. They conjecture that there may be a reverse causation from that put forward by Calvo. In this alternative hypothesis, foreign investors see events that lead them to predict a future drop in output, and as a result they refuse to lend more to the country. Thus it is the falls in expected output that cause the sudden reversals of capital flows, not the reverse (Chari, Kehoe, and McGrattan 2005b, p. 387).

11.1.2   Simulating a Reversal in Capital Flows

We can check out the CKM (Chari, Kehoe, and McGrattan) and Calvo hypotheses by simulating the model described in chapter 10. We model the sudden stop by imposing an abrupt jump of the risk premium to an exogeneously predetermined value of 0.01 and by freezing the evolution of foreign debt. We also stabilize the growth in productivity to highlight the effects of sudden stops.

In figure 11.1 simulated paths are compared for the case where an abrupt stop occurs to foreign lending at observation 100 (dashed line) with the base case where no sudden capital reversals occur (solid lines). A message here is that sudden stops do not cause falls in output when the government is in a position to provide the necessary finance to support the adjustment process (in this case, the necessary increase in domestic prices and the fall in consumption). A quick run through of the countries affected by the tequila crisis of Mexico in 1994, the Asian

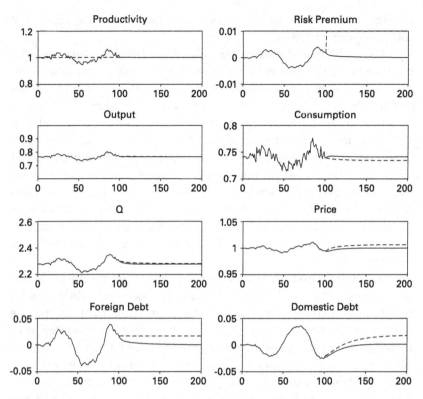

Figure 11.1
Simulated data: with sudden stop (*dashed line*) and base case (*solid line*)

flu of Thailand, Indonesia, and South Korea in 1997, and the Russian virus in 1998 would suggest that this is indeed the case.

11.2 Continuing Inflows

11.2.1 Current Account Deficits and Asset-Price Inflation

In chapter 8 we drew attention to the great moderation in 1983 to 1984 that coincided, as Fogli and Perri (2005) note, with the start of a deterioration in the US current account balances. In essence this is the reverse or mirror image of the sudden stop effect that has plagued emerging market countries. The United States had been experiencing large capital inflows, leading to mounting external debt–GDP ratios and to a very large asset-price boom.[1]

Mendoza, Quadrini, and Ríos-Rull (2006) link the large US current account deficits (along with the global imbalances) to heterogeneity in

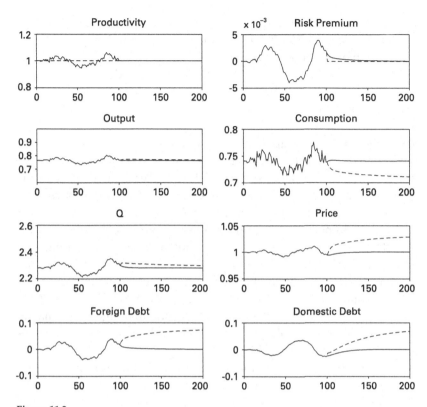

Figure 11.2
Simulated paths: with endogenously determined capital inflows (*solid line*) and with exogenously determined capital inflows (*dashed line*)

financial markets across countries rather than to any particular moderation within the United States. Using a two-country model, they find global financial integration to favor the more financially developed country. In other words, the financial depth of the United States attracted huge capital inflows from countries with surplus funds looking for investment opportunities.

11.2.2   Simulating Continuing Capital Inflows

In this scenario we compare the case of a sudden abrupt drop in the risk premium in conjuction with an exogenously determined increase in capital inflows with the base case of no sudden changes. The simulated paths are shown in figure 11.2. The solid lines represent the adjustment paths to the endogenously determined inflows (our standard base case) and the dashed lines represent the case with exogenously determined capital inflows. The sharp rise in the foreign debt is as expected, and likewise the rise in the Q variable and in prices. Note, however, the rise in domestic debt as well; this twin-deficit phenomenon is what is being currently observed in the United States.

11.3   Future Research

The questions we take up in this chapter center on the usefulness of the model we have developed so far, for assessing macroeconomic adjustment, under a wider set of stochastic shocks. Clearly, many interesting questions can be asked. What happens if the Calvo mechanism for wages and domestic prices becomes even more sticky so that prices and wages do not rise very much? Alternatively, what happens if the monetary authority targets asset-price inflation as well as domestic-price inflation? What happens if the exogenous capital inflows stimulated a growth in productivity? The message we wish to impart here is that the subject matter of the book—computational methods for DSGE modeling—is part of an active research agenda to design better macroeconomic models to enhance our understanding of the economy as well as to provide better guidance for policy.

There are many avenues for future research. For example, we did not specify within any of our models expectational frictions or *bounded rationality*, in which the agents, be they household, firm, or central bank decision makers, have to learn the laws of motion for key macroeconomic variables, such as inflation or Tobin's Q. We have also only concentrated on the single-country model. When discussing financial openness, a more complete treatment would involve at least a two-country model, in which residents of either country hold shares or claims on capital as well as the bonds of the other country. We have not explored this fuller type of financial openness.

Another avenue for research is to incorporate housing into the household consumption and asset portfolio decision. Piazzesi, Schneider, and Turzel (2007) show that the introduction of housing in a general equilibrium model induces a lower risk-free rate of return, while the share of housing expenditures can be used to predict excess returns. Davis and Heathcoate (2005) note that the percentage standard deviation of residential investment is about twice that of nonresidential investment. Both studies used closed economy models. The effects of adding housing consumption and investment in an open economy will have implications for real exchange-rate and current account dynamics.

This chapter and book concludes with an observation made by Cochrane (2008), in his survey "Financial Markets and the Real Economy." The dynamic stochastic general equilibrium approach, especially when applied to open economies, is still relatively unexplored territory. Like explorers, missionaries, and adventurers, the task ahead is to explore, expand, and enrich our existing knowledge of computational macroeconomics for the open economy.

Appendixes

A   Definitions of Symbols

Symbol	Calibrated value	Definition
α, α_1	0.15	Share of capital in production of home or manufactured goods
α_2	0.3	Share of capital in production of export or resource goods
β	0.99	Households' discount factor
γ_1	0.3	Share of foreign goods in aggregate consumption
γ_2	0.15	Share of export goods in domestic consumption
δ	0.025	Depreciation rate (quarterly)
ζ	6	Elasticity of substitution between differentiated goods
η	1.5	Coefficient of relative risk aversion
θ_1	2.5	Elasticity of substitution between domestic and foreign goods
θ_2	1.5	Elasticity of substitution between home and export goods
$\kappa, \kappa_1, \kappa_2$	0.1	Elasticity of substitution in production
Ψ	0.025	Adjustment cost parameter for production
μ_1, μ_2	0.2	Proportion of wage bill supported by bank loans
ξ	0.85	Price and wage stickiness factor
ρ	0.90	Autoregresive coefficient
σ		Standard deviation error of productivity shock
τ_1	0.2	Tax rate on labor income
τ_2	0.1	Tax rate on consumption
ϕ_1, ϕ_2	1.5, 0.9	Taylor coefficients on inflation, smoothing parameter
χ_1	0.1	Sensitivity of G to deviations of B
χ_2	1.0	Sensitivity of X to changes in the real exchange rate (S/P)
φ	0.01	Risk premium parameter associated with the exchange rate
ψ_1	0.005	Reserve deposit ratio associated with the deposits
ψ_2	0.005	Default ratio associated with loans
ω	0.25	Elasticity of marginal disutility with respect to labor
Φ		Risk premium

B   Definitions of Variables

Variable	Definition
A	Auxiliary variables in the Calvo pricing formula
B	Government bonds
C	Consumption C, C^d, C^f, C^h, C^o
D, d	Index for domestically produced goods
F, f	Foreign debt, index for foreign goods
G	Government expenditures
H, h	Index for home nontraded manufactured goods
I	Imported capital/investment goods, I^h
J, j	Index for differentiated goods
K	Capital K^h, K^o
L	Labor services L^h, L^o
M	Money—deposits of households in banks
N	Loans to firms
O, o	Index for traded-export goods
P	Prices P, P^d, P^f, $P^{m*} P^{o*}$, P^o, P^h, P^a
Q	Tobin's Q
R	Interest rate, R, R^m, R^n, R^*
S	Exchange rate
T, t	Index of time
W	Wage rate
X	Exports
Y	Output, Y^h, Y^o
Z	Productivity index, Z^h, Z^o

C   The Computer Algorithm

- Generate the productivity shocks:

$$\ln(Z_t) = \rho \ln(Z_{t-1}) + (1-\rho) \ln(\bar{Z}) + \varepsilon_t, \qquad \varepsilon_t \sim N(0, \sigma_z^2)$$

- Set up the approximating functions for the forward variables C, S:

$$\Delta_t^c = \Omega_1^c(Z_t - \bar{Z}) + \Omega_2^c(F_{t-1} - \bar{F}) + \Omega_3^c(R_{t-1} - \bar{R})$$

$$\hat{C}_t = \bar{C}\left(\frac{1}{1 + \exp(-\Delta_t^c)} - 0.5\right)$$

$$\Delta_t^s = \Omega_1^s(Z_t - \bar{Z}) + \Omega_2^s(F_{t-1} - \bar{F}) + \Omega_3^s(R_{t-1} - \bar{R})$$

$$\hat{S}_t = \bar{S}\left(\frac{1}{1 + \exp(-\Delta_t^s)} - 0.5\right)$$

- Solve for the endogeous variables Y, L, K, P^k, P, W, R, F:

$$Y_t = \hat{C}_t + \bar{G} + \bar{X}$$

$$L_t^{1+\varpi-\kappa_1} = 0.5(1 - \alpha_1)(Z_t)^{\kappa_1}(Y_t)^{1-\kappa_1} C_t^{-\eta}$$

$$K_t^{\kappa_1} = \frac{1}{\alpha_1}\left[\left(\frac{Y_t}{Z_t}\right)^{\kappa_1} - (1 - \alpha_1)(L_t)^{\kappa_1}\right]$$

$$P_t^k = P_t^* S_t$$

$$f_t^l = (1 - \alpha_1)(Z_t)^{\kappa_1}\left(\frac{Y_t}{L_t}\right)^{1-\kappa_1}$$

$$f_t^k = \alpha_1 (Z_t)^{\kappa_1}\left(\frac{Y_t}{K_t}\right)^{1-\kappa_1}$$

$$P_t = \frac{W_t}{f_t^l} + \frac{P_t^k}{f_t^k}$$

$$W_t = L_t^\varpi P_t C_t^\eta$$

$$\pi_t = 0.25\left[\left(\frac{P_t}{P_{t-1}}\right)^4 - 1\right]$$

$$R_t = \phi_2 R_{t-1} + (1 - \phi_2)[R^* + \phi_1(\pi_t)]$$

$$\Phi_t = sign(F_{t-1}^*) \cdot \varphi[e^{(|F_{t-1}^*| - \bar{F}^*)} - 1]$$

$$\hat{S}_t F_t^* = (1 + R_{t-1}^* + \Phi_{t-1})\hat{S}_t F_{t-1}^* + (\hat{S}_t P_t^* I_t - P_t X_t)$$

- Obtain the Euler errors:

$$\epsilon_t^c = \Lambda_t \beta(1 + R_{t-1}) - \Lambda_{t-1}, \qquad \Lambda_t = \frac{C_t^{-\eta}}{P_t}$$

$$\epsilon_t^s = \Lambda_t \beta(1 + R_{t-1}^* + \Phi_{t-1} + \Phi_{t-1}' F_{t-1}^*)S_t - \Lambda_{t-1}S_{t-1}$$

- Sample MATLAB Program for Chapter 2:

```
% Chapter 2: Base Flexible Price Model
%_____
% Start with a clean workspace
%_____
   clear all;
%_____
% Define global variables and parameters
%_____
   global eta omega beta alpha1 kappa rho phi0 phi1 chis
   global Rstar PFstar PXstar
   global Blam_ss C_ss F_ss G_ss K_ss L_ss P_ss Pk_ss R_ss S_ss W_ss X_ss Y_ss Z_ss
   global nstart T1 T2 zshock nstatevar neuronx neuler
%_____
% Nominate the function that sets out the model
%_____
   fun = 'chapter2_netfun';
%_____
% Define the exogenous variables and the calibrated parameters
%_____
   Rstar = 0.01;
   PFstar = 1.0;
   PXstar = 1.0;
   eta = 1.5;
   omega = 0.25;
   beta = 1/1.01;
   alpha1 = 0.15;
   kappa = 0.1;
   chis = 0.1;
   rho = 0.9;
   phi0 = 0.9;
   phi1 = 1.5;
%_____
% Set out the initial steady-state values
%_____
   Blam_ss = 3.22696890071349;
   C_ss = 0.45793462256871;
   F_ss = 0;
   G_ss = 0;
   K_ss = 0.02729049017873;
```

```
   L_ss = 0.74732008502373;
   P_ss = 0.99999998539410;
   Pk_ss = 1.0000;
   R_ss = 0.0100;
   S_ss = 0.99999999315490;
   W_ss = 0.28812562001981;
   X_ss = 0.02729049020372;
   Y_ss = 0.48522511277243;
   Z_ss = 1;
%_____
% Determine the nature of the approximating function
%_____
   nstatevar = 3; neuler = 2; neuronx = 1;
   neuronx1 = neuronx + 1;
   nparm = nstatevar*neuler*neuronx;
%_____
% Create the shocks
%_____
   T1 = 200; %length of simulated data
   T2 = 50; %number of simulations
   randn('state', 888); %random seed
   se_shock = 0.01; %std.of shock
   zshock = randn(T1,T2)*se_shock;
   nstart = 4;
%_____
% Call up an optimizing algorithm
%_____
   options = optimset('Display', 'iter', 'MaxFunEvals', 100, 'MaxIter', 100, 'TolFun',
   0.0001);
   gammaf = [2.8342 −1.6406 −0.0868 0.5264 −0.0000 3.0591]; % starting values
gammaf = fminsearch(fun, gammaf, options);
[ERROR, C, F, K, L, P, R, S, W, Pk, Y, Z, trade, ERR_C, ERR_S] = feval(fun,gammaf);
%_____
% Generate impulse-responses
%_____
   T1 = 200;
   T2 = 1;
zshock = [zeros(24,1); 0.1; zeros(T1-25,1)];
   [ERROR, C, F, K, L, P, R, S, W, Pk, Y, Z, trade, ERR_C, ERR_S] = feval(fun,gammaf);
   figure(1);
   subplot(5,2,1); plot(Z); title('Z')
   subplot(5,2,2); plot(C); title('C')
   subplot(5,2,3); plot(S); title('S')
   subplot(5,2,4); plot(Y); title('Y')
   subplot(5,2,5); plot(K); title('K')
   subplot(5,2,6); plot(L); title('L')
   subplot(5,2,7); plot(W./P); title('W/P')
   subplot(5,2,8); plot(P); title('P')
   subplot(5,2,9); plot(R); title('R')
   subplot(5,2,10); plot(F); title('F')
   saveas(1,'c:\eg1.eps','eps');
```

```
% Chapter 2: Function
    function [ERROR, C, F, K, L, P, R, S, W, Pk, Y, Z, trade, ERR_C,
    ERR_S] = chapter2_netfun(gamax);
    global eta omega beta alpha1 kappa rho phi0 phi1 chis
    global Rstar PFstar PXstar
    global Blam_ss C_ss F_ss G_ss K_ss L_ss P_ss Pk_ss R_ss S_ss W_ss X_ss Y_ss Z_ss
    global nstart T1 T2 zshock nstatevar neuronx neuler
%_____
% Create the vector space
%_____
    Blam = Blam_ss*ones(T1,T2);
    C = C_ss*ones(T1,T2);
    F = F_ss*ones(T1,T2);
    K = K_ss*ones(T1,T2);
    L = L_ss*ones(T1,T2);
    P = P_ss*ones(T1,T2);
    R = R_ss*ones(T1,T2);
    S = S_ss*ones(T1,T2);
    W = W_ss*ones(T1,T2);
    Pk = Pk_ss*ones(T1,T2);
    Y = Y_ss*ones(T1,T2);
    Z = Z_ss*ones(T1,T2);
    Zrisk = zeros(T1,T2);
    ERR_C = zeros(T1,T2);
    ERR_S = zeros(T1,T2);

    jk = nstatevar*neuler*neuronx;
    jj = 1:nstatevar:jk;
    kk = nstatevar:nstatevar:jk;
%_____
% The model simulated for length T1 and T2 times
%_____
    for j = 1:T2;
    for i = nstart + 1:T1,
%_____
% Defining the shock process
%_____
    Zz = rho*log(Z(i − 1,j)) + (1 − rho)*log(Z_ss) + zshock(i,j);
    Z(i,j) = exp(Zz);
%_____
% Demeaning the state variables
%_____
    ZZ(i,j) = Z(i,j) − Z_ss;
    FF(i,j) = F(i − 1,j) − F_ss;
    RR(i,j) = R(i − 1,j) − R_ss;
    xstate = [ZZ(i,j) FF(i,j) RR(i,j)];
%_____
% Setting the approximating functions
%_____
    for nn = 1: neuler*neuronx;
    neuron(1,nn) = 1./(1 + exp(−gamax(jj(nn):kk(nn))*xstate')) − 0.5;
    end;
```

```
pea_C = [([neuron(1, 1: neuronx)])];
pea_S = [([neuron(1, neuronx + 1:2*neuronx)])];
C(i,j) = exp(pea_C)*C_ss;
S(i,j) = exp(pea_S)*S_ss;
%
```

%_____
% Generating the endogeous variables
%_____

```
Y(i,j) = C(i,j) + G_ss + X_ss;
LL = 0.5*(1 - alpha1)*(Z(i,j)^kappa)*(Y(i,j)^(1 - kappa))*(C(i,j)^-eta);
L(i,j) = LL^(1/(1 - kappa + omega));
L(i,j) = real(L(i,j));
KK = ((Y(i,j)/Z(i,j))^kappa) - (1 - alpha1)*L(i,j)^kappa;
K(i,j) = (KK/alpha1)^(1/kappa);
K(i,j) = real(K(i,j));
mpl = (1 - alpha1)*(Z(i,j)^kappa)*(Y(i,j)/L(i,j))^(1 - kappa);
mpk = (alpha1)*(Z(i,j)^kappa)*(Y(i,j)/K(i,j))^(1 - kappa);
mpl = real(mpl);
mpk = real(mpk);
Pk(i,j) = S(i,j)*PFstar;
P(i,j) = 2*Pk(i,j)/mpk;
W(i,j) = (L(i,j)^omega)*(C(i,j)^eta)*P(i,j);
W(i,j) = real(W(i,j));
Zinf(i,j) = 0.25*((P(i,j)/P(i - 4,j)) - 1);
R(i,j) = phi0*R(i - 1,j) + (1 - phi0)*(Rstar + phi1*Zinf(i,j));
trade(i,j) = P(i,j)*X_ss - S(i,j)*PFstar*K(i,j);
trade1 = trade(i,j)/S(i,j);
F(i,j) = F(i - 1,j)*(1 + Rstar + Zrisk(i - 1,j)) - trade1;
Blam(i,j) = (C(i,j)^-eta)/P(i,j);
Blam(i,j) = real(Blam(i,j));
Zrisk(i,j) = sign(F(i - 1,j))*chis*(exp(abs(F(i - 1,j))) - 1);
Zder(i,j) = chis*(exp(abs(F(i - 1,j))));
%
```

%_____
% Obtaining the Euler errors
%_____

```
MUC = Blam(i,j)*(beta*(1 + R(i - 1,j)));
MUCLAG = Blam(i - 1,j);
ERR_C(i,j) = (MUC/MUCLAG) - 1;
MUS = S(i,j)*(1 + Rstar + Zrisk(i - 1,j) + Zder(i - 1,j)*F(i - 1,j));
MUSLAG = (1 + R(i - 1,j))*S(i - 1,j);
ERR_S(i,j) = (MUS/MUSLAG) - 1;
end;
end;
%
```

%_____
% Defining the errors function to be minimized
%_____

```
err1 = reshape(ERR_C,T1*T2,1);
err2 = reshape(ERR_S,T1*T2,1);
ERROR = mean(err1.^2) + mean(err2.^2) + 2*mean(err1.*err2);
```

Notes

Acknowledgments

A quick introduction to MATLAB code by Winistörfer and Canova (2006) may be found on the Web ⟨http://crei.cat/people/canova/teaching%20pdf/intro%20to%20matlab .pdf⟩.

Chapter 1

1. A special issue of the *Journal of Business and Economic Statistics* in 1991, edited by John Taylor and Harold Ulig, found that even for a model with a fairly simply nonlinear structure, simulated series displayed different dynamic properties depending on the solution methods used. Canova (2007) quite rightly advocates caution when assessing the results from any one method.

2. The computational literature refers to these decision rules for variables that depend on their own and other expected future variables as policy functions. The word "policy" in this case is not to be confused with the interest rate policy function given by the Taylor rule. The terms "policy function" or "decision rule" refer to functional equations (functions of functions) that we use for the forward-looking control variables.

3. Similar limitations apply to linear quadratic approximations. Woodford (2003), for example, confines his analysis to cases in which "steady-state growth" is perturbed by "small stochastic variations" in the exogenous variables (Woodford 2003, p. 77).

4. At the 2006 Meetings of the Society of Computational Economics and Finance in Cyprus, the title of Kenneth Judd's plenary session was "O Curse of Dimensionality, Where Is Thy Sting?"

5. When there are more than one error, we use a robust method for estimating the parameters of the decision rules, where we weight the errors at each observation by the inverse of the Euler error variance-covariance matrix (similar to GLS in econometrics). The advantage of using this robust method is that it puts less weight on errors that have higher volatility and more weight on errors with lower volatility.

6. Den Haan and Marcet (1994) recommend a sample size of $T = 30,000$.

7. Good starting values help speed up the optimization process. For this reason we sometimes use the genetic algorithm (GA) to obtain sensible initial values. As Sirakaya,

Turnovsky, and Alemdar (2006) note, the GA does not require continuity and the existence of derivatives. The GA is a global search algorithm that starts "completely blind" and learns gradually. Regardless of the initial parameter values, they converge to an approximate global optimum within the domain space and continue to improve through genetic operators such as selection, breeding, and mutation. The drawback of the use of the genetic algorithm for optimization, of course, is that it is much slower than gradient-based methods. But despite this limitation, Sirakaya, Turnovsky, and Alemdar (2006) stress that the GA can solve many problems that otherwise are both analytically and computationally intractable (Sirakaya, Turnovsky, and Alemdar 2006, p. 187). A detailed description of the genetic algorithm for nonlinear estimation appears in McNelis (2005, pp. 72–75).

8. In addition to the basic Matlab package, users who wish to reproduce the results found in this book (and, of course, extend them) will need the Optimization and Statistics toolboxes.

Chapter 2

1. The functional form adopted in this book assumes that risk is symmetric. However, in our nonlinear approach we can easily suppress this symmetry. For example, we can allow the sensitivity of the risk premium to foreign debt and the sensitivity of the risk discount to foreign assets to be different.

2. The utility function with habit persistence becomes: $U_t(.) = [(C_t - \varrho C_{t-1})^{1-\eta}/(1-\eta)] - [L_t^{1+\varpi}/(1+\varpi)]$, where $\varrho > 0$ is the habit persistence parameter. We assume that $\varrho = 0$.

3. The utility function can be modified to impose an upper limit on labor services L at unity (and a lower limit greater than zero):

$$U_t(.) = \frac{C_t^{1-\eta}}{1-\eta} + \frac{(1-L_t)^{1+\varpi}}{1+\varpi}, \qquad 0 < L \leq 1.$$

4. See Orphanides (2000) and Perez (2001), for studies on the Taylor rule using real-time data, meaning data available at the time when the policy decisions were made.

5. We note at the outset that all models in the book are specified and calibrated for the case where the steady-state inflation rate is assumed to be zero.

6. See Bullard and Mitra (2002) for a study with private sector learning, and see Evans and Honkapohja (2003) for a study with central bank learning where the learning relates to obtaining structural parameters needed in the policy rule. See also Lim and McNelis (2004, 2007) for studies where the central bank generates forecasts of inflation using a VAR model.

7. For the case, with no Taylor rule, since the policy variable is fixed to the world rate, $R_t = R^*$, we would not include the interest rate in the information set.

8. A commonly used procedure to study the time-series property of variables is to first filter the simulated artificial data using, for example, the Hodrick-Prescott (1980) method to filter the data for trend and cyclical effects (see Cooley 1995, pp. 27–29). Since the data are stationary in these simulations, we have not applied the filter here. We describe this application in chapter 3 in the context of the output gap.

9. Note, however, that the persistence, for price, is in the levels and not the first differences. A more complicated model is needed to generate persistence in inflation.

Chapter 3

1. Goodfriend and King (1997) point out that monetary policy cannot eliminate the distortion caused by the markup, since it has a steady-state effect. Since we are evaluating monetary policy rules and wish to compare the dynamics of the model under sticky prices with the dynamics and welfare effects under flexible prices, we follow the common practice of eliminating this steady-state distortion by assuming an optimal tax or subsidy scheme to offset the markup effect on pricing and production.

2. These results are further elaborated in Canzoneri, Cumby, and Diba (2004).

3. It should also be noted that the Calvo pricing mechanism is the foundation for the more familiar new Keynesian Phillips curve, relating the current inflation rate to marginal costs and the discounted future inflation rate: $\pi_t = \lambda \cdot h_t + \beta \mathbf{E}_t \pi_{t+1}$, where $\lambda = (1 - \xi)(1 - \xi\beta)/\xi$ and h_t represents the logarithmic transformation of marginal costs relative to the steady-state value of zero inflation. However, Ascari (2003) notes that this log-linearized version of the Calvo pricing model is misleading (Ascari 2003, p. 3).

4. For further discussion of the price dispersion index and resource costs, see Schmidt-Grohe and Uribe (2004), Yun (1996), and Goodfriend and King (1997). Yun (2004) rewrites the dispersion index, in terms of Calvo relative prices, as the following law of motion: $\Delta_t = (1 - \xi)[p_t^*]^{-\zeta} + \xi[1 + \pi_t]^{\zeta} \cdot \Delta_{t-1}$. In the steady state this also implies that $\Delta_t = [P_t^{j*}/P_t]^{-\zeta} = 1$. This is the benchmark welfare model. Overall, the major implication of price stickiness is that it creates distortion, and hence it generates resource allocation costs.

5. As an aside, we note that in both cases, of fully flexible prices as well as sticky prices, the monetary policy followed an inflation targeting rule. The operating assumption is that monetary policy is following a zero inflation target and that productivity shocks are both positive and negative. The welfare costs of a positive steady-state inflation may be much higher with the sticky price system.

6. Policy attentuation could be continued, however, when large positive changes in the output gap, or deceases in unemployment, are accompanied by falling inflation. In this case the policy makers could reasonably assume that that the natural rate of unemployment is falling, or potential output is increasing, since normally a large increase in the output gap or a sharp fall in unemployment should be accompanied by accelerating inflation. See Lim and McNelis (2007) for a study with state-contingent Taylor rules.

7. See Canova (2007, ch. 3) for a fuller discussion of the HP filter and related hybrid decompositions for time-series analysis.

Chapter 4

1. Alternatively, we could let the tax rates, either on income or consumption, be state contingent, rising and falling (slightly) with domestic debt levels (see Hughes Hallet 2005), or productivity (as suggested by Kim and Kim 2005).

Chapter 5

1. See also Kollmann (2004) for a study with a tax rate on household income that responds to public debt.

2. This formulation can be made more complicated by embedding foreign habit persistence. We leave it to the reader to introduce this, but we will be taking up domestic habit persistence in chapter 10.

Chapter 6

1. This shadow price of new capital is known as Tobin's Q since it was introduced by Tobin (1969) in his article "A General Equilibrium Approach to Monetary Theory" and later developed by Brainard and Tobin (1977) in their analysis of assets markets and the cost of capital.

2. We have abstracted from adjustment costs on labor, but we will introduce wage stickiness in chapter 9.

3. Of course, we recognize that it would not be straightforward to include the rate of growth of Tobin's Q as a target for monetary policy because most central banks do not know the underlying true model driving investment and thus cannot measure the rate of growth of this fundamental variable with accuracy, much less on a current quarter-to-quarter basis. For this reason alone we are not likely to see this variable as a target for monetary policy, at least in the simple Taylor-rule framework, which is the way we have characterized the operating procedure for monetary policy in this chapter. Lim and McNelis (2007) have drawn attention to the role of Q growth in a monetary rule in a learning environment. Since Q growth is not known with accuracy, Lim and McNelis have shown that replacing the Taylor rule with a nonlinear threshold rule, in which the interest rate response to changes in Q growth only if it reaches critical positive or negative values, is welfare enhancing.

Chapter 9

1. Note that lowering ϖ affects the utility through the denominator as well as the exponent. A fall in ϖ in this case increases the disutility of labor. For large initial values of ϖ the opposite effects take place.

Chapter 11

1. Anna Schwartz reports that from 1995 to 1999, the US stock markets had their biggest boom ever, with the Dow Jones rising from 3484 at year-end 1994 to 11,145 at the end of 1999, while the Standard and Poor index went from 460 to 1327 and the NASDAQ from 752 to 4069 for the same period (Schwartz 2002).

Bibliography

Aiyagari, S. Rao, Albert Marcet, Thomas J. Sargent, and Juha Seppala. 2002. Optimal taxation without state-contingent debt. *Journal of Political Economy* 110: 1220–54.

Arellano, Cristina, and Enrique G. Mendoza. 2002. Credit frictions and sudden stops in small open economies: An equilibrium business cycle framework for emerging market crises. Working paper 8880. National Bureau of Economic Research, Cambridge, MA.

Aruoba, S. Borağan, Jesús Fernández-Villaverde, and Juan F. Rubio-Ramírez. 2006. Comparing solution methods for dynamic equilibrium economies. *Journal of Economic Dynamics and Control* 30: 2477–2508.

Ascari, Guido. 2003. Staggered prices and trend inflation: Some nuisances. Bank of Finland discussion paper 27/2003. Available at SSRN: http://ssrn.com/abstract=501743.

Backus, David K., Patrick J. Kehoe and Finn E. Kydland. 1992. International real business cycles. *Journal of Political Economy* 100: 745–75.

Balassa, Bela. 1964. The purchasing power parity doctrine: A reappraisal. *Journal of Political Economy* 72: 584–96.

Benhabib, Jess, and Stefano Eusepi. 2005. The design of monetary and fiscal policy: A global perspective. Working paper, Department of Economics, New York University. Available at http://www.econ.nyu.edu/user/benhabib/globalfinal32.pdf.

Benigno, Pierpaolo, and Michael Woodford. 2004. Optimal monetary and fiscal policy: A linear-quadratic approach. Working paper series 345. European Central Bank. Available at http://www.ecb.int/pub/pdf/scpwps/ecbwp345.pdf.

Bernanke, Ben S. 2004. The great moderation: Speech at Eastern Economic Association meetings. Washington, DC: Board of Governors of the Federal Reserve System.

Betts, Caroline, and Michael B. Devereux. 2000. Exchange rate dynamics in a model of pricing-to-market. *Journal of International Economics* 50: 215–44.

Blanchard, Olivier Jean, and Charles M. Kahn. 1980. The solution of linear difference models under rational expectations. *Econometrica* 48: 1305–12.

Boldrin, M., L. Christiano, and J. Fisher. 2001. Habit persistence, asset returns, and the business cycle. *American Economic Review* 91: 149–66.

Bollerslev, Timothy. 1986. Generalized autoregressive conditional heteroskedasticity. *Journal of Econometrics* 31: 307–27.

Bollerslev, Timothy. 1987. A conditionally heteroskedastic time series model for specula-tive prices and rates of return. *Review of Economics and Statistics* 69: 542–47.

Bullard, J. and Mitra, K. 2002. Learning about monetary policy rules. *Journal of Monetary Economics* 49: 1105–29.

Caballero, Ricardo J. Emmanuel Farhi, and Pierre-Olivier Gourinchas. 2006. An equilib-rium model of "global imbalances" and low interest rates. Working paper 11996. Depart-ment of Economics, Massachusetts Institute of Technology.

Calvo, Guillermo A. 1983. Staggered prices in a utility-maximizing framework. *Journal of Monetary Economics* 12: 383–98.

Calvo, Guillermo A. 2005. *Emerging Capital Markets in Turmoil*. Cambridge: MIT Press.

Campbell, John Y., and John H. Cochrane. 1999. By force of habit: A consumption-based explanation of aggregate stock market behavior. *Journal of Political Economy* 107: 205–51.

Canova, Fabio. 2007. *Methods for Applied Macroeconomic Research*. Princeton, NJ: Princeton University Press.

Canzoneri, Matthew B., Robert E. Cumby, and Bhezad T. Diba. 2004a. The cost of nominal inertia in NNS models. Available at http://www.georgetown.edu/faculty/canzonem/Costs_02_04_05.pdf.

Canzoneri, Matthew B., Robert E. Cumby, and Bhezad T. Diba. 2005. Price and wage in-flation targeting: Variations on a theme by Erceg, Henderson and Levin. In Jon Faust, Athansious Orphanides, and David Reifschneider, eds., *Models and Monetary Policy: Research in the Tradition of Dale Henderson, Richard Porter and Peter Tinsley*. Washington, DC: Board of Governors of the Federal Reserve System.

Carroll, Christopher D., Jody Overland and David N. Weil. 2000. Saving and growth with habit formation. *American Economic Review* 90: 341–55.

Chang, Roberto, and Andres Velasco. 2001. A model of financial crises in emerging markets. *Quarterly Journal of Economics* 116: 489–517.

Chari, V. V., and Patrick J. Kehoe. 1999. Optimal fiscal and monetary policy. In J. B. Taylor and M. Woodford, eds., *Handbook of Macroeconomics*, vol. 1C. Amsterdam: North Holland.

Chari, V. V., Patrick J. Kehoe, and Ellen R. McGrattan. 1992. Current real-business-cycle theories and aggregate labor-market fluctuations. *American Economic Review* 82: 430–50.

Chari, V. V., Patrick J. Kehoe, and Ellen R. McGrattan. 2000. Sticky price models of the business cycle: Can the contract multiplier solve the persistence problem? *Econometrica* 68: 1151–79.

Chari, V. V., Patrick J. Kehoe, and Ellen R. McGrattan. 2002. Can sticky price models generate volatile and persistent exchange rates? *Review of Economic Studies* 69: 533–63.

Chari, V. V., Patrick J. Kehoe, and Ellen R. McGrattan. 2005a. A critique of structural VARs using business cycle theory. Working paper 631. Minneapolis: Federal Reserve Bank of Minneapolis.

Chari, V. V., Patrick J. Kehoe, and Ellen R. McGrattan. 2005b. Sudden stops and output drops. *American Economic Review: Papers and Proceedings* 95: 381–87.

Christiano, Lawrence J., and Jonas D. M. Fischer. 1999. Algorithms for solving dynamic models with occasionally binding constraints. Available at http://www.faculty.econ.northwestern.edu/faculty/christiano/research/PEA/final99.pdf.

Christiano, Lawrence J., Martin Eichenbaum, and Robert Vigfusson. 2003. What happens after a technology shock? Working paper 9819. National Bureau of Economic Research, Cambridge, MA. Available at http://www.nber.org/papers/w9819.

Christiano, Lawrence J., Martin Eichenbaum, and Charles Evans. 1997. Sticky prices and limited participation models of money. *European Economic Review* 41: 1201–49.

Clarida, Richard, Jordi Gali, and Mark Gertler. 2001. Optimal monetary policy in open versus closed economies: An integrated approach. *American Economic Review* 91: 248–52.

Cochrane, John. 2008. Financial frictions and the real economy. In Raijnish Mehra, ed., *The Handbook of the Equity Rich Premium*. Amsterdam: Elsevier, pp. 239–330.

Cogley, Timothy, and Thomas J. Sargent. 2005. The conquest of U.S. inflation: Learning and robustness to model uncertainty. *Review of Economic Dynamics* 8: 528–63.

Collard, Fabrice, and Michel Julliard. 2001a. Perturbation methods for rational expectations models. Manuscript. CEPREMAP, Paris.

Collard, Fabrice, and Michel Julliard. 2001b. Accuracy of stochastic perturbation methods: The case of asset pricing models. *Journal of Economic Dynamics and Control* 25: 979–99.

Cooley, Thomas F. 1995. *Frontiers of Business Cycle Research*. Princeton, NJ: Princeton University Press.

Davis, Morris, and Jonathan Heathcoate. 2006. The price and quantity of residential land in the United States. Available at http://www9.georgetown.edu/faculty/jhh9/land-final.pdf.

De Long, B. 2004. John Taylor blasts off for the gamma quadrant. Brad De Long's Semi-Daily Journal: A Weblog.

Den Haan, Wouter J., and Albert Marcet. 1990. Solving the stochastic growth model by parameterizing expectations. *Journal of Business and Economic Statistics* 8: 31–34.

Den Haan, Wouter J., and Albert Marcet. 1994. Accuracy in simulations. *Review of Economic Studies* 61: 3–17.

Devereux, Michael B. 2001. Monetary policy, exchange rate flexibility, and exchange rate pass through. Working paper. Department of Economics, University of British Columbia.

Dixit, Avinash K., and Joseph E. Stiglitz. 1977. Monopolistic competition and optimum product diversity. *American Economic Review* 67: 297–308.

Dunlop, John T. 1938. The movement of real and money wage rates. *Economic Journal* 48: 413–34.

Efron, B. 1979. Bootstrap methods: Another look at the jackknife. *Annals of Statistics* 7: 1–26.

Efron, B., and R. Tibshirani. 1993. *An Introduction to the Bootstrap*. New York: Chapman and Hall.

Erceg, Christopher J., Dale W. Henderson, and Andrew T. Levin. 2000. Optimal monetary policy with staggered wage and price contracts. *Journal of Monetary Economics* 46: 281–313.

Erceg, Christopher J., Luca Guerrieri, and Christopher Gust. 2005. Expansionary fiscal shocks and the trade deficit. International Finance Discussion Paper 825. Board of Governors of the Federal Reserve System. Available at http://www.federalreserve.gov/pubs/ifdp/2005/825/ifdp825.pdf.

Evans, G. W., and Honkapohja, S. 2003. Adaptive learning and monetary policy design. *Journal of Money, Credit and Banking* 35: 1045–72.

Evans, Martin D. D., and Viktoria Hnatkovska. 2005. International capital flows, returns and world financial integration. Working paper. Department of Economics, Georgetown University.

Faia, Ester. 2005. Financial frictions and the choice of exchange rate regimes. Working paper. Universitat Pompeu Fabra, Barcelona.

Feldstein, Martin. 2006. Central banking: Is science replacing art? Comments at European Central Bank Conference in Honor of Otmar Issing. Available at http://www.nber.org/feldstein/issingcomments.html.

Fernandez-Villaverde, Jesus. 2006. Nonlinear and non-gaussian methods in DSGE models. Manuscript. Department of Economics, Duke University.

Fernandez-Villaverde, Jesus, and Juan Rubio. 2006. Solving DSGE models with perturbation methods and a change of variables. *Journal of Economic Dynamics and Control* 30: 2509–31.

Feynman, R. R. Leighton, and M. Sands. 1963. *The Feynman Lectures on Physics*, vol. 1. Reading, MA: Addison-Wesley.

Fogli, Allesandro, and Fabrizio Perri. 2006. The great moderation and the US external imbalance. Working paper 2006-E-22. Institute for Monetary and Economic Studies, Bank of Japan, Tokyo.

Franses, Philip Hans, and Dick van Dijk. 2000. *Non-linear Time Series Models in Empirical Finance*. Cambridge: Cambridge University Press.

Frenkel, Jacob A., Assaf Razin, and Chi-Wa Yuen. 1996. *Fiscal Policies and Growth in the World Economy*. Cambridge: MIT Press.

Friedman, Milton. 1968. The role of monetary policy. *American Economic Review* 58: 1–17.

Galí, Jordi. 1999. Technology, employment, and the business cycle: Do technology shocks explain aggregate fluctuations? *American Economic Review* 89: 249–71.

Galí, Jordi. 2004. Trends in hours, balanced growth, and the role of technology in the business cycle. *Review of Federal Reserve Bank of St. Louis* 87: 459–86.

Galí, Jordi, and Tommaso Monacelli. 2005. Monetary policy and exchange rate volatility in a small open economy. *Review of Economic Studies* 72: 707–34.

Goodfriend, Marvin. 2002. Monetary policy in the new neoclassical synthesis: A primer. Available at http://www.blackwellpublishing.com/pdf/goodfriend.pdf.

Galí, Jordi, and Robert G. King. 1997. The new neoclassical synthesis and the role of monetary policy. *NBER Macroeconomics Annual* 12: 231–83.

Granger, Clive, and Y. Jeo. 2004. Thick modeling. *Economic Modeling* 21: 323–43.

Gray, Jo Anna. 1978. On indexation and contract length. *Journal of Political Economy* 86: 1–18.

Gregory, A., and G. Smith. 1993. Calibration in macroeconomics. In G. Maddala, ed., *Handbook of Statistics*, vol. 11. Amsterdam: Elsevier Science, pp. 703–19.

Hansen, Lars Peter, and Thomas J. Sargent. 2000. Wanting robustness in macroeconomics. Working paper. Department of Economics, New York University. Available at http://homepages.nyu.edu/~ts43/.

Harrod, R. F. 1933. *International Economics*. Cambridge: Cambridge University Press.

Heer, Burkhard, and Alfred Maußner. 2005. *Dynamic General Equilibrium Modelling: Computational Methods and Applications*. Berlin: Springer-Verlag.

Hendry, Scott, Wai-Ming Ho, and Kevin Moran. 2003. Simple monetary policy rules in an open-economy limited participation model. Working paper 2003-08. Bank of Canada.

Hodrick, Robert J., and Edward C. Prescott. 1980. Post-war U.S. business cycles: An empirical investigation. Mimeo. Carnegie-Mellon University.

Hornik, Kurt, Maxwell Stinchcombe, and Halbert White. 1989. Multilayer feedforward networks are universal approximators. *Neural Networks* 2: 359–66.

Hughes Hallet, Andrew. 2005. Fiscal policy coordination with independent monetary policies: Is it possible? Working paper. Department of Economics, Vanderbilt University.

Jensen, J. L. W. V. 1906. Sur les fonctions convexes et les inégalités entre les valeurs moyennes. *Acta Mathematica* 30: 175–93.

Judd, John P., and Glenn D. Rudebusch. 1998. Taylor's rule and the Fed: 1970–1997. *Economic Review: Federal Reserve Bank of San Francisco* 3: 3–16.

Judd, Kenneth L. 1992. Perturbation solution methods for economic growth models. In Hal Varian, ed., *Economic and Financial Modelling with Mathematica*. New York: Springer-Verlag, pp. 80–103.

Judd, Kenneth L. 1996. Approximation, perturbation, and projection solution methods in economics. In Hans M. Amman et al., eds., *Handbook of Computational Economics*, vol. 1. Amsterdam: Elsevier, pp. 509–86.

Judd, Kenneth L., and Jess Gaspar. 1997. Solving large-scale rational-expectations models. *Macroeconomic Dynamics* 1: 45–75.

Justiniano, Alejandro, and Giorgio Primiceri. 2006. The sources of macroeconomic stability: Good luck or good policy? Available at http://www.nottingham.ac.uk/economics/res/media2006/surico%20et%20al.pdf.

Kara, Amit, and Edward Nelson. 2002. The exchange rate and inflation in the UK Bank of England, External MPC Unit. Discussion paper 11. Available at http://www.bankofengland.co.uk/publications/other/externalmpcpapers/extmpcpaper0011.pdf.

Kim, Jinill, and Sunghyun Henry Kim. 2005. Welfare effects of tax policy in open economies: Stabilization and cooperation. Working paper. Department of Economics, Tufts University. Available at http://www.tufts.edu/%7Eskim20/paper/kk2.pdf.

Kollmann, Robert. 2004. Welfare-maximizing operational monetary and tax policy rules. Working paper 4782. Center for Economic Policy Research. Available at http://www .robertkollmann.com/MonFisc_240705.pdf.

Kydland, Finn E., and Edward C. Prescott. 1982. Time to build and aggregate fluctuations. *Econometrica* 50: 1345–70.

Lahiri, Amartya, Rajesh Singh, and Carlos Végh. 2005. Segmented asset markets and optimal exchange rate regimes. *Journal of International Economics*, forthcoming.

Laxton, Douglas, and Paolo Pesenti. 2003. Monetary rules for small, open, emerging economies. *Journal of Monetary Economics* 50: 1109–46.

Lim, G. C., and Paul D. McNelis. 2004. Learning and the monetary policy strategy of the European Central Bank. *Journal of International Money and Finance* 23: 997–1010.

Lim, G. C., and Paul D. McNelis. 2007. Inflation targeting, learning and Q volatility in small open economies. *Journal of Economic Dynamics and Control* 31(11): 3699–3722.

Lubik, Thomas, and Frank Schorfheide. 2005. A Bayesian look at new open economy macroeconomics. Working paper. Department of Economics, Johns Hopkins University, Baltimore. Available at http://www.econ.jhu.edu/people/lubik/nber05.pdf.

Lucas, Robert E., Jr. 1976. Econometric policy evaluation: A critique. *Carnegie-Rochester Conference Series on Public Policy: The Phillips Curve and Labor Markets* 1: 19–46.

Lucas, Robert E., Jr. 1993. On the welfare costs of inflation. Manuscript. Department of Economics, University of Chicago.

Marcet, Albert, and Juan Pablo Nicolini. 2003. Recurrent hyperinflations and learning. *American Economic Review* 93: 1476–98.

Marcet, Albert. 1988. Solving nonlinear models by parameterizing expectations. Working paper. Graduate School of Industrial Administration, Carnegie Mellon University.

Marcet, Albert. 1993. Simulation analysis of dynamic stochastic models: Applications to theory and estimation. Working paper. Department of Economics, Universitat Pompeu Fabra, Barcelona.

Marcet, Albert, and G. Lorenzoni. 1998. The parameterized expectations approach: Some practical issues. In R. Marimon and A. Scott, ed., *Computational Methods for the Study of Dynamic Economies*. Oxford: Oxford University Press, pp. 143–71.

McCallum, Bennett T. 1981. Price level determinacy with an interest rate policy rule and rational expectations. *Journal of Monetary Economics* 8: 319–29.

McCallum, Bennett T. 2001. Analysis of monetary transmission mechanisms: Methodological issues. In Deutsche Bundesbank, ed., *The Monetary Transmission Process: Recent Developments and Lessons for Europe*. New York: Palgrave Macmillan, pp. 11–43.

Mehra, Rainjish, and Edward J. Prescott. 1985. The equity premium: A puzzle. *Journal of Monetary Economics* 15: 145–61.

Mendoza, Enrique G., Vincenzo Quadrini and José-Victor Ríos-Rull. 2006. Financial integration, financial deepness and global imbalances. Working paper. Department of Economics, University of Maryland.

Miranda, Mario J., and Paul L. Fackler. 2002. *Applied Computational Economics and Finance*. Cambridge: MIT Press.

Obstfeld, Maurice, and Kenneth Rogoff. 2002. Risk and exchange rates. In Elhanan Help-man and Efraim Sadka, eds., *Economic Policy in the International Economy: Essays in Honor of Assaf Razin*. Cambridge: Cambridge University Press, pp. 74–117.

Obstfeld, Maurice, and Kenneth Rogoff. 2006. The unsustainable current account position of the United States revisited. Working paper. Deparment of Economics, University of California, Berkeley.

Olivera, J. 1967. Money, prices and fiscal lags: A note on the dynamics of inflation. *Banca Nationale del Lavoro Quarterly Review* 20: 258–67.

Orphanides, Athanasios, and John C. Williams. 2002a. Imperfect knowledge, inflation expectations, and monetary policy. Working paper. Finance and Economics Discussion Series, Board of Governors of the Federal Reserve System. Available at http://www.federalreserve.gov/pubs/feds/2002/200227/200227pap.pdf.

Orphanides, Athanasios, and John C. Williams. 2002b. Robust monetary policy rules with unknown natural rates. *Brookings Papers on Economic Activity* 2002: 63–118.

Oviedo, P. Marcelo. 2005. World interest rate, business cycles, and financial interme-diation in small open economies. Manuscript. Department of Economics, Iowa State University.

Piazzesi, Monika, Martin Schneider, and Selale Tuzel. 2006. Housing, consumption, and asset pricing. *Journal of Financial Econometrics* 83: 531–69.

Razin, Assaf. 2005. Globalization and disinflation: A note. Working paper 10954. Na-tional Bureau of Economic Research. Available at http://papers.nber.org/papers/w10954.pdf.

Samuelson, Paul A. 1964. Theoretical notes on trade problems. *Review of Economics and Statistics* 46: 145–54.

Sargent, Thomas J. 1979. *Macroeconomic Theory*. 2nd ed. New York: Academic Press.

Sargent, Thomas. 1991. Two difficulties in interpreting vector autoregressions. In *Rational Expectations Econometrics*. Underground Classics in Economics. Boulder, CO: Westview Press.

Sargent, Thomas J., and Neil Wallace. 1975. "Rational" expectations, the optimal mone-tary instrument, and the optimal money supply rule. *Journal of Political Economy* 83: 241–54.

Schmitt-Grohé, Stephanie, and Martín Uribe. 2003. Closing small open economy models. *Journal of International Economics* 61: 163–85.

Schmitt-Grohé, Stephanie, and Martín Uribe. 2004a. Optimal simple and implementable monetary and fiscal rules. Working paper 10253. National Bureau of Economics Re-search, Cambridge, MA. Available at http://www.econ.duke.edu/~uribe/simple.pdf.

Schmitt-Grohé, Stephanie, and Martín Uribe. 2004b. Solving dynamic general equilib-rium models using a second-order approximation to the policy function. *Journal of Eco-nomic Dynamics and Control* 28: 755–75.

Schmitt-Grohé, Stephanie, and Martín Uribe. 2005. Habit persistence. In Steven Durlauf and Lawrence Blume, eds., *The New Palgrave Dictionary of Economics*, forthcoming.

Schmitt-Grohé, Stephanie, and Martín Uribe. 2006. Comparing two variants of Calvo-type wage stickiness. Working paper 12740. National Bureau of Economic Research, Cambridge, MA.

Schwartz, Anna J. 2002. Asset price inflation and monetary policy. Working paper 9321. National Bureau of Economic Research, Cambridge, MA.

Sims, Christopher A. 1980. Macroeconomics and reality. *Econometrica* 48: 1–48.

Sims, Christopher A. 2001. Solving linear rational expectations models. *Computational Economics* 20: 1–20.

Sirakaya, Sibel, Stephen Turnovsky, and M. Nedim Alemdar. 2006. Feedback approximation of the stochastic growth model by genetic neural networks. *Computational Economics* 27: 185–206.

Smets, Frank, and Raf Wouters. 2002. Openness, imperfect exchange rate pass-through, and monetary policy. *Journal of Monetary Economics* 49: 947–81.

Smets, Frank, and Raf Wouters. 2003. An estimated dynamic stochastic general equilibrium model of the euro area. *Journal of the European Economic Association* 1: 1123–75.

Smith, Anthony A., Jr. 2004. Computational methods in economics: General points. Class materials. Available at www.econ.yale.edu/smith/econ561b/compute5.pdf.

Summers, Lawrence. 2003. Address on the bubble in asset prices, Davos World Economic Forum, annual meeting 2003. Available at www.weforum.org/site/knowledgenavigator.nsf/Content/_S7593?open.

Summers, Peter M. 2005. What caused the great moderation? Some cross-country evidence. *Economic Review*, Federal Reserve Bank of Kansas, pp. 5–31.

Svensson, Lars E. O. 2000. Open-economy inflation targeting. *Journal of International Economics* 50: 155–83.

Swanson, Eric T. 2006. Optimal nonlinear policy: Signal extraction with a non-normal prior. *Journal of Economic Dynamics and Control* 30: 185–203.

Tanzi, V. 1978. Inflation, real tax revenues, and the case for inflationary finance: Theory with an application to Argentina. *IMF Staff Papers*.

Tarshis, Lorie. 1939. Changes in real and money wages. *Economic Journal* 49: 150–54.

Taylor, John B. 1979. Staggered contracts in a macro model. *American Economic Review* 69: 108–13.

Taylor, John B. 1993. Discretion vs. policy rules in practice. *Carnegie-Rochester Conference Series on Public Policy* 39: 195–214.

Taylor, John B. 2000. Using monetary policy rules in emerging economies. In *Stabilization and Monetary Policy: The International Experience*. Mexico City: Bank of Mexico, pp. 441–58.

Taylor, John B. 2004. The U.S. current account: Recent trends and policies. JS 2084, Office of Public Affairs, United States Department of the Treasury. Available at http://www.treas.gov/press/releases/js2084.htm.

Uribe, Martín. 2003. Real exchange rate targeting and macroeconomic instability. *Journal of International Economics* 59: 137–59.

Walsh, Carl E. 1998. *Monetary Theory and Policy*. Cambridge: MIT Press.

Winistörfer, Patrick, and Fabio Canova. 2006. Introduction to Matlab. Available at http://crei.cat/people/canova/teaching%20pdf/intro%20to%20matlab.pdf.

Wolkenhauer, Olaf. 2001. *Data Engineering: Fuzzy Mathematics in Systems Theory and Data Analysis*. New York: Wiley.

Woodford, Michael. 2003. *Interest and Prices: Foundations of a Theory of Monetary Policy*. Princeton, NJ: Princeton University Press.

Wright, Brian D., and Jeffrey C. Williams. 1982. The economic role of commodity storage. *Economic Journal* 92: 596–614.

Wright, Brian D., and Jeffrey C. Williams. 1984. The welfare effects of the introduction of storage. *Quarterly Journal of Economics* 99: 169–92.

Wright, Brian D., and Jeffrey C. Williams. 1991. *Storage and Commodity Markets*. Cambridge: Cambridge University Press.

Yun, Tack. 1996. Nominal price rigidity, money supply endogeneity, and business cycles. *Journal of Monetary Economics* 37: 345–70.

Index

Printed in the United States
by Baker & Taylor Publisher Services